SO THIS IS DEPRAVITY

Books by RUSSELL BAKER

Washington: City on the Potomac
An American in Washington
No Cause for Panic
All Things Considered
Our Next President
Poor Russell's Almanac
The Upside-down Man

SO THIS IS DEPRAVITY

RUSSELL BAKER

Congdon & Lattès, Inc.
New York

"The Flag" appeared in Esquire. *"Moods of Washington" and "Letter from Washington" appeared in* The New York Times Magazine, *copyright © 1974 and 1976 respectively by The New York Times Company; reprinted by permission. All other material appeared in the author's "Observer" column in* The New York Times *and his "Sunday Observer" column in* The New York Times Magazine. *Copyright © 1973, 1974, 1975, 1976, 1977, 1978, 1979, and 1980 by The New York Times Company; reprinted by permission.*

Library of Congress Cataloguing in Publication Data

Baker, Russell, 1925–
So this is depravity and other observations.

Most of the articles originally published in the New York times, 1973–1980.
I. Title.
PS3552.A4343S6   814'.54   80–67859

Distributor's ISBN: 0-312-92782-7
Distributor's ISBN: 0-312-92783-5 (Limited Edition)
Publisher's ISBN: 0-86553-000-9
Publisher's ISBN 0-86553-008-4 (Limited Edition)
Published by Congdon & Lattès, Inc.
Distributed by St. Martin's Press
Published simultaneously in Canada by Thomas Nelson & Sons Limited
Copyright © 1980 by Russell Baker
All Rights Reserved
Printed in the United States of America
Designed by Barbara Huntley
First Edition

Nemo repente fuit turpissimus.
—JUVENAL

*The publisher wishes to thank those named below,
for their suggestions of favorite Baker pieces and
for their eloquent enthusiasm.*

Jack Anderson
Carlos Baker
Clive Barnes
Jacques Barzun
A. Scott Berg
George Borchardt
Marshall Brickman
Tom Brokaw
John Brooks
Art Buchwald
John Chancellor
Schuyler Chaplin
Craig Claiborne
Frank Conroy
Norman Cousins
Malcolm Cowley
Jane Curtin
Ralph Ellison
Avery Fisher
Frances Fitzgerald
Leonore Fleischer
John Kenneth Galbraith
Brendan Gill
Doris Grumbach
Robert L. Heilbroner
Joseph Heller
Rust Hills
Edward Hoagland
Arthur Hoppe
John Jay Iselin

E. J. Kahn, Jr.
Alfred Kazin
Alan King
Larry King
Edward I. Koch
Seymour Krim
Fran Lebowitz
John Leggett
Robert Lekachman
John V. Lindsay
Martin Mayer
Ved Mehta
Charles Michner
Herbert Mitgang
Edward P. Morgan
Robert Motherwell
Daniel P. Moynihan
Sidney Offit
Robert Osborn
George Plimpton
Peter S. Prescott
Dan Rather
Arthur Schlesinger, Jr.
William V. Shannon
Roger W. Straus, Jr.
Gay Talese
Evan Thomas
Hunter S. Thompson
Alice Trillin
Calvin Trillin

Asylum

Recently I discovered that I was going sane. It was surprisingly pleasant. There were weeks unbroken by fits of melancholia, rage, anxiety, despair, hypochondria or terror. Life, inexplicably, seemed worth living again, and I went through my daily rounds whistling "Redwing" instead of bristling with hostility and perspiring with fear that my deodorant might not keep me safe all day long.

Pleasant, yes. But—

"If you permit yourself to sink into sanity and continue whistling 'Redwing' like this," the doctor explained, "you will be unfit to function in American society. You could very well end up in—"

"In a sane asylum?"

He gravely fingered commitment papers.

I had placed myself in his hands after being found in a traffic jam whistling "Redwing" at the steering wheel. It seemed obvious that no car locked into that vast immobilized ocean of machinery would escape before the next weekend, and whistling seemed a pleasant way to pass the time.

All around me, other motorists were mashing their horns, grinding their fenders and bursting blood vessels. The notes of "Redwing" intensified their rage. "What's the matter? Aren't you crazy or something?" they shouted at me.

A policeman came. "If everybody just sat here whistling 'Redwing,' " he said, "how would we ever get any fenders smashed while nobody's going anyplace? You mustn't be some kind of nut."

One must function, after all. How else can America fulfill its destiny? How else can fenders be smashed while going noplace? The doctor prescribed strong treatment—television and newspaper immersion.

All of one day I sat straitjacketed at the tube being doused periodically with torrents of newspaper. Hypochondria burst into full flower almost immediately.

"You'd better quit whistling 'Redwing,' Buster, and get your blood pressure checked," said the box. "And while you're at it, don't forget—you could be diabetic, have muscular dystrophy, be suffering from alcoholism without even knowing it and drop dead any instant of heart disease, stroke or failure to contribute to the Arthritis Fund."

The newspapers suggested that early death was probable unless I jogged five miles a day in unpolluted air (presumably in the Antarctic), quit eating beef (bowel cancer), stopped sleeping more than eight hours at a stretch (cerebral hemorrhage) and quit kissing women (influenza).

Tension. Fear. Anxiety. Only by changing an entire way of life could I survive to old age. Could I do it? Not likely. Why not? Too set in my ways, perhaps? More sinister than that—maybe, subconsciously, I wanted to kill myself.

Feelings of self-loathing and misery. Then—another dousing of newspapers. Ah, what despair! "So you live to old age," the newspapers laughed. "Know what that means? Unemployment. Sleazy pension boardinghouses. Shuffled off to play shuffleboard, starved on Social Security peanuts, ground down by inflationary cost rises, stuffed away in fire-trap nursing homes."

Intense desire to weep, melancholia rampant. Sense of hopelessness.

"Ah, there is bad news tonight." (The box has taken over again.) "The ozone layer of the atmosphere is being destroyed by gases emitted from aerosol cans."

Despair, sense of imminent doom. Guilt. Who is emitting those doomful aerosol gases? Me. And for what? Shaving. Destroying the earth for whisker removal.

Intolerable sense of futility to go with guilt. After all, why give up beef, kissing and eight and a half hours' sleep, why move to the Antarctic to jog in good air, if the ozone layer is going to be wiped out anyhow by shaving cream?

The box attacks from the blind side. That graying hair—yes, it could indeed cost me my job as well as the love of ungray women. That early evening fatigue—could it really be iron-poor blood?

I shall not go on. I require only the first hour of television and newspaper immersion, but the full therapy lasts all day and, in some cases, a full lifetime. At the end, one is normal again. Depressed, enraged, anxiety-ridden, desperate, terrorized—normal.

I no longer whistle "Redwing." I have forgotten the tune. The doctor says this is because I am again well adjusted to society.

Hey, I know an island far away. Let's go.

Cooped Up

I go to the movies. Gary Cooper is in the next seat as usual, wearing his badge and Stetson. I am sick and tired of him. He grins and offers popcorn. "What are we going to see tonight?" he asks. *"The Sting,"* I say, "and this time stay out of it, Coop."

"Shucks," says Cooper. "You know me."

I know Gary Cooper all right. The previous week he embarrassed me at *Chinatown.* The unprincipled cop was just about to let John Huston get away with murder, on account of Huston's being a millionaire, when Coop threw his popcorn box on the floor, strode down the aisle and drew his six-shooter on Huston and the cop.

"Get off the screen," the audience yelled, but Gary Cooper paid them no heed. "I'm takin' you both down to the U.S. marshal's office," he said.

"You can't do this," Jack Nicholson objected. "The whole point of this picture is that good guys never win."

"You better get on your buckboard and get out of town fast, son," Cooper told him, "before I take you in for interfering with an arrest."

It was a long speech for Cooper, so without another word he marched Huston and the cop off the screen and the movie ended with Nicholson heading for Laramie.

"I hear this is a real good one," Cooper says of *The Sting.*

"Just stay out of it, Coop," I say.

After a while he begins stirring unhappily. "These fellows are nothing but a bunch of crooks," he whispers.

"They happen to be Robert Redford and Paul Newman," I say. "Even if they are crooks, they're charming and lovable, and the audience loves them, so stay out of it."

It is too late. He is already striding down the aisle and is up on the screen with the drop on the whole roomful of swindlers, before Newman can get away with the loot.

"Get those hands up," he says. "We're all going to take a little walk down to the marshal's office."

The audience boos as Cooper rides them all off into the sunset, manacled aboard cayuses. I am fearful that someone will know Cooper was with me and beat me for being an accessory to the triumph of law.

My analyst is no comfort.

"You are merely hallucinating Cooper as an agent for fulfilling a childish desire for heroes who are honest," he says. He suggests staying away from movies in which criminality and corruption prevail until I become less infantile.

Cooped Up

So I go to *Deep Throat.* Cooper is there. After ten minutes he says, "Whew."

"Stay out of it, Coop," I plead. Futilely, of course.

"Miss Lovelace," says Cooper, towering over her on the screen, "you need a little church training."

He throws her over his shoulder, covers her with his badge and says, "I'm taking you down to the schoolmarm so she can introduce you to the Ladies Aid Society."

The audience pelts the screen with comic books and dark glasses.

My analyst loves this report. He asks me to commit myself for study at the Institute of Incredible Sexual Repressions in Zurich. I run.

To the movies, of course. But this time it's *The Apprenticeship of Duddy Kravitz,* which I know in advance is merely about an ambitious young man.

Cooper is there. He even likes the movie. "This is okay," he grins as Duddy goes into the business of making home movies of bar mitzvahs. But what is this? Duddy is behaving rudely to grown-ups. Yes, very rudely. He is laughing at them and ordering them off his land. Cooper is in the aisle before I can stop him. "Stay out of it, Coop."

It is useless. Up on the screen Cooper has Duddy under his gun arm and he is saying, "Young fellow, I'm taking you over to old Judge Hardy's book-lined den for a man-to-man talk about good manners." End of picture.

Quickly, I run to see *Going Places,* figuring Cooper will be tied up giving Andy Hardy some quick-draw tips, but he arrives in time to see the movie's two utterly charming heroes engage charmingly in burglary, kidnapping, car theft and casual thuggery. "Those fellows are nothing but a pair of skunks," he says, striding down the aisle.

"Stay out of it, Coop!"

The audience is enraged to see him rescue a lovely mother from ravishment, but Cooper takes the charmers to the marshal's office anyhow.

My analyst says Gary Cooper is dead and I am too immature to accept reality. Cooper looks at the analyst without expression. "I could take him down to the marshal's office for taking money for useless explanations," says Cooper.

"Stay out of it, Coop," I plead.

The Great Forgetting
[1973]

What the country needs now at the end of the Vietnam war is not amnesty but amnesia.

It is time to put the whole thing up in the attic, to store it away up there with the snapshot of Granddaddy as a young man, foot up on the running board of his Model T Ford. Up there where we keep the old Blue Eagle (NRA, kiddies) window decal, the 1945 newspaper with the headline about Roosevelt's death, the stamp collection we started that year we had the mumps and couldn't leave the house. The Vietnam war ought to go up there very first thing in the morning, so we can start forgetting about it right away. The sooner the better.

What a protest that's going to produce, what an overpoweringly reasoned lecture of right thought, summoning Freud, history, Founding Fathers, "The Star-Spangled Banner," Joseph Pulitzer and the memory of Heinrich Himmler, among others, to prove that forgetting is bad for you, particularly if you are a heavily muscled superpower half mesmerized between Cotton Mather and Krafft-Ebing.

The great forgetting wouldn't be forever, though. The attic isn't for things we want to forget forever. Things get put up there because we don't know what else to do with them this year, or because they are in the way right now, or because we want to get them out of our lives for a while without throwing them away.

Later, when we have changed and become different people, we

our house, the last of the people who used to be our kids is finishing high school, and most of us who will sit there in the heat for the last commencement speech know the rest of the truth.

We young marrieds have become somebody else, too. We feel it in the knees when we start to stand after sitting too long, which, like the wheezing and lower martini capacity, is discouraging. The better side of the coin compensates for that. Whoever we are now, most of us have probably learned that it is better to have people than kids, that people, in fact, are much easier to live with, once you grow up and quit screaming at them for not being kids anymore.

Gaudeamus igitur!

The Way It Was

Thomas Jefferson and George Washington sat silently in a Philadelphia drawing room waiting for Benjamin Franklin. It was 10:30 P.M. and George Washington, who had eaten too much apple pandowdy at dinner, was suffering the distress of acid indigestion.

He was wishing someone would invent a powder that gave fast, fast, fast relief, but it was still only 1775, and, since acid indigestion hadn't yet been discovered, Washington thought he was probably having a heart attack. It wasn't easy living in the eighteenth century, Washington reflected. Dentistry still in the Dark Ages. No football on television. Heart attacks after dinner every night of the week. Finally, to relieve the silence, Washington addressed Jefferson, who he thought was Button Gwinnett. "Do you often have an after-dinner heart attack, Button?" he asked.

"I am sorry, sir," said Jefferson, who was awed at being in the presence of the Father of His Country and genuinely sorry about having to sound like an ignoramus, "but I do not know what an after-dinner heart-attack button is, sir."

Washington scowled at Jefferson. An impertinent lout, Washington thought. What are the colonies coming to? Ask a man a civil question and he makes an asinine joke. Still, what could you expect of anybody named Button?

Jefferson, who wanted to make a smart impression, said, "I do know, however, about certain inalienable rights with which man is endowed by his Creator."

"Some other time," said Washington, who had heard footsteps outside. It would be Benjamin Franklin and John Adams, he reflected, come at his request to discuss the Declaration of Independence. Washington liked Franklin, but wished he wouldn't drink and pinch barmaids because it was bad for the image of the Revolution.

Like everybody from Massachusetts, Adams gave Washington a pain. He was one of those know-it-alls who thought it was a waste of time listening to anybody who hadn't gone to Harvard. Washington liked to get under his skin by humming "Boola Boola" whenever Adams was making a speech to the Continental Congress, but just now he would need Adams's approval for calling off the Revolution.

When the newcomers entered, Washington smelled the applejack on Franklin's breath and the superiority on Adams's education. Franklin noticed the pain on Washington's brow and immediately diagnosed a simple case of acid indigestion. He dissolved a spoonful of powder in a glass of water and urged Washington to drink. A moment later, Washington belched.

"You are a genius, Dr. Franklin," he said. "Tush," said Franklin, "merely a small discovery I stumbled on between my research on electricity and inventing the Franklin stove."

"I'm not kidding," Washington said. "This powder can do more for mankind than any revolution ever made. If we could produce and market large quantities of it, we could wipe out after-dinner heart attack all over the world."

Adams gave Washington a look of such contempt that Washington began humming "Boola Boola." Franklin diplomatically suggested that it would be better to complete the Revolution before going into the bicarbonate-of-soda business, since otherwise the ruling tyrants in London would tax away all their profits.

Washington said, all right, it was the Revolution he wanted to talk about. He thought they were making a mistake. Adams became furious. "If you don't want to be the Father of Our Country, step aside," he cried.

Jefferson interrupted. "Are you saying," he asked Adams, "that you are going to become the Father of Our Country? What about me?"

"You!" said George Washington. "That's ridiculous. Can you imagine a great country governed from a capital called Button, D.C.?"

Franklin suggested everyone calm down and hear Washington's case. Washington put it succinctly. "If we go ahead with the revolt," he said, "200 years from now, our countrymen will have to celebrate its bicentennial. Do you know what that means for us, gentlemen?"

Adams was ashen: "Boston will be overrun with tourists watching reenactments of old battles." Franklin said: "The whole history of my sex life will be exhumed and displayed on television." Washington said: "Plastic replicas of my false teeth will be sold at every roadside frozen-custard stand in the country."

Jefferson saved the Revolution. "I will go it alone," he declared. The other three reluctantly joined him. Washington, because he couldn't bear to have his country fathered by a man named Button. Adams and Franklin, because they thought Jefferson was Gouverneur Morris and believed the country would be a laughingstock if its first leader was called President Gouverneur.

Portrait of a Great Man

Here is a series of vignettes attempting to answer that most difficult question, Why was George Washington a great man?

One day in the 1790's word spread through the capital that
George Washington was sick and tired of Thomas Jefferson's
constant bickering with Alexander Hamilton. That afternoon a
man named J. Edgar Hoover was admitted to George Washington's office.

"I have been keeping an eye on this Jefferson," said the visitor,
"and have here ye goods to justify giving him ye heave-ho from
ye Cabinet." He offered George Washington a dossier.

George Washington recoiled and asked what was in it. "Ye
transcripts of Jefferson's activities while wenching," said Hoover,
"as well as recordings of his dinner-table criticism of ye Government." George Washington took the dossier and deposited it in
his fireplace where it burned to ashes while he was having Hoover
thrown into the street.

"It would have been unworthy of my office," he told Martha
Washington afterwards, "to do ye throwing myself."

George Washington's spelling was terrible. Everybody in the
Government was laughing about it. "Ye President," went the
joke, "cannot chew gum and spell at ye same time."

One day Alexander Hamilton suggested that he hire a ghost-
speller, who would make sure that George Washington didn't
spell anything indiscreetly.

George Washington had Hamilton thrown out of his office
with orders not to show his face there for a week. In his explanation to Hamilton, he wrote, "If I begin by hirring a gost to spel
for me, I shall next higher gosts to rite my speches, and then gosts

to do my thinkkeng, and then gosts to construck an immidge for me, and I shal end up with nuthing to do but travl around ye contry makynge foollish speches and eating chiken diners."

Early in his Presidency George Washington was told that he should get out of the office and exercise more. James Madison urged him to take up golf and buy a summer house on Martha's Vineyard, where he could go on summer weekends, and a winter house in South Carolina where he could go on winter weekends.

"One could be called Ye Summer White House and ye other Ye Winter White House, and you could pay for them by taking a loan from—"

George Washington had Madison thrown into the street before the sentence was completed.

All through his later years George Washington was afflicted with a nagging mother. She would go around Virginia telling neighbors that George Washington was a merciless tightwad who never came to visit his old mother and wouldn't send her enough money to live on.

One day a man passionately devoted to George Washington came to see him. His name was Charles Colson. He had heard the stories told by George Washington's mother and thought something should be done to shut the old lady up. George Washington recoiled. "For you," Colson told him, "I would walk over your mother."

George Washington had Colson thrown out of the country.

Tom Paine came to see George Washington about spreading freedom all over the world. Paine was particularly worried about Asia, which he feared would go monarchist unless George Washington committed the United States to stopping the spread of Royalism.

If that occurred, Paine warned, the free world would be outflanked by monarchism in both the Pacific and Atlantic. Paine proposed a vast intelligence agency to destabilize hostile governments, a standing army prepared to fight anywhere on earth, a highly mobile Secretary of State and—

George Washington interrupted to ask Paine if he was feeling well. "Never better," Paine said. George Washington said, "In that case," and had Paine thrown into the street.

George Washington, who was always angry with the press, was furious one morning when the papers reported that he intended to change his image and, for this purpose, had ordered a new shoulder-length wig. Martha, who was in the office, said, "Somebody has been leaking to ye press, and I will bet it is John Adams."

George Washington said, well, there was nothing he could do about it. "Nonsense, George," said Martha. "You are ye President—ye only President ye country has. You could create a Federal police force and have footpads trail this Adams to catch him while committing ye leaks."

George Washington had Martha thrown out of his office.

Why Being Serious Is Hard

Here is a letter of friendly advice. "Be serious," it says. What it means, of course, is "Be solemn." The distinction between being serious and being solemn seems to be vanishing among Americans, just as surely as the distinction between "now" and "presently" and the distinction between liberty and making a mess.

Being solemn is easy. Being serious is hard. You probably have to be born serious, or at least go through a very interesting childhood. Children almost always begin by being serious, which is what makes them so entertaining when compared to adults as a class.

Adults, on the whole, are solemn. The transition from seriousness to solemnity occurs in adolescence, a period in which Na-

Why Being Serious Is Hard

ture, for reasons of her own, plunges people into foolish frivolity. During this period the organism struggles to regain dignity by recovering childhood's genius for seriousness. It is usually a hopeless cause.

As a result, you have to settle for solemnity. Being solemn has almost nothing to do with being serious, but on the other hand, you can't go on being adolescent forever, unless you are in the performing arts, and anyhow most people can't tell the difference. In fact, though Americans talk a great deal about the virtue of being serious, they generally prefer people who are solemn over people who are serious.

In politics, the rare candidate who is serious, like Adlai Stevenson, is easily overwhelmed by one who is solemn, like General Eisenhower. This is probably because it is hard for most people to recognize seriousness, which is rare, especially in politics, but comfortable to endorse solemnity, which is as commonplace as jogging.

Jogging is solemn. Poker is serious. Once you can grasp that distinction, you are on your way to enlightenment. To promote the cause, I submit the following list from which the vital distinction should emerge more clearly:

1. Shakespeare is serious. David Susskind is solemn.
2. Chicago is serious. California is solemn.
3. Blow-dry hair stylings on anchormen for local television news shows are solemn. Henry James is serious.
4. Falling in love, getting married, having children, getting divorced and fighting over who gets the car and the Wedgwood are all serious. The new sexual freedom is solemn.
5. *Playboy* is solemn. *The New Yorker* is serious.
6. S. J. Perelman is serious. Norman Mailer is solemn.
7. The Roman Empire was solemn. Periclean Athens was serious.
8. Arguing about "structured programs" of anything is solemn. So are talking about "utilization," attending conferences on the future of anything and group bathing when undertaken for

the purpose of getting to know yourself better, or at the prescription of a swami. Taking a long walk by yourself during which you devise a foolproof scheme for robbing Cartier's is serious.

9. Washington is solemn. New York is serious. So is Las Vegas, but Miami Beach is solemn.

10. Humphrey Bogart movies about private eyes and Randolph Scott movies about gunslingers are serious. Modern movies that are sophisticated jokes about Humphrey Bogart movies and Randolph Scott movies are solemn.

Making lists, of course, is solemn, but this is permissible in newspaper columns, because newspaper columns are solemn. They strive, after all, to reach the mass audience, and the mass audience is solemn, which accounts for the absence of seriousness in television, paperback books found in airport book racks, the public school systems of America, wholesale furniture outlets, shopping centers and American-made automobiles.

I make no apology for being solemn rather than serious. Nor should anyone else. It is the national attitude. It is perfectly understandable. It is hard to be Periclean Athens. It is hard to be Shakespeare. It is hard to be S. J. Perelman. It is hard to be serious.

And yet, one cannot go on toward eternity without some flimsy attempt at dignity. Adolescence will not do. One must at least make the effort to resume childhood's lost seriousness, and so, with the best of intentions, one tries his best, only to end up being vastly, uninterestingly solemn.

Writing sentences that use "one" as a pronoun is solemn. Making pronouncements on American society is solemn. Turning yourself off when pronouncements threaten to gush is not exactly serious, although it shows a shred of wisdom.

Sociologists could probably catalogue us all into our distinctive cultures by studying the people we are willing to read about on days when there is nothing worth reading about them. There are hordes of people in this country who will read about Johnny Carson's wardrobe, others who cannot sate an appetite for news of Mick Jagger's diet, and others who can sit through the night watching pictures of Hugh Hefner at the Playboy Pad. It is all a question of what you think is important enough to care about when there is nothing going on worth caring about.   **—American Olympians**

The Congress is 535 people, mostly men, mostly white, mostly lawyers and mostly out when you need them.
         —The House Is a Home

The best thing about being President is that it gets you out of American life. I don't know what the theory is behind this, but it is a fact. The first thing we do with a President is shunt him off on a siding where nothing American can ever happen to him. This is why you never see a President waiting in the rain at a bus stop. Somebody decided a long time ago that this was too American for Presidents to be subjected to. After a while, Presidents quite naturally forget that there are such things as bus stops, and if they stay in office long enough they even forget that it rains.
         —The President's Plumbing

What a splendid time to be alive. Everybody holding down cholesterol intake, everybody reading *The Complete Book of Running.* Has there ever been another period in American cultural history when you had the choice of four movies, all playing simultaneously, about people inhabited by evil spirits?
         —Count Your Blessings

Minions of Morality

I was having a martini. It was good. The gin was excellent, the vermouth ratio was just right and the chilling was perfect, but the best thing about it was the annoyed expression it produced on the face of one of the other guests.

Like the others, he was holding a glass of white wine. He approached with policeman's tread. "You realize, of course," he said, "that nobody drinks martinis anymore."

"Nobody but me."

"Do you have any idea how many brain cells it's destroying?"

"Billions," I said.

"And yet," he said, "you go ahead and drink it anyhow. Isn't that rather juvenile?"

"That isn't the worst of it," I said. "I don't jog either."

"Well, it's your heart attack," he said, "provided your brain doesn't go first." The thought of my imminently ghastly demise seemed to improve his day.

I recognized him now. He was one of the agents of physical and moral uplift, the new American tyranny that was determined to bully everybody into living the fully uplifted life whether they wanted to or not.

"As long as you're here," I said, "maybe you could tell me who you have to see in this town to get a parking ticket fixed."

"Aren't you ashamed of being a party to the corruption of public officials?" he asked.

"I am, indeed," I said, "but I'd be twice as ashamed if I contributed to a situation in which it was impossible to get a parking ticket fixed in America. That's one of the things democracy is about."

He rallied the other guests to combat. "Look," he said, "at this symbol of American folly. Busily engaged in destroying himself with his vices, he would pollute the system by trading his vote for a parking-ticket fix. He probably drives three blocks when he wants to go to the drugstore instead of walking."

"And in a gas guzzler," I said. "I used to walk, but joggers kept jeering at me for not jogging, and doctors kept stopping me to warn me off eggs and marbled beef, and excessively decent young people scolded me for flirting casually with divorcees. They said I should establish healthy permanent sexual relationships. The only way I could get any privacy was to drive."

The group moaned unhappily. "Hear that moan?" asked the agent of the uplift police. "That is the cry of an outraged America demanding that a law be passed to take care of people like you."

"No," I said. "That is the moan of people who have been drinking white wine too long in hopes of attaining physical and social uplift. They are moaning for martinis."

The agent turned upon the moaning crowd. "Anybody who would drink a martini would eat eggs," he said. The crowd recoiled in terror. "Anybody who would drink a martini," he said, "would take saccharin."

The crowd retreated rapidly. Several persons dashed to their doctors for emergency injections of fear to help them resist vice and achieve senility intact.

"Anybody who would drink two martinis," I said, finishing my second, "would break up the furniture."

"How juvenile," said the uplift agent as I broke up a lamp and an oak table in very respectable time. It was excellent exercise and far more fun than jogging. It also created a thirst for another martini, which I resisted, as I did not want to give this man the satisfaction of seeing me break up my gas guzzler. I knew there was no hope of bribing Congress into letting Detroit make me a new one. Uplift had cast such a blight over Washington that you could scarcely find a dishonest Congressman anymore.

The commotion had drawn a large crowd outside. They were threatening to pass a law that would require me to be sold over the counter as a prescription drug, but the martinis' fleeting gift of genius enabled me to get rid of them. "Disperse at once," I shouted, "or I shall do something dreadful."

"He's going to smoke," shrieked a voice.

"Worse than that," I said, "I'm going to say a good word for Richard Nixon." They scattered. Of course it was perverse, but at times uplift has to be beaten across the snout to keep it in its place. It made me feel so good I had the third martini after all. Now I need a new car.

Richly Deserved

New York's financial trouble apparently left most Americans rather pleased. Many seemed downright delighted, and salesmen trying to find buyers for Municipal Assistance Corporation bonds reported a positive emotional hostility, suggesting a desire to see the place plowed with salt like conquered Carthage.

The reason for this antipathy is easily explained and easily removed. It is the rich and the poor. The rich of New York are mostly people who left Main Street for Gomorrah-by-the-Bronx and ended up on top of the world.

Few people who have stayed home and watched an old school pal go on to tailored suits, hip flasks and long-stemmed beauties on distant boulevards are spiritually elevated by the spectacle of the hero's success. Many experience twinges of pleasure upon hearing that he is mired in a fen.

New York is filled with these human successes we all went to school with before they began lunching on expense accounts and dictating memoranda in limousines. Only a person with a heart of mush could weep upon hearing that their milieu has gone sour.

To compound the problem, New York is also filled with the poor, the incompetent and the wretched. It is the national conven-

Richly Deserved

tion center for life's losers, and while everybody may not love a winner, this is a country where most people believe nobody can really lose unless he tries to. The high concentration of these misfits in New York is accountable partly to the intelligence spread across the land that New York treats them less abominably than most places.

Thus, Americans have a distorted impression of New York. It is perceived as a city of arrogant successes and coddled failures.

If it is a pleasure to despise such an urban perversion of the American code, it is also a cruel injustice to the great majority of New York's population who will never lunch at Lutèce or cash a welfare check.

A solution becomes obvious. If the successes and the failures were both removed, Americans would again see New York as a place much like Kansas City or Des Moines, full of earnest white-collar toilers and purposeful yeomanry. New York's problems would then be seen to be the same problems everyplace else faces, and a creative spirit of brotherhood untainted by ugly regional and economic envy would prevail.

Disposing of the troublesome element in New York would, moreover, vastly increase the city's per capita wealth and possibly dissolve its financial problem. If all the successes and all the failures were moved elsewhere the population decline would be about 1.5 million persons, the great majority of whom would be people who merely drain the city's wealth.

Relocating a million poor people is relatively easy. One month very soon, they could be mailed, instead of welfare checks, bus tickets to Chicago, or perhaps to Washington. It is a difficult choice. Chicagoans boast that Chicago knows how to cope with poor people but, on the other hand, constant suggestions from Washington that the Federal Government could teach New York a thing or two about handling money argue in favor of letting the Federal city give these wretched losers the benefit of Washington's superior fiscal know-how.

Alternatively, they might be shipped to a suburb. The future of America lies in the suburbs, everyone says. That's where the old virtues abide and people still understand about work, dedication and commitment to American values. Surely, a million losers from New York would profit from the salubrious ethical atmosphere of, say, Armonk, New York, or Chevy Chase, Maryland, which would doubtless be proud to give New Yorkers a lesson in how to deal with such people.

Disposing of the rich will not be so easy. No other city will wish to take them all, lest the new host city incur the same kind of enmity these successes brought upon New York. They must be spread around. Television people might be assigned to Buffalo and the theater crowd to East St. Louis, which could use brighter lights.

The gangster community could be relocated in Roanoke, Virginia, which needs excitement. The beautiful-people set, which flies to the Alps, could go to Salt Lake City, which has a good airport, and the bankers and market kings could be moved to Baltimore, where East Pratt Street would doubtless soon make the world forget Wall Street had ever existed.

Afterwards, no American would dislike New York again, and anyone from anywhere visiting New York would feel so perfectly at home standing on a street corner on a Saturday night eating a piece of cheese that nobody probably would think it worth a visit.

So This Is Depravity
[1976]

With the Democrats coming to New York for their convention, everyone is suddenly worried about sheltering them from the depravity of Times Square, 42nd Street and Eighth Avenue.

Sheltering a Democrat from depravity has always seemed to me to be an offense against nature, like sheltering a fish from water, but a friend in the city government insists that what goes on in

So This Is Depravity

the midtown depravity zone makes Friday night at the typical Democratic Club seem, by comparison, like a Girl Scout picnic.

To persuade me of the degradation which will imperil Democrats unless the area is cleaned up, he took me to a pornographic film parlor off Seventh Avenue, which will lie right in the Democrats' line of vision.

Admission was $5. "You've got nothing to worry about," I told my friend. "You'll never catch a Democrat laying out five bucks for a movie when he can hang out in the convention bars and cadge free drinks from the candidates' 'bag men.'"

"They could be forced to take sanctuary in places like this to escape the prostitutes on Eighth Avenue," he said.

We watched some of the movie. It was shocking. Sex is apparently hard labor. Various persons supported crushing weights in agonizing positions for what seemed endless blocks of time. Exhausted men grunted and toiled like movers trying to get a refrigerator into a fifth-floor walk-up.

"Should Democrats be forced to look at stuff like that?" my friend demanded.

"As friends of the laboring man, they should not only look at it, they should stand up and cheer," I told him.

After a while, the movie dramatized the thankless lot to which woman has been reduced in the sexual labor force. A wan, dispirited woman, obviously defeated by years of sweatshop labor, trudged about naked in a kitchen cooking a chicken dinner.

"Disgusting," murmured my friend.

"But politically powerful," I whispered. "If every Democrat in Congress could see this there'd soon be legislation guaranteeing that poor creature enough pay for her labor to buy a housecoat and put some sirloin on the table."

We fell quiet then, for the woman—small thanks for her toil over a hot stove—had been hung by ropes from the ceiling and was being severely whipped.

From the start of the picture I had realized that sex was a harsh

[25]

and thankless business, but I hadn't guessed it treated its work force like this.

"Every Democrat in the country ought to see this," I said. "Then maybe there'd be legislation forcing sex to treat its workers at least as well as chain-gang prisoners."

"Shut up," said my friend.

We watched in dismay while a giggling, deformed man, who appeared to be an idiot, struggled to move several hundred pounds of listless female furniture that had been placed in awkward positions.

"Exploitation of the mentally defective for the vicious purpose of perpetuating a system of human labor that should have been automated years ago," I said. "If the Democrats see this, you can bet there'll be new fair-labor legislation to bring sex into the twentieth century."

"You're spoiling the movie for me," said my friend.

I subsided, for the movie had switched themes. Having dramatized the odious toil and punishment of sex, the movie now began illustrating various machine operations. It had become essentially an industrial training film designed to instruct sex workers in industrial processes.

For this purpose, seven or eight human bodies were employed. By example, the film demonstrated various functions of machinery. In sex, I gathered, the human body is not regarded as a human body, but as plant equipment.

Now the laborers, who had toiled so dispiritedly in the earlier sequences, took turns demonstrating sundry mechanical processes their machines could perform, and we had a lengthy, didactic illustration of generator upkeep, valve timing, lubrication maintenance, clutch disengagement and other such engineering matters.

I was disgusted and hauled my friend out of the theater. "That cuts it," I told him. "When the Democrats see that sex is turning people into machines, I think we can count on fast action."

"They'll outlaw it," said my friend, somewhat sadly.

"And why not?" I demanded. "Who wants their life afflicted with something like that?"

Caesar's Puerile Wars

Among treasures recently uncovered by Italian workmen excavating for a new discothèque in Rome is an essay entitled "How I Spent My Summer Vacation," written by Julius Caesar at the start of his junior year in Cato the Elder High School. At the request of the Italian Government and the classics faculty of Oxford University, I have translated it from the Latin into English. The text reads as follows:

These things thus being so which also, from the nones to the ides, the impediments having been abandoned, Caesar constituted on the rostrum to exhort his comrades to joy. "No more lessons, no more parchment scrolls, no more teacher's dirty looks," Caesar hortated.

Ten days having subsided, of which the maximum was the first Sunday, Caesar, of whom the parents having to a villa in Capri passed from the injurious sun of Rome to that lambent insular quiescence. Which, therefore, Caesar, being abandoned solely to the urbans of the Rome, he gave himself illicit custody of his father's chariot and hied it through the Roman routes and streets in quest of frumentum.

Between those all which conjoined with Caesar in the paternal chariot, thus to harass the maximally beautiful feminine youth of the city and to make the ejection of empty wine jugs onto the lawns of quaestors, censors, tribunes and matrons, were Cassius and Marc Antony.

Brutus noble was superior to the omnibus, however, of others between Caesar's cohorts. That one opposed his stance to the puerile search for frumentum, stating which things thusly: primary, that harassings of femininity from a moving chariot and ejectings of empty wine jugs had not been predicted by the Cumae Sibyl. Fourthly, that Caesar was a reckless driver which would wreak ire, not only of the gods, but also of Caesar's father, by the arrogance of which he burnt the iron from the paternal chariot wheels.

The which made much risibility itself between Cassius, Marc Antony and Caesar. "Friends, Romans, countrymen," said Brutus, "evince respect to the public thing unless you will have forgotten to obviate too long our patience, O Catiline."

These things having been exhorted, Marc Antony asked Caesar to lend him his ear and declared into it, "Brutus is a sissy. For two denariuses I'd whip his gluteus maximus."

Caesar's ear whence, by forced march, having been manumitted to Cassius, this one, his lips having been juxtaposed to the lobe, uttered, "Brutus thinks too much about the public thing. Such schoolboys are stuffy."

Twelve nights having marched, Caesar and his amiables having collected a six-pack of Falernian wine and three frumentums from South Tiber Girls' Latin School, these made strategems to effectuate nocturnal sport on Capitoline Hill.

To which speeding full of equitation, the chariot encountered an opposing chariot adjoined in much agitation, having debauched from the superior route without attention to the whiffletree connection.

After brusque externalization from Caesar's chariot in a shower of frumentum, Caesar, Cassius and Marc Antony, their wounds being inferior, hurled themselves furioso with epithet upon the two passengers of the intersecting chariot shattered in regard to the right wheel.

"Tacit your puerile abuse," said the younger of those there two. "You are speaking to Cato the Younger and this one here of us two is Pliny the Elder."

Thus which then Caesar being aware, without days of wrath and being recognized by Cassius and Marc Antony as the without whom none, Caesar sent pleas to Cato the Younger and Pliny the Elder lest they make him under arrest for driving a chariot without a license.

Of which indeed it would have been made, the more thus also by which that inspection of Caesar's chariot would have unopened the essence of a can of paint, revealing his juvenilian strategy to paint a graffito on the statue of Romulus and Remus. By high fortune joined the dispute Cicero, having been awakened from his oration by the crash.

"How long, O Julius, will you continue to abut our patience?" asked Cicero. Then was Caesar full of dolor, by which he made the oath to work hard all summer and respect the public thing, whomever would Cicero lend him the money to repair the two ruinous chariots before his father got back from Capri.

"I shall make it thus to be so which," said Cicero, "because of the respect I support for your old genitor."

Thus came Caesar to toil his summer vacation in labored makings and to ponder the glory of the public thing, of which the which is such that there is no posse to improve it, although Caesar is determined to study hard this year so he can grow up and improve it anyhow, whichever is of what.

Pr-s-d-nt--l Sex

Revelations about the sex lives of Thomas Jefferson, John F. Kennedy, and Franklin and Eleanor Roosevelt have prompted many questions about sex and the Presidency. Because of the new public demand for lubricious political disclosure, it is now vital to answer them with full candor. Here are the answers to the questions Americans most commonly ask:

Q: Is it true that President Zachary Taylor liked to be spanked by older women?

A: This is a base canard, which arises from the fact that President Taylor was known as "Old Rough and Ready." Actually, Taylor abhorred spanking, as well as French postcards.

Q: Wasn't George Washington once treated for an Oedipus complex?

A: Yes, but it was accidental. Washington had gone to have his dental plate adjusted and was inadvertently shown into a psychiatrist's office and told to lie on the couch. The doctor began by asking, "How long have you had these feelings about your mother?" Washington was so embarrassed by the hour which followed that he never went to the dentist again. This is why George Washington's false teeth still didn't fit when Gilbert Stuart painted him.

Q: I have always heard that Rutherford B. Hayes wore shiny black leather underwear throughout his Presidency. Is this true?

A: Anyone who knows how hot it gets in Washington in July will realize that this is nonsense. President Hayes, in fact, was an exceedingly prudish President, who blushed when he had to go into a haberdashery and ask to see some long woolen union suits.

Q: Wasn't Abraham Lincoln a foot fetishist?

A: During his career in Illinois politics, Lincoln liked to have women members of the Legislature step on his corns, but he had conquered this vice by the time he became President.

Q: Who was the famous "horse-faced woman" who was brought into the White House nights during the Grant Administration and led out shortly before dawn through secret underground passages?

A: President Grant's famous "horse-faced woman" was not a woman at all, but a horse cleverly got up to look like a woman. Grant devised this scheme to deceive journalists into believing that he was leading a colorful sex life, thus preventing them from discovering that the horse's saddle bags were being used to carry whiskey into the White House and empties out.

Q: How do men as busy as Presidents find so much time for adultery?

A: They don't. This is a common complaint among women summoned to the White House for adultery. They are kept waiting for hours and then squeezed in between the Secretary of Commerce and lunch at the desk. If war breaks out, they may be left forgotten in secret antechambers for months. The great amount of time available to Vice Presidents for adultery has always been bitterly envied by Presidents, and is a major source of so much of the bad feeling traditional between the two offices.

Q: Is it true that Martin Van Buren was a very poor lover?

A: President Van Buren felt the cold more acutely than most men. For this reason, he went to bed every night with two huge hot-water bottles, one on either side of him. These made it difficult to effect intimacies and led to rumors that he was a hard man to get close to. Van Buren's sex life gradually dwindled down to nothing, and he was not elected to a second term.

Q: How often should the ideal President have sexual relations?

A: Never. It is painful for parents to concede that their children have sexual relations and even more painful for children to concede that their parents have sexual relations, but the most painful thing of all is for the American people to concede that their Presidents have sexual relations. Ideal Presidents don't.

Q: I have heard that President William Henry Harrison's nickname—"Old Tippecanoe"—actually derives from a particularly flamboyant and disgusting sexual practice in which he frequently indulged. What was this?

A: The limitations of family-paper journalism preclude an answer to this question here, but it will be fully described in my forthcoming book, *Inside the White House Drawers*, which will be even more incredible than *Jaws* and, I hope, twice as successful.

Cultivated Killing

In Washington I was put in a room with thin walls.

A great killer was being entertained in the next room. From time to time laughter was audible through the wall, but the wall was not so thin that you could hear the conversation and know what the laughter was about. I am certain, nevertheless, that the laughter was civilized, and not about killing, for afterwards I went into the corridor and looked at the members of the party, and they were cultivated men.

Washington, after all, is not Chicago. Although it is a city of great killers, its great killers are cultivated men. You can walk into the corridor and stare at them without fear.

This particular great killer was no great shakes. Washington has plenty of bigger ones. This one was not even very famous. His name would probably not mean a thing to you. It is unlikely that many of his victims had ever heard of him.

One could become mawkish about this aspect of it, could argue that being done in by a man you have never heard of is unfair. "But why should this particular man in faraway Washington have been the agent of our deaths?" the slain might ask. "Is it not unfair for such final effect to have no recognizably human cause?" In this instance, however, there is a rough justice, for the author of their dispatch would think it unfair to be thought a killer. Thus is unfairness compounded in the great world at Washington's disposal.

My killer was, of course, a Government man. Not a soldier. It is doubtful that he has ever killed in person. Maybe he has never seen blood fall in violence. He wears a business suit to work, a conservative necktie in good taste.

The laughter he occasions through thin walls would be in good taste, too. He has wit, good education, excellent taste. He would consider it very bad taste for anyone to describe him as a great killer. In Government service a man does his duty, and for small pay, too, considering what his old college classmates are making in corporation boardrooms.

A good man, you would say. The sort you would like for a neighbor. Civilized, neat, hard-working, cares about the neighborhood, keeps his lawn up, lights out before midnight, works hard for his country.

Goes to the office and spends the day devising programs for killing people. And not soldiers, either. "Enemy," he would call them, in the air-conditioned conference room, among colleagues in their good-taste haberdashery.

Killing "enemy" is decent work, even if they aren't always in uniform. The famous better world a-coming will a-come that much sooner if good men can steel themselves against false squeamishness and face the ordeal of ordering the disposal of those who long for a worse world.

Or so, at any rate, the national security bureaucrats tell themselves. President Nixon once referred to the bombing of Hanoi, which he had ordered, as *his* ordeal.

It is the easy availability of power in Washington that makes these Government people behave so badly in spite of their commendable neckties. Some years back, all the best people came to bipartisan agreement that the most shameful thing a person could do with power was not use it.

Since then everybody who wants to get ahead in Washington has made a great show of being a fierce fellow when left alone in the room with a little power. There seems to be a fear that if there is somebody around so low that it is all right to dump the garbage on him, and you hesitate, everybody will call you a sissy, and you will never be invited to lunch with Professor Kissinger.

Strange values result. Great killers are esteemed for good citizenship. "Not afraid to use power," people say of them.

They are entertained by cultivated men in rooms with thin walls. You can hear their laughter. It is civilized. Everything is in good taste. Such good taste.

As it should be, of course.

In the nation's capital.

Moods of Washington
[1974]

I came to Washington in the high afternoon of the imperial American Presidency, although we did not recognize it as such at the time. Eisenhower, two years into his peaceful occupation of the White House, was a gentle Caesar, more a homespun Marcus

Aurelius than great Julius, certainly no Caligula, but the imperial machinery was already in place awaiting the dynamic *imperatores,* Kennedy and Johnson, and after them the Whittier brooder doomed to inherit the whirlwind.

Washington today is a far world removed from that pastoral age of simple-minded follies and small-bore Rasputins. We were placid and smug with Eisenhower and, Lord!, life was dull here then, but the sense of stability was overwhelming, and under its slumberous ease we took permanence for granted, deplored pessimists and looked forward to an even more golden age when our children would inherit the good life assured by American wealth and power.

And now—panic, dismay, fever, despair. The world is turned upside down. The Huns are at the city gates. The Presidency is a ruin, the Congress a dilapidation. Power is ebbing. The good life is flowing away through our fingers. Everything comes unstuck and nothing works. We sit in the gasoline lines and curse, and seek comfort in sour mirth.

Despite the air of collapse and spoilation, however, or perhaps because of it, the city is also infected with a morbid exhilaration. Washington, after all, is built for murder and cheap melodrama concocted under the shroud. It goes with the imperial territory. Nasty though it is, a taste for it is in the marrow, and Washington can no more resist the appetite than a piney-woods mob can resist attending a lynching.

Nixon apologists have noted the cruel assiduity with which the Washington reporters have undone their tormented captain, peeling away the once impenetrable imperial flesh layer by layer, stripping him down to the bare bones of Haig, Ziegler, Kissinger and Shultz.

Dreadful it may be to the fastidious and the gentlemanly, but, ah, is it not exciting? After the bland porridge of the first Nixon term this garish and awful circus has its compensations. In the Haldeman-Ehrlichman reign, Washington was Des Moines on a Sunday in February. Now it has celebrities again.

The great celebrities are those with the smell of rascality on them. To see someone who has been indicted, to meet a man who wakes in the night with the clank of jail doors echoing out of his dreams—that is the new delight.

Rubbernecks lunching at Sans Souci now strain for a glimpse of Jeb Magruder or Maurice Stans. That splendid showcase room falls into reverential awe for a rare appearance by James McCord. Not an archbishop ascending to the altar, but the famous Watergate burglar himself, who first spilled those fateful beans to Judge Sirica.

Charles Colson, who used to pride himself on such loyalty to Richard Nixon as might stamp his boot marks on his grandmother, is one of Sans Souci's dependable attractions. Coarse japes circle the room as Colson sits to order, for everyone is mindful that he has publicly turned to Jesus since the likelihood of criminal indictment began to trouble him, and cynicism about timely conversions is part of the city's adaptation to the disagreeable new reality.

I do not report this with approval or satisfaction. No great sensitivity is required to recoil from it, but there, nevertheless, are the facts. The obscene and the grotesque have become the commonplace. I was strolling Pennsylvania Avenue past the White House one day recently when the driver leaned from the window of a speeding car and screamed a string of unimaginative sailor's obscenities at our absent President. A few days earlier, a madman had been killed at the Baltimore airport in the act of stealing an airliner which he had planned to dive, suicidally and homicidally, into the White House.

Omens of a civilization coming unhinged are not associated exclusively with the Watergate affair. Unrelated breakdowns of the system add to the general sense of Gotterdämmerung just around the corner. The Government has surrendered before inflation, and has nothing to suggest but prayer.

The Federal Energy Office has six new pronunciamentos every day, and each conflicts with the one before. William Simon, ordering dramatic emergency allocations of gasoline that may or may not exist, is like absurd Glendower boasting, "I can call spirits from the vasty deep," to whom fierce Percy—the oil cartel?—replied, "Why, so can I . . . but will they come when you do call for them?"

The Pentagon thunders blindly on out of all human control. In this celebrated first year of peace with honor it will spend more money than during any year of the Vietnam war. When peace has become more expensive than war, does it not follow that to cut the budget we must go to war? And if so, can anybody, anybody at all, possibly be in charge here?

Wild ironies abound. It has been duly observed that Mr. Nixon's staunchest remaining defenders are those very same heathen Communists he used to denounce as scourges of the planet. The paradox, while amusing, is not inexplicable. His power was once greater than theirs, and the example of its ruin, of how quickly such steel can turn to ash, must wake them in the Kremlin night with visions of rioting in the G.U.M. and graffiti on Lenin's tomb. At such times the brotherhood of power is more affecting than old theological Billingsgate.

I went to the Rayburn Building the other day on trifling business. It was an appalling experience. I had forgotten how preposterous the thing is with its pretentious megatonnage of rock and steel spreading acre after acre down the slope of Capitol Hill in sullen defiance to eternity and man.

It dwarfs the forum of the Caesars. Mussolini would have sobbed in envy.

Inside, one is compelled to dwell upon the insignificance of humanity. Not a single tiny wisp of beauty, nothing that is graceful, or charming, or eccentric, or human presents itself to the senses. Trying to imagine Clay and Webster in this celebration of the death of the spirit, erected to the glory that was Congress, is an exercise in comic despair.

What do we have? Banks of stainless-steel elevators. Miracles of plumbing. Corridors of cemetery marble stretching to far horizons under the most artificial light unlimited millions of dollars can create, a light that abides no shadow, grants no privacy, tolerates nothing that is interesting in the slightest degree.

Moods of Washington

Occasionally a small figure appeared in the distance, grew larger, then larger, then assumed human proportion, then passed and became smaller, and smaller, and smaller. Two ants had passed in a pyramid.

And for what? Why, for office space for our House of Representatives. Not for all 435 of them either, although it is big enough for all 435, as well as the Senate's 100, and the resident population of Syracuse, New York, with room left over in the basements for the Parthenon and the tomb of King Victor Emmanuel.

I go on about the Rayburn Building because it is such an eloquent expression of the sterile grandiosity which has beset Washington since the modest days of the Eisenhower pastorale. One sees efforts everywhere to emulate its arrogance.

The Kennedy Center nearly succeeds for barefaced oppression of the individual spirit. Poor Lincoln, down the road a piece in his serene little Greek temple, would be crumpled like a candy wrapper if the Kennedy Center could flex an elbow. The Pentagon of the warlike forties is matched by a monstrous new Copagon, home for the FBI, astride Pennsylvania Avenue. The vast labyrinths bordering the Mall would make a Minotaur beg for mercy.

My misgivings are not about the wretched architects, who must give Washington what it pays for, but about their masters who have chosen to abandon the human scale for the Stalinesque. Man is out of place in these ponderosities. They are designed to make man feel negligible, to intimidate him, to overwhelm him with evidence that he is a cipher, a trivial nuisance in the great institutional scheme of things.

Those most likely to be affected are men who work in such arrogant surroundings. And so, it is not surprising that of late we have seen a curious tendency for Government people to differentiate between duty to Government and duty to country in a most ominous way.

It is as if the United States Government were a separate power to which Washington owes prime loyalty, and the people at large an obstreperous ally, a less truculent France, perhaps, to be guardedly eyed and kept in line.

Government is revered for itself, is conceived even outside Washington among much of the population as a sort of private, almost sacred entity whose business is not necessarily any of the public's business. Like some vast industrial combine in the soap or processed-food business, the Government now spends hundreds of millions of dollars in public relations and advertising to persuade us of the excellences of its products (war, tax forms, détente, etc.) and to engineer our agreeability to its policies.

An adventurer like Daniel Ellsberg who betrays the sacred scrolls and the secret handshake is hounded and tormented to give example to potential heretics of the price the Government can exact from whoever dares step out of the lodge.

At the very top we see President Nixon engaged in public veneration of the office of the Presidency. When he speaks of it as an institution beyond common public obligation to submit to law, one thinks of a bishop contemplating the Trinity.

John Ehrlichman's reluctance, under Senator Talmadge's questions, to draw the line at murder as a proper presidential activity in stringent cases suggests how detached from people Government has become. When it was merely giving itself airs by showing us through Internal Revenue how it could terrorize us out of our last cent it was still tolerable; when it starts telling us it might even have the right to murder us for its own good—national security—one starts to wonder.

Yet much of the public and even distinguished thinkers hesitate to side with people when the question involves Government's rights. No less a philosopher than Chief Justice Burger was outraged by Ellsberg's publication of classified documents. They belonged to the Government, Burger reasoned, and Ellsberg had no more right to give them to the people than he would have had to filch another man's private property off a taxicab seat.

The Government, of course, commonly leaks classified documents when it deems publication convenient to manipulate public opinion to its advantage. Ellsberg's documents threatened to manipulate opinion adversely. Only the Government, it seems, has a legal right to manipulate opinion with hot documents.

The Rayburn Building, for all its monstrosity, contains, finally, a mouse. It is a monument to Congress, and as Eugene McCarthy used to observe before forsaking the Senate for poetry, monuments exist to memorialize the dead.

Completed in the 1960's when Congress had become a spare tire on the imperial presidential machine, the building tells us something about congressional envy of executive power. If Congress was to have little say about which Asiatic countries we would ravage, about how many billions were to be thinned from the citizenry's purse, about whether we would build a civilized or a barbaric order in the United States or whether we should all risk incineration to save presidential face, it could at least have the biggest house in town.

A sad and touching monument to impotence. And now, of course, it confronts the monumental question of the age: impeachment.

It is endlessly fascinating to watch the terror with which Congress edges toward its dreadful trial. One thinks of an old heavyweight, retired these many years, coming out of his easeful dotage to fight the champion. He has no stomach for it, or more correctly, too much stomach for it. Training is an agony, his legs have forgotten how to work, he gasps and pants and chuffs at the big bag, and has nightmares about the moment when he must finally be alone on his own in the ring.

His hangers-on struggle to infuse him with courage. They shower him with press clippings attesting to the champion's enfeeblement, revealing that the champion's jab has lost its sting, that his hook is gone, that he has been knocked down by sparring partners, that Las Vegas is dropping the odds to even money.

Congress is not persuaded. It has soaked so long in the juices of its own mediocrity that its confidence has withered. It is fearful of Presidents and, therefore, deferential to a fault. It knows how to vote its powers away to Presidents, and how to complain when they use them, but it has been a long time since it seriously considered itself in the imperial weight class with Presidents.

Congress is not suited for this sort of work. In its declining years it has adapted itself for unambitious service chores. These days it is fitted principally for servicing the powerful and the rich, who repay the obligation by picking up the bills for reelecting Congressmen, who repay the obligation by assuring a perpetually rising standard of living for the rich and the powerful, the labor unions among them.

Will Congress deprive their bankrollers and themselves of this sweetheart contract by adopting reforms cutting off their special friends from private access to public lawmaking? Despite Watergate, there is no evidence that the idea has crossed any important congressional minds.

Congress likes things as they are. It likes leaving heavy Government duties to Presidents, and would happily see Gerald Ford assume all the powers of imperial Caesar to be rid of the Nixon awkwardness. It likes its role of slopping more gravy to the hogs. It likes being reelected by constituencies who do not know, and do not much care, who their Congressmen are.

Impeachment imperils everything. It is a congressional act of insolence to an office the electorate venerates. Being urged to strike the king is a disagreeable suggestion to a man happily tending fat sheep. Indeed, the view of President as king is so extensive that Congressmen frequently discuss a Nixon defenestration in terms of royal head chopping.

"History does not look kindly on regicides," Senator Scott, the Republican leader, has observed, thinking no doubt of how the English exhumed the dead Puritans who had beheaded Charles I and hanged their corpses at Tyburn when the crown was restored.

The luckiest member of the House on the day an impeachment vote was taken, Senator Robert Byrd said recently in a singularly congressional metaphor, would be the man anesthetized at Bethesda Naval Hospital undergoing a hemorrhoidectomy.

Nothing would make Congress happier than a Nixon resignation, although cannier Democrats would sorrow at the premature loss of such a splendid political bogey for putting the fear of Republicanism into the masses. In the main, however, Congress prays that the cup may pass and writhes in misery with each new presidential assurance that Nixon will sit it out as unbudgeably as Molotov.

Having penetrated to the heart of the Aztec kingdom and occupied the center of the capital, Tenochtitlán, Hernando Cortes and his tiny conquering army found themselves hopelessly entrapped when the Aztecs perceived that they were not agents of heaven after all, but only a gang of boodlers. At this stage, writes the great Prescott, "there was no longer any question as to the expediency of evacuating the capitol."

Cortes's plight in Mexico foreshadowed Richard Nixon's plight in Washington. Having penetrated to its heart with a tiny band of captains, he rapidly cultivated the sense of a conquest turned to beleaguerment. Beyond the White House fortress he saw a city peopled with an envious and bloodthirsty multitude.

Although he had lived in Washington through the Truman and Eisenhower years, Nixon returned in 1969 with small appetite for the place. His taste runs to palm fronds and hot sand. Washington saw nothing of him, heard little and knew less. We know now that his craving for Florida and California rose in some measure from the sort of edginess that must have affected Cortes over the altar of Huizilopochtli. From inside the White House, Washington appeared to be a murderous confusion of mutinous bureaucrats, jealous and malicious newsmen, raving demonstrators and senile congressional bumblers.

To protect himself, Cortes kidnapped Montezuma, who, dying a captive in his own kingdom, left Cortes locked in his trap with nothing to save him but Spanish courage. Accounts of Cortes's bloody extrication read less like history than like an Errol Flynn screenplay, and like Flynn, Cortes made it. President Nixon's extrication struggle is scarcely less melodramatic, but the outcome is in grave doubt.

"What agitating thoughts must have crowded on the mind of

[Cortes] as he beheld his poor remnant of followers thus huddled together in this miserable bivouac!" Prescott wrote of the escape's denouement. "And this was all that survived of the brilliant array with which but a few weeks since he had entered the capitol of Mexico! Where now were his dreams of conquest and empire? And what was he but a luckless adventurer, at whom the finger of scorn would be uplifted as at a madman?"

Cortes, it may comfort the President to reflect, came back to Tenochtitlán in conquering glory. The President looks forward to glory in the history books. Although his polls are miserable, his men are fond of observing that Harry Truman's were worse, and that now Truman is widely viewed as a great success in the office.

They do not point out that the Democrat Truman's term also ended in a Republican landslide, but, then, they are not much interested in politics anymore. They are fighting now for the judgment of history.

Is there any accounting for this neurotic obsession with being well reviewed, first in the press, then in the history texts, which has characterized our past three Administrations? Is there no reward in the toil of Government more satisfying than seeing oneself flattered by drones and hacks?

The press's surly reluctance to award President Nixon four stars and the blue ribbon with palms has eaten into the soul of good Republicans here, as everywhere, but none of them are more passionate about it than the President himself. In one of his rare unofficial Washington appearances outside the White House, he went up Connecticut Avenue a few weeks ago to attend Alice Roosevelt Longworth's ninetieth birthday party.

Encountering reporters after the party, he fired one of those off-the-top-of-the-head shots at the newspapers which disclose how bitterly he feels the press to be the cause of all his woe.

If Mrs. Longworth "had spent all her time reading *The Post,* she'd be dead now—or *The Star,* for that matter," he said, referring to the two local papers. "She stays young by not being

obsessed by miserable political things all of us unfortunately think about in Washington, instead of the great things which will affect the future of the world—which *The Post* unfortunately seldom writes about in a responsible way."

The daughter of Theodore Roosevelt, Mrs. Longworth has lived in close communion with political Washington for most of this century. Informed later of Mr. Nixon's explanation for her longevity, Mrs. Longworth said, "Nonsense."

In those early Eisenhower years the elite of the governing classes dined each other with minuet precision. Week in and week out, one made the rounds of appointed tables to sit glassy-eyed with boredom while the officially approved dinner conversation ran its tedious course.

We talked about the Communist menace and cold war, about Eisenhower's golf and his passion for Zane Grey. Then a tidbit of gossip, some dreary news from the Capitol about Senator Lyndon Johnson's latest coup, a rumor of a new ambassadorial appointment to the Court of Zippity Zap.

Afterward, we would rise and divide sexually, the women retreating to a boudoir to discuss matters presumably too feminine for mixed conversation, the men to another chamber to hear some old Princetonian from CIA warn us against imminent Communist penetration of the Crocodile Zones, or something equally hair-raising and fatuous.

With Kennedy the ritual of Washington dining became briefly giddy. It was chic to raise a voice now and then at table. If sufficiently well connected at New Frontier headquarters, one could even throw a soft roll at a fellow diner to express disagreement and exhibit fashionable vigor. The Middle Empire was already experiencing the collapse of manners which always accompanies the onset of decadence.

Assassination, Johnson and Vietnam occurred. Now we went to dine with dread and horror. It was certain that before the meal was out men would exchange accusations of treason, Fascism and

related barbarities, that as the result of this dinner one's name would be entered in secret dark books known only to secretive dark men.

With Watergate, dinner went on for hours. Everybody was astounded and delighted by everything. After the total pseudo event of the first Nixon term, there was genuine news again and genuine people behaving like genuine people. One night last fall a group of us sat down at 8 o'clock, fell onto Watergate three seconds later and were still marveling at it when a collapsed wife murmured across the tablecloth that it was 2 o'clock in the morning.

Now the elite still dine each other with minuet precision. Week in and week out, they make the rounds of appointed tables to sit glassy-eyed with boredom about the collapse of civilization and the Huns at the city gates.

At dinner the other night a guest interrupted the talk at the salad course, declaring, "It's time for somebody to say something outrageous."

Everyone pondered a moment, but could think of nothing. "When the outrageous has become commonplace," someone finally observed, "nothing can possibly be outrageous anymore."

I do not entirely agree. Something so unspeakable will eventually happen in Washington that it will strike us as outrageous. I cannot guess what such an event might be. It would have to be something bigger than the thermonuclear holocaust.

American Fat

Americans don't like plain talk anymore. Nowadays they like fat talk. Show them a lean, plain word that cuts to the bone and watch them lard it with thick greasy syllables front and back until it wheezes and gasps for breath as it comes lumbering down upon some poor threadbare sentence like a sack of iron on a swayback horse.

American Fat

"Facilitate" is typical of the case. A generation ago only sissies and bureaucrats would have said "facilitate" in public. Nowadays we are a nation of "facilitate" utterers.

"Facilitate" is nothing more than a gout-ridden, overstuffed "ease." Why has "ease" fallen into disuse among us? It is a lovely little bright snake of a word which comes hissing quietly off the tongue and carries us on, without fuss and French horns, to the object which is being eased.

This is English at its very best. Easing is not one of the great events of life; it does not call for Beethoven; it is not an idea to get drunk on, to wallow in, to encase in multiple oleaginous syllabification until it becomes a pompous ass of a word like "facilitate."

A radio announcer was interviewing a doctor the other day. The doctor worked in a hospital in which he apparently—one never really hears more than 3 percent of anything said on radio —controlled the destinies of many social misfits. The announcer asked the purpose of his work.

The doctor said it was "to facilitate the reentry into society as functioning members"—the mind's Automatic Dither Cutoff went to work at this stage, and the rest of the doctor's answer was lost, but it was too late. Seeds of gloom had been planted.

The doctor's passion for fat English had told too much. One shuddered for the patients at his hospital—"institutional complex," he probably called it—for it must be a dreadful thing to find oneself at the mercy of a man whose tongue drips the fatty greases of "facilitate." He doubtless, almost surely, says "utilize" too, when he means "use," and "implement" when he means "do."

Getting his patients out of the hospital and back home has become for this doctor "the reentry into society," a technological chore of the sort performed in outer space. Having facilitated their reentry into society, he will be able to greet them as "functioning members."

How dreadful it must be, caged up and antisocial in a beauti-

[45]

fully sterilized container for misfits, for a patient to find himself at the mercy of men whose English is fat, who see him as an exercise in engineering and who are determined to turn him into "a functioning member."

Peace, doctors! Of course it is merely a manner of speaking, although the "merely" may not be quite so mere as it sounds.

We are what we think, and very often we think what we say rather than what we say we think.

Long words, fat talk—they may tell us something about ourselves. Has the passion for fat in the language increased as self-confidence has waned? We associate plain talk with the age of national confidence. It is the stranger telling the black hat, "When you call me that, smile." It is the campaign of 1948 when a President of the United States could open a speech by saying, "My name's Truman, I'm President of the United States and I'm trying to keep my job."

Since then campaign talk has become fatter and more pompous, as though we need sounds that seem weighty to conceal a thinness of the spirit from which they emanate. But politicians are not our corrupters here; we are all in love with the fat sound.

There is the radio disk jockey who cannot bring himself to say that the temperature at the studio is "now" forty-five degrees but must fatten it up, extend it, make more of it, score it for kettle drums, by declaring that the temperature at the studio is "currently" forty-five degrees, and often, carried into illiteracy in his passion for fat talk, "presently" forty-five degrees.

Newspapers seem to be the father and mother of fat. The bombing is never the stark, dramatic "intense," but always the drawled, overweight "intensive." Presidents are rarely allowed to "say" the weather is improving; the papers have them "declare" it, "state" it, "issue a challenge for the Weather Bureau to deny" it.

Why do we like our words so fat but our women so skinny?

One of the CIA's few endearing traits is its penchant for making headlines. It is the world's most fully headlined secret agency.
—Our Uncle Is Now Dorian Sam

Inability to get results back at the plant doesn't seem to matter anymore. Nowadays, to get results you go to Washington.

Can't-do guys do all right in Washington, perhaps because lobbying is one thing the can't-do guys almost always can do, and magnificently. Detroit may not be able to dispose of exhaust very neatly, but it can build a beautiful lobbying machine for selling Government the story of its own inadequacy.

What is it in the Washington air that restores the energies of these once dynamic American manufacturers? Something there is that brings out all the old latent half-forgotten ingenuity that seems to have abandoned them back in the home plant.
—The Can't-Do Guys

The decent thing for an inanimate object in America to do is wear out. Most inanimate objects understand and do their duty. Light bulbs are particularly good about it.
—Wearing

Americans treat history like a cookbook. Whenever they are uncertain what to do next, they turn to history and look up the proper recipe, invariably designated "the lesson of history."
—All Right, Jerry, Drop the Cookbook

The truest Pentagon stories are never believed until it is too late. Remember the C-5A? Remember TFX? Remember the electronic wall around Vietnam? Remember Vietnam?
—The Honker at the Pentagon

[47]

Mr. Black Thumb

This is a geranium. Notice the slimy brown gelatinous blooms. Notice the green leaves. In a closed room with cigar smoke, geraniums smell like Germany between the wars.

Geraniums make people want to play Brahms on the cello, but only when the blooms are red. These blooms are slimy, brown and gelatinous to the touch. They evoke no old German parlors, no Brahms, no cello urge.

Why are these particular geranium blooms so disgusting? They have been watered too much. Too much water affects geraniums the way too much gin affects commuters. They lose their fragrance, turn unpleasant colors and dare you to throw them out.

The geraniums got too much water because they were put right here beside these dissolute-looking plants called impatiens. Impatiens, you see, are aquaholics. They start drinking at breakfast and keep right on lapping it up until the last guest is gone at night.

Notice how the greenish-white stalk of the impatiens suggests an unwholesome human membrane. It reaches everywhere and sucks up water. At night it can turn itself into a bat and fly around the country in search of ponds, rivers and rain barrels.

Was not the gardener who placed geraniums and impatiens here, side by side, a fool about gardening? Ah! Do not be so fast to judge gardeners, you urban cliff people, until you have gardened for yourselves. For now, be quiet and learn.

This ruin here, this botanical dilapidation, this wreck, this holocaust of thorns and crinkled brown leaves—this is a rose bed. It was a rose bed very much like this of which Heinrich Himmler, in his black Himmler suit with the state-trooper puttees, was thinking when he smiled ever so tinily and said: "We will make life for the whole world a bed of roses."

Almost all beds of roses look like this between the tenth of June

Mr. Black Thumb

and the second of May in the following year. Rose bushes make us think of June mornings in Appalachian valleys in 1932, for these were the last places and last time that roses looked and smelled like roses. In July of 1932 the rose tycoons discovered how to make them with monosodium glutamate.

We can see from the existence of this brown, thorny eyesore that the gardener here is a sentimentalist. He refuses to believe that the Appalachian roses of June mornings will never come back. Listen carefully. Do you hear the roses whispering among themselves in their black Himmler suits with the canker rot where their state-trooper puttees should be?

They're planning to stick thorns into the gardener's thumb and right index finger when he comes later today to lavish more fertilizer on them.

Here is something less cruel. It is a giant marigold. It is two feet tall and has no leaves and no bloom. People plant them because they remind us of miniature television transmission towers. If we were Japanese we could probably make billions of yen exporting giant marigold stalks to underdeveloped countries starving for television transmissions.

No human labor is required to raise a giant marigold that is all stalk and no leaf or flower. All the work here has been done by bugs. These are probably the same bugs who created that sad brown clump there where the lawn borders the flower bed.

The sad brown clump is actually a beautiful five-foot strip of velvety purple petunias as they appear three weeks after leaving the flower merchant's showroom. These petunias were used as supplemental feeding for the women and children bugs that were not strong enough to compete with the swinish men bugs eating the giant marigold.

Before moving on to the delphiniums, which are going to require good nerves and a strong stomach, perhaps we should go inside for some tea. Maybe even some gin. It must be 5 P.M. somewhere in the American sphere of influence. And even if it is not, the impatiens wouldn't hesitate, would they?

Hesitate and you are lost, they say in the gardening game. Of course, they also say you are lost whether you hesitate or not.

That yellow flower you just snapped off with your heel there —that was a lily. For some reason a lily grows here every so often. It doesn't make any sense, does it?

Bomb Math
[1973]

Wearing his Secretary of Defense hat, Elliot Richardson gave Congress the other day a fascinating glimpse into the mathematics of saving the hearts and minds of remote peoples from whatever our bombers save them from when they bomb their countries.

During one quarter of this year (February, March, April), he said, the United States dropped 145,000 tons of bombs on Cambodia and Laos.

Population of the two countries is about 10 million persons.

Changing tons to pounds, we begin to see light. Territory containing 10 million people has been struck with 290 million pounds of bombs, or, to put it another way, the United States has been bombing at the rate of 29 pounds per person per quarter.

Extrapolating over a full year, we get a more useful mathematical formulation; to wit, that the United States is bombing the average Laotian/Cambodian at the rate of 116 bomb pounds per year.

The interesting question then arises, What is the weight of the average Laotian/Cambodian?

Here we lack data. We know them to be small people physically. We can only guess at what proportion of them is too young to have attained adult weight. Conceding these data deficiencies, it is still not unreasonable to hypothesize that our average Laotian/Cambodian weighs 87 pounds—or three-quarters of the annual bomb poundage used by the United States to save his heart and mind.

Secretary Richardson suggested that the bombing has done its

Bomb Math

job (which is to preserve the Government of a man named Lon Nol) and says it must go on in order to continue preserving this Government. Thus, for those of us interested solely in the mathematics of the thing, Mr. Richardson may fairly be said to have stated the proposition that the present bombing level is sufficient for the saving of hearts and minds.

If so, then we may state a general mathematical formula for determining the bomb poundage the United States will have to drop to save the hearts and minds of any given nation.

This formula is: $HM = (4W/3)P$, where HM represents hearts and minds, W represents weight of the average body containing the heart and mind to be saved and P represents total population of the bombed country.

Example: Suppose it is necessary to save the hearts and minds of Italy. How many pounds of bombs will we need? To get the answer we multiply the average Italian's weight (111 pounds) by 4 and divide the result (444) by 3, which gives us the hearts-and-minds-winning factor number, 148.

To save the hearts and minds of Italy we would have to drop 148 pounds per year per Italian, of whom there are about 55 million. This means we would have to drop 8.14 billion pounds of bombs or, to put it more manageably, about 4 million tons.

"All very well," the taxpayer will say, "but what will it cost me?" Here Mr. Richardson's figures are helpful.

The 63,000 tons dropped on Laos in three months, he reported, cost $99.2 million, or $1,574 per ton.

In Cambodia 82,000 tons were dropped at a cost of $159.5 million, or $1,945 per ton.

In short, it costs 97 cents a pound to bomb Cambodia, but only 79 cents a pound to bomb Laos.

Of the two countries, Cambodia is relatively more advanced economically and has much the larger population. Thus, it appears that per-pound bombing cost must increase in proportion as size and economic complexity of the target country increases.

The bombing of Italy, which is much more advanced than

Cambodia and much more populous, might cost as much as $2.50 a pound. At this price the 4 million tons needed to save Italy's hearts and minds for one year would cost slightly over $20 billion. Expensive perhaps, but who would say it is not worth it to save Venice for the free world?

These figures may improve taxpayer morale, for they give a clear idea of the useful tasks performed with the money we pay our Government.

If, for example, you have paid taxes of $1,000, you may very reasonably tell yourself that your contribution has made it possible to drop 1,266 pounds of bombs (at 79 cents per pound) on Laos, thereby saving the hearts and minds of 10 and 53/58ths Laotians for a whole year. (It takes 116 bomb pounds per year, remember, to save a single heart and mind there.)

With figures like these, you do not have to ask your country what it will do for you. You can tell Laos and Cambodia what you have done for them.

Communicate, Dear Romeo

Everybody is so enlightened these days about relations between the sexes that relations between the sexes hardly seem like relations anymore.

It is sad to see them going the way of baseball, but the hardest part is composing the letters to notify old friends of their obsolescence. I have just mailed such a note to poor dear Othello.

My dear old friend, I said, you can be no more distressed than I to learn that jealousy is regarded by the great majority of young people interviewed for *The New York Times* as hopelessly passé and definitely tiresome.

To have killed dear Desdemona for jealousy—how cruel are the whims of time. In the ultimate enlightenment at which we have now arrived your "tragedy"—will Othello ever forgive me those quotation marks?—your "tragedy" no longer merits the attention of sexually mature youth.

Demanding fidelity was selfish of you. Did you not see that trying to own another's body would make you nothing better than a slave master? I regret, dear misguided old Moor, that you would seem relevant to us today only if you had had the wisdom to share her liberally with Cassio and the Venetian Senate, and to release your own suppressed desires more healthily by bedding Iago.

It will be harder writing to Caesar. He can be vindictive in reply. It will never do to cut the case plainly, to tell him outright that it is simply old hat for anybody, but especially Caesar, to have a wife—much less a wife who is above suspicion.

"Julius," I might say, "enlightenment must eventually overtake us all—even Caesar."

Writing to Penelope was rather fun. Ulysses, as you know, has been caroming around the Mediterranean for years having a ball while poor, simple-minded Penelope sits home in Ithaca resisting suitors. I told her about swinging.

Let us face it, my dear old straight Penelope, I told her, the day when wives sit home at Ithaca while hubby cuts up at conventions from one end of the Mediterranean to the other—those days have given way to enlightenment.

Unless you want to be the joke of the late twentieth century you had better tear the suits off a few of those suitors this coming weekend and stop being so uptight about your natural healthy desires.

If the tone of this note seems brassy and coarse, it may be because I have just finished writing to my great old friend and idol, Romeo Montague. My greatest ambition had always been to burn with a monogamous passion so fierce that I might climb the highest balcony.

Forgive this embarrassing confession. I intruded it only to indicate how hard it was to break the news to Romeo.

It was all just damned childish silliness, Romeo, I told him, trying to strike a virile note. Machismo is important to Romeo with his Latin blood. His favorite writer was Ernest Hemingway.

You made too much of sex, Romeo, I told him. And what is sex? As we now perceive, thanks to our enlightenment, sex is only sex, a sigh is just a sigh. A handshake can be far more vital, Romeo, because as we now know, the important thing in life is not sex but communicating, and there can be more communicating in a simple handshake than in all the balcony climbing in Verona.

Oh, Romeo, oh, Romeo! It was so—so—so *straight of you* to insist on getting married. I mean, Lord! A friar even! A church ceremony!

If you had wanted to speak to us here in the enlightened lavender twilight of the twentieth century, Romeo, you could have done it so beautifully, just by getting together with Mercutio and Tybalt and Paris and Juliet and some of the other Verona girls who hung out around the fountain, and gone off to Rimini and lived in a commune. But married!

That was the hardest letter to write. To the idol after whom one's own life had been patterned. It had not seemed a bad life until then. Not so deep as a well, nor so wide as a church door, perhaps, but it seemed likely to do. And now, the enlightenment . . .

Ah, well. Who gets the bad news next? Emma Bovary.

"Poor dear Emma: Dreadful news—"

Small Kicks in Superland

I often go to the supermarket for the pure fun of it, and I suspect a lot of other people do too. The supermarket fills some of the same needs the neighborhood saloon used to satisfy. There you can mix with neighbors when you are lonely, or feeling claustrophobic with family, or when you simply feel the urge to get out and be part of the busy, interesting world.

Small Kicks in Superland

As in the old neighborhood saloon, something is being sold, and this helps clothe the visit in wholesome material purpose. The national character tends to fear acts performed solely for pleasure; even our sexual hedonists usually justify themselves with the thought that they are doing a higher duty to social reform or mental hygiene.

It is hard to define the precise pleasures of the supermarket. Unlike the saloon, it does not hold out promise of drugged senses commonly considered basic to pleasure.

There is, to be sure, the brilliant color of the fruit-and-vegetable department to lift the spirit out of gray January's wearies, provided you do not look at the prices.

There are fantastic riches of pointless variety to make the mind delight in the excess that is America. In my neighborhood supermarket, for example, there are twenty or thirty yards of nothing but paper towels of varying colors, patterns and thicknesses.

What an amazing country that can make it so hard for a man to choose among things designed for the purpose of being thrown away!

The people, however, are the real lure. As in the traditional saloon, there are many who seem determined to leave nothing for anybody else. These sources prowl the aisles with carts overflowing with excesses of consumption. Twenty pounds of red meat, backbreaking cartons of powdered soap, onions wrapped lovingly in molded plastic, peanut butter by the hundredweight, cake mixes, sugar, oils, whole pineapples, wheels of cheese, candied watermelon rind, preserved camel humps from Persia . . .

Groaning and sweating, they heave their tonnage up to the checker, see it packaged in a forest's worth of paper bags and, the whole now reassembled as a tower of bags pyramided on another cart, they stagger off to their cars, drained of their wealth but filled with pride in their awesome capacity for consumption.

At times, seeing such a customer trying to buy up the whole supermarket, one is tempted to say, "Come now, my good woman, you've had enough for the day." Unfortunately, the ambience of supermarkets does not encourage verbal exchanges. In this it is inferior to the saloon.

Urban people, of course, are terribly scared nowadays. They may yearn for society, but it is risky to go around talking to strangers, for a lot of reasons, one being that people are so accustomed not to have many human contacts that they are afraid they may find out they really prefer life that way.

Whatever the reason, they go to the supermarket to be with people, but not to talk with people. The rule seems to be, you can look but you can't speak. Ah, well, most days there is a good bit to see. The other day in my own supermarket, for example, there was a woman who was sneakily lifting the cardboard lids on Sara Lee frozen coffee cakes and peeking under, eyeball to coffee cake, to see if—what?

Could she have misplaced something? Did she suspect that the contents were not as advertised? Whatever her purpose, she didn't buy.

Another woman was kneading a long package of white bread with her fingertips, rather like a doctor going over an abdomen for a yelp of pain that might confirm appendicitis. I had seen those silly women in the television commercial squeeze toilet paper, and so was prepared for almost anything, but this medical examination of the bread was startling.

The woman, incidentally, did not buy. She left the store without a single purchase. This may have been because she looked at the "express checkout" line, saw that it would take forty-five minutes to pay for her bread and decided bread was not worth the wait.

(I am making a study of how supermarkets invariably manage to make the "express checkout" line the slowest in the store, and will report when interviews are completed.)

I suspect that woman who left empty-handed never intended to buy. I think she had simply become lonely sitting alone in her flat, or had begun to feel claustrophobic perhaps with her family, and had decided to go out to the supermarket and knead a loaf of white bread for the pure fun of feeling herself part of the great busy world.

Careless, Careless

It was in the late 1940's that the United States finally succeeded in losing an entire country. In those years it lost China. It was an astounding feat, comparable to losing a bull elephant in a studio apartment.

Many Americans did not even know we had China until we lost it. I remember at the time meeting a politician. "Doesn't it make your blood boil that we've lost China?" he said. He said that if elected he would find it and, what's more, would punish the people who had lost it. I was too terrified to admit that I didn't even know we had had China.

I tried to bluff through my ignorance. "Where was it the last time you saw it?" I asked.

"Where was what?" he demanded.

"China," I said. "Are you sure we didn't leave it in the garage?"

"You must be an imbecile," he said, smiling happily and plastering a bumper sticker on my lapel. "Vote for me."

I did. After a while I heard we had lost Cuba. The politician came back and asked if my blood wasn't boiling. I told him I hadn't been so mad since my wife lost the car keys. People ought to be more careful with things like Cuba, I said.

"What an idiot you must be," he smiled. "Don't forget to vote."

I voted him back to Washington and, sure enough, he came knocking at the door again. "They've lost Cambodia," he said. "Doesn't it make your blood boil?"

Actually, I didn't think losing Cambodia was anywhere near the same class as losing China, or even Cuba, but I said it was terrible and would certainly vote for him if he would give me some information. He agreed.

I asked him what other countries we had. "I never know we have these countries until you come around to announce that we've lost them," I explained. "I'd like to know what we've got in safekeeping so I'll know what to expect next time."

"We could lose Turkey, Portugal or South Vietnam any day unless I am elected," he said.

"Could we lose Russia?" I asked.

"What a half-wit!" he said with delight, and urged me to vote several times.

Shortly afterwards, I went to Washington to see if he had heard of anyplace interesting being lost. His secretary, hearing the reason for my call, sent me instead to the White House Lost and Found Nations Office. "Lost any good countries lately?" I asked a brilliant, hard-working director with an impeccable dossier at the FBI.

He was outraged. "You don't just lose countries, you simpleton," he said. "A country is not like your eyeglasses. You have to work and plan for years in order to lose one."

"It must be fascinating work," I suggested. "Do you think I could do it?"

"You amateurs!" he snorted. "Tell me, what would you do if you were assigned to lose England?"

I told him I would take it up to the attic in my hip pocket and then get distracted going through some old trunks, during which time it would probably sneak out of my pocket, crawl downstairs and hide itself in the garage rafters.

"That's not the way to lose a country," he said. "The first thing you do is find out what the English people want. Then you locate a general who believes they have all been duped by Communism, and you finance him to pull a coup, suppress the newspapers, ship the Queen to Switzerland, jail the House of Commons and then hold free elections which give every Englishman the chance to vote for the general.

"If you're lucky, some farmers will take down their guns and start shooting at his headquarters in Windsor Castle. You then ship him a billion tons of bombs and bullets to defend himself against rebel strongholds in York, Manchester, Birmingham, Leeds, Canterbury and Bognor Regis.

"When England is starved and decimated, you ship the general several millions for pin money, so he can build a heated swimming pool for himself and an unheated prison for anybody he doesn't like. As the populace rises en masse against him, you send him more bullets to honor your commitment, and in ten or fifteen years England is lost."

"Does it always work?"

"We've been doing it for twenty-five years, and it hasn't failed yet."

It made my blood boil, which didn't help those poor, lost countries one bit, but somewhere, I know, a politician smiled.

Betrayed

In *Love and Death,* Woody Allen gets the girl again. It is becoming a bad habit of his. Woody Allen should never get the girl. It is bad enough to go to the movies and have to watch Robert Redford get the girl. Or Paul Newman. Even Jack Palance. A man can take that. One accepts the American reality, realizes that the getting of the girl is inevitable if blessed with Redford's masculine beauty, Newman's insouciance, Palance's magnificent cheekbones. The getting of the girl is their cinematic due.

Before them, Gable, Cooper, Grant and a pack of irresistible leading men extending back to Valentino taught us resignation to our inferiority. Yes, such charming devils would always get the girl. It would be useless to compete.

One felt gray, puny, lifeless, slow-witted, heavy-footed, dense and timid sitting there in the dark watching them always get the girl. Feminists now say that women who grew up on these films were scarred, that they came to view themselves as despicable sex objects because movie women existed only to be gotten by leading men. But what of the men who grew up on them? Were they not also scarred? Were they not cursed with a lifelong sense of masculine inferiority?

If the movies created a sense of inferiority in men, they did occasionally compensate with a character so timid, so incompetent, so awkward, absurd and inconsequential, that the dreariest mouse of a man could sit in the dark and feel like a prince of lovers. Men tired of seeing Valentino get the girl could recover their self-esteem by watching Chaplin's tramp, a man so inferior he could get nothing but a nightstick over the skull. The tramp did occasionally wind up with the girl, but he was so inept at the techniques of amour that one knew he would immediately lose her to the first passing Valentino.

Woody Allen has some of Chaplin's power to make us feel superior by playing the loser. He makes us laugh by being more miserable in almost every respect than the most miserable specimen of humanity in his audience. We sit laughing in contentment with our own superiority while he fails tests of manhood which the meekest of us could pass without exertion.

Then he betrays us. He gets the girl. And not just any girl. She is the ultra sex-symbol girl, the fantasy girl displayed full-length in men's daydream magazines. In *Love and Death,* she is the most desirable courtesan in Russia, a girl brave men have died for, a girl whom Gable, Cooper, Grant or even Valentino might not have been able to get without adding a bit of brilliantine to their locks.

No problem for Woody Allen. All it takes him to reduce her to jelly is a bit of eye-rolling at the opera house.

It is appalling. Allen has been traveling under false colors. We have been gulled, made to feel like one of the schlemiels Woody Allen has been impersonating. He is not a schlemiel at all, but a Valentino in schlemiel's eyeglasses, and he has made fools of us by luring us into feeling superior and then sneaking away to get the most desirable girl in the house.

All right, we suspend judgment. After all, Groucho Marx often almost got the girl, but we were always saved by Harpo and Chico parading through the love nest, thereby establishing that Groucho was no more apt at amour than the rest of us. W. C. Fields once came very close to getting the girl, if the term can be applied to Mae West, but when he cuddled up under the blanket, Mae had substituted a goat, and our sense of superiority was saved.

Surely Woody Allen, setting off for the courtesan's boudoir, is setting himself up for similar humiliation.

Alas, he is not. The betrayal only becomes worse. Woody Allen goes ahead and shamelessly gets the girl. Bad enough, but the twist of the knife is still to come. In the following scene the girl, this empress of passion, notifies the audience that Allen is the greatest lover she has ever embraced, and she is not kidding.

I couldn't have been more crushed if Hopalong Cassidy had announced he was joining Gay Liberation.

Woody Allen has done this in earlier movies, and I wish he would stop it. It is one thing when the full-time girl getters— Newman, Redford and company—send you out into the street feeling like a schlemiel. When America's leading schlemiel sends you out feeling like a schlemiel, that, friend, is having schlemiel-hood ground into your soul.

Come on, Woody—be a lousy lover.

Religion, or Possibly Gin

Here were people with a lust to know everything. They had a vision of total information. They believed in intelligence with a faith which bordered on religion.

Intelligence. One still senses a vocal genuflection when the word passes over their lips. God may be love, but knowledge is power. They were like their predecessors in exulting in the very special, inside, eyes-only, supersecret, pried-out-with-latest-electronic-miracle-device, ultra-classified information which was theirs alone, as they believed. Faith in intelligence was very presidential, like "Ruffles and Flourishes," the Secret Service men with the heaters under their jackets, the airplanes, clicking heels, vacation White Houses. Johnson had had the faith. Kennedy. Maybe Eisenhower.

"Only the President can have all the facts." Who said that? Johnson probably. Certainly his apologists, sycophants, public-relations flunkies, who may even have believed it. Whether they ever said it or not, the Nixon men surely had it engraved on the back walls of their minds, for they pursued intelligence with the intensity and pure devotion of true believers.

Theirs was a faith in Total Intelligence. In their dream of ultimate fulfillment, absolutely everything was knowable. But could the FBI be trusted to bring about the ultimate fulfillment? Not half likely. Not with old Hoover there. Hoover sat on information, kept it for himself, wouldn't share.

Total Intelligence was impossible under such conditions. Accordingly, retired gumshoes from the CIA and the New York police force were brought in. The miracle workers of electronics were summoned to sow secret ears through the country.

Johnson's pride in exclusive knowing centered upon the delusion that he had all the facts about Vietnam. The new crowd wanted more than that. They wanted all the facts about everything. When somebody obtained some facts the new crowd had wanted to keep for themselves, they wanted the facts about who let the inside facts out of the bag, and why, and what he was telling his psychiatrist, and whether he ever read comic books, went to the movies, could help his kids with the new math.

One imagines Washington in that new electronic age of faith, its air filled with tiny little amplified conversations bleeping through the night, out of bugged telephones and wired martini olives, into the incessantly rotating spools of the tape-recording machines. One fancies thousands of nodding monitors, earphones clamped to skulls, nodding over a thousand miles of slowly moving tape.

Were these monitors chosen because they had no tongues, because they could not understand English, because they were willing to submit afterwards to execution to protect the sanctity of Total Intelligence? An excessive flight of fantasy perhaps. And yet—

Was not the President himself submitting to total bugging and total wiretapping? Were his closest advisers not having their own closest advisers bugged to add to the fund of Total Intelligence? Were the President's agents not toiling to add to the sum of Total Intelligence information about whether his political opponents liked girls and whether they preferred scotch or bourbon?

The astounding thing, of course, was that the harder the White House labored to know absolutely everything, the less it knew about the relatively few things that were its business to know about.

Prodigies of intelligence-gathering were being performed; the tapes were turning night and day; yet it took months and months and months for the President to learn something he could have found out by buying a newspaper; to wit, that he had a problem down at the Watergate.

The Administration's information was flawless on Senator Muskie's 1972 handshaking scheduling, yet nobody at the top was able to find out that the Air Force was bombing Cambodia 3,500 times during 1969 and 1970 when U.S. policy was to treat that country as a neutral.

Intelligence may have become Presidents' gin. A little of it taken discreetly can ease life along more gently. If one becomes hooked on it, however, it becomes hard to find out what day it is.

In the Absence of
Serious Men

The confession by the President's man, H. R. Haldeman, that he was responsible for intelligence during the Nixon campaign of

1972 must have been hard to make for intelligence was the one commodity in which the campaign was poverty-stricken.

It had millionaires in surplus and hard-hats in the side pocket, and as soon as President Nixon decided not to campaign he could have been declared the winner by forfeit, for in George McGovern the Democrats had contributed a candidate who could have beaten no one except the Mr. Hyde whom Richard Nixon becomes when he takes to the stump.

Nixon said afterwards it was all over the night the Democrats nominated McGovern. One wonders why he didn't tell Haldeman. Perhaps he thought a man responsible for campaign intelligence would not have to be notified of the obvious.

Whatever the case, the Nixon campaign was permitted to proceed at peak output as though up against a Roosevelt or an Eisenhower. Maybe the President didn't have the heart to call it off. Everybody, after all, had been looking forward to a fight, and now if there was to be no fight there could at least be a picnic.

Intelligence failure was rampant. First off, somebody decided that the White House front organization for the campaign would be called the Committee to Re-elect the President. Where was the intelligence division at this point? Why didn't Haldeman say, "But if we call it that, somebody with an eye for a cheap acronym is going to call it CREEP?"

The spirit of Laurel and Hardy was stalking the landslide. Intelligence failed, and CREEP it became.

Enter Maurice Stans, the greatest squeezer of the rich since the estate tax. On behalf of CREEP, Stans amassed a pile of campaign swag big enough to reelect the President for the rest of the twentieth century. This was typical of the pointlessness of things. The President was constitutionally blocked from running for the rest of the century and didn't need any money to win in 1972.

Whether the satchels full of cash, the Mexican money-laundering operation, the Arab bazaar in ambassadorships—whether

[64]

In the Absence of Serious Men

these are symptoms of a new low in political rot or merely low comedy in slightly bad taste will depend on the observer's political bias. Nobody, on the other hand, will disagree about their dumbness.

At the top there had been intelligence failure. Nobody had thought to send CREEP a note saying, "What's the point of embarrassing ourselves? We've got it won."

There was not even much thought given, apparently, to splitting the money with Republicans running for Congress. Another intelligence failure. When the landslide was over the Republicans had gained not a dime at the Capitol, and the President had lost a few friends in his own party because of CREEP's sitting on that superfluous hoard.

Everything was superfluous in the best Laurel and Hardy tradition. Stans's millions. The Mexican laundry. ITT's $400,000, or $100,000, depending upon which superfluous figure you choose to believe.

The Watergate business, the well poisoning, the electronic eavesdropping, the gumshoe surveillance of important Democrats—it is too kind to dismiss all this as merely superfluous dumbness. It is all too strongly suggestive of overgrown boys playing at a fantasy of government, instead of men at work on the intractable complexities of the state's business.

Haldeman opened the question when he said he was responsible for intelligence. Intelligence? Why in the world does a political party require a big White House mucky-muck to play CIA and KGB when any respectable newspaper reporter in Washington can spend three hours on the telephone and learn more about the Democratic Party than even a Republican President wants to know?

This suggestion of men enacting boyish fantasies is more worrisome than whatever crimes may have been committed in the heat of game playing. Serious men do not carry on the way these people did. It is disturbing to discover that this huge, potentially demonic superstate in which we abide can fall so readily into the hands of unserious men.

The Days They Used to Make

"Have a nice day" has replaced "This is a stickup" as the most frequently spoken four-word sentence in the American language.

Give a waitress a tip and she says, "Have a nice day." "Have a nice day," advises the cabdriver collecting his fare. Say, "Fill her up" to the gas pumper and he replies, "Have a nice day." The other morning after I had paid the bakery woman for a coffee cake and been urged to have a nice day, I asked, "Where do I get one?"

"What?" asked she.

"A nice day," said I.

"What are you talking about?" she asked.

"You just advised me to have a nice day. The idea appeals to me. I wonder if you know where I can get one."

The baker had come out of his oven and was watching as if he expected to hear, "This is a stickup."

"This dude making trouble out here?" he asked.

"Have a nice day," I told him, departing.

I went to Cromley & Swotts. ("Everything for the man who can afford anything. Bumbershoots, stuffed elephants, decorated rooms and silver barstools our specialties.")

"May I help you?" asked the clerk.

"I'd like to see something in a nice day."

"Right this way," he said, entering the Day department and taking a gray, windy day off the rack. "Our standard model," he said. "It has seven bills in the morning mail, a two-hour breakdown in the subway, a traffic ticket, a fresh spaghetti-sauce stain on the necktie and a notice that your auto insurance has been canceled."

"You don't understand. I said I wanted a nice day."

He was miffed. "Our days," he said, "are the nicest in the

The Days They Used to Make

trade. This is only an average day, I'll admit, but it is one of the nicest average days made and the wind and grayness are very high quality."

"I'd rather have something with sunshine in it and no bills at all."

He said he had just the thing. It was dazzling. "Isn't that sunshine splendidly woven?" he asked. "And look. Not a bill anywhere in it."

"I like it."

"You've seen nothing yet," he went on. "Look, it has a trip to the ball park where the home team loses by a score of 12 to 1. The air conditioning at home breaks down and when you get back it is 110 degrees in your house and the telephone is ringing and —beautiful detailed workmanship here—your children are calling for you to wire $75 immediately."

"It's a nice enough day," I said. "But not really a nice day. What do you have with flowers in it and a luscious fat check nobody had been expecting and a smile from a charming woman?"

"Our special," he said, taking down a day embroidered with wild roses and popcorn. "It comes complete with this remarkably lovely woman in this quite exclusive restaurant and a luncheon bill for $68. And here is a delightful surprise. At the bus stop outside the restaurant door, as you leave you run into your wife."

"And I suppose, to cap it off, the dog is run over by a truck just at dinnertime," I said.

"Nothing that elegant," he demurred. "The cat comes in with a dead bird in its jaws."

It wasn't my idea of a nice day. "For one thing, there isn't any music," I complained.

"Music," he said. "Why didn't you say so? Look at this." He took down a lovely quiet Saturday. Delicious breakfast. Strains of Haydn on the phonograph wafted through the morning. "And in the afternoon," he said, "notice the children coming to visit with their electric trumpets, amplified drums and brand-new rock records."

The whole lower half of the day pulsated with thunderous blare and roar. "Note the magnificent headache with which it ends," he urged, "right after the magnificent quarrel with the neighbors."

"Don't you have just an ordinary, nice, quiet day?"

"Something with a funeral, perhaps?"

"Nice! Nice! I want a nice day! Not a nice day for a funeral! What kind of junk are you trying to sell here?"

The manager appeared with armed men in uniform. "Is there some problem?"

"He doesn't like our nice-day selection," said the clerk.

"Really?" said the manager. "Was there something particular you had in mind?"

"Just a plain, ordinary, sweet, uneventful, serene, inexpensive, old-fashioned nice day with no bills, no dead birds and a victory for the home team."

The manager smiled through veils of contempt. "They don't make them anymore," he said. "Can we show you something in a stuffed elephant?"

I walked out. "Have a nice day," said the manager.

Hand an American a problem and he immediately takes it to court. Half the population over the age of thirty is at law because it lacks the ingenuity to solve such humdrum problems as how to live with somebody who snores or dislikes your taste in television, and how to divide up the dishes, the children, the house and the jewelry before plodding on into middle age.

As a result, these people are often well advanced toward senility before the law has straightened out their problems for them. Everybody knows some aging bankrupt who got that way because he and his former wife didn't think they could solve the problem of what to do on Saturday night without hiring lawyers.

—The Courts of First Resort

Watergate left Washington a city ravaged by honesty.
—Honestly

One development in the American pursuit of happiness is the feelgood movement. The country is swarming with swamis from Asia, quacks from California and evangelists of sexual joy, narcotic paradise, communal contentment and dining ecstasy. My misgivings about feelgoodness are heightened by the origins of its preachers. Asia, California and the psychological sciences do not have an impressive record at making people feel good. In Asia nobody has felt good for centuries.

The feelgoodists are heretics who have turned the pursuit of happiness into a search for the endless smile, the total serenity, the complete fulfillment of self, the supreme orgasm and the perfect doughnut. Society becomes a service station to supply fuel and spark plugs for easy motoring from womb to tomb. Just thinking about it makes you feel bad.

—The Pursuit of Unhappiness

[69]

One Very Smart Tomato

I had coffee with Dr. Irving Slezak, the brilliant genetics researcher. He brought some genes and a chopping knife. Working with the skill of a master salad chef, he chopped one of the genes into dozens of tiny parts, threw half of them away and tossed the rest into a salad bowl.

He repeated the process with the second gene, then stirred the bowl vigorously, at the same time explaining. One gene, he said, belonged to a truck driver and the other to a state policeman. By blending the two, he hoped to produce a brand-new form of life —a truck driver who, immediately upon exceeding the fifty-five-mile-an-hour speed limit, would pull himself over and give himself a ticket.

This was but a small example of the new fuel-saving developments possible through research in recombinant DNA. He had bigger projects afoot in the lab. He became confidential.

"Would you believe a topless go-go dancer crossed with a seal?" he whispered.

"You're mad, Slezak, mad," I said.

"They won't think I'm mad when I produce a topless dancer who can perform without a single goose pimple in a room heated to a mere thirty-six degrees Fahrenheit," he said.

So far he had succeeded only in producing a seal that liked to take off its brassiere and twitch to loud records, he confessed. But, in the meantime, other miraculous gene stews were being cooked.

Even now he was combining the genes of a midget with the genes of an interstate highway to produce a smaller turnpike which would force people to drive smaller cars.

"Impossible," I said. "Turnpikes don't have genes."

"If that's right," he asked, "how come I've already got seventeen midgets with 'Do Not Cross Median Strip' signs growing in their navels?''

No wonder so many people were opposed to recombinant DNA projects. Slezak speared a coffee gene in his cup and held it up, then dropped it on the table and before it could wiggle to safety chopped it into tiny pieces.

"Now give me one of your genes," he said.

"What for?"

"By blending a human gene with a coffee gene," he said, "I shall reduce the outrageous price of coffee by producing a man with built-in caffeine. He will no longer need coffee."

"But he'll need constant infusions of milk and sugar."

"Then I'll cross him with a cow and a sugar beet," said Slezak.

"Use your own gene," I said.

"It's too dangerous," he said. "America isn't ready for a mooing beet that's absolutely brilliant. It still doesn't know what to do with Henry Kissinger."

I edged a safe distance from the great scientist's chopping blade and switched the subject. "Is it true, Dr. Slezak, that you are actually a clone?"

"A canard," he snorted. "A distortion of truth spread by my enemies who would have the world believe that the great Irving Slezak had himself cloned from a wart on his ear, that this clone overpowered him one dark night in a frenzy of wartish rage, hurled his genes into a Venus's-flytrap and assumed Slezak's identity. A vicious fiction."

The truth was far more botanical, he explained. He, Irving Slezak, had for years been enslaved by a two-pack-a-day cigarette habit. Being unable to abandon his brilliant work for the two years it would take him to break the habit, he decided to outwit it.

"And so," he said, "I spent two weeks locked in the lab crossing myself with a tobacco plant."

"Brilliant," I cried. "Once you became partly tobacco, you immediately lost the desire to take tobacco into your system."

"Not quite," said Slezak. "Unfortunately, an imbecilic lab assistant had supplied tomato genes instead of tobacco genes. The two plants are related, of course, but that was no excuse for the slipup. The result was that I lost all hunger for tobacco but developed an insatiable appetite for salt and pepper, Worcestershire sauce, bacon, lettuce and vodka."

Aha, I thought: this explains why Slezak takes his coffee with two heaping teaspoons of mayonnaise.

"A pity," I said, as he brushed a tomato worm off his lapel and rose to return to the service of science.

"Not at all," he said. "Once I have crossed myself with toasted whole wheat I'll be a B.L.T. and never have to wait again for a stool at the lunch counter."

May Day Commune

The number of people who love nature is astonishing. You see them in overalls sitting on the ground playing banjos and combing each other's hair. Their songs tell of glorious sunsets and of finding love on a glacier while the moon whispers of a full harvest.

Others, wearing gray suits and blank faces, walk in the flora on the magic eve of May doing nothing so far as the eye can tell, but those pipes give them away. They are up to their old tricks. They are communing with nature.

Confront a pipe smoker with nature on a spring day and he becomes helpless. He must commune with it. Pipe smokers may be the most relentless communers in the culture. No wonder the wives of pipe smokers are such a suspicious lot.

The worst trait of the entire nature-communing breed, however, is their insistence on boasting about themselves. "You won't believe how much nature I communed with today," they are always saying. Thoreau was the worst of these chest thumpers. He went about the country badgering people because they were not in his weight class when it came to nature communing, and then he wrote books boasting about his boasting. He was the Muhammad Ali of nature communing.

Thoreau's example survives unpleasantly in most of the otherwise excellent people who love nature today. They are intolerant of all who do not share their passion for leaf mold and northeast gales.

In this vice, they are like certain blessedly graceful people who will not leave the clods of the world alone until they have been mounted on skis and made a laughingstock for coming down with comminuted compound fractures.

There is nothing wrong with skiing if you are built like elastic, and there is nothing wrong with nature if you are one whom nature loves. Unfortunately, nature loves few and dislikes many.

The metaphor about Mother Nature is wrong. There is nothing motherly about nature. Nature is more like one of those ugly drunks you are always in danger of encountering in a strange bar —short-tempered, quixotic, dangerous.

Some people have an instinct for cozying up to such characters. For them, he may be a giver of boons, picking up the tab, offering the use of his car, extending a $20 loan. Some people are blessed by nature.

When they sit on the ground to play their banjos, nature does not saturate their overalls with lumbago-producing dews and muds, or dispatch a mosquito to bleed an exposed ankle.

Nature likes these people. When they go to some wretchedly frigid glacier, nature does not open a crevasse under them and suck them into her maw. Nature heats them with passion, and then propels a similarly warmed party of the other sex up onto that same glacier, and then orders the moon to start whispering of harvest.

Such people are highly favored. I would hold nothing against them but envy if they would stop twitting me for not visiting glaciers and sitting on the ground with a banjo. Nature does not favor us all equally.

Over the years, I have come out of paranoia about nature and into reason. I no longer believe that nature is stalking me, that nature sits up nights organizing seventy-two-hour rainstorms to spoil my weekend, planning termite invasions of my house, preparing 1,000 miles of rough air at 30,000 feet simply because I am about to fly to Chicago.

I am persuaded now that I do not matter that much to nature, and that so long as nature doesn't notice me nature will not do anything particularly beastly. When nature does notice me, of course, things become rough.

If, for example, I were to go into the woods and start communing with nature, there can be little doubt how nature would commune back. Having called attention to my existence, I should be attacked by poison ivy, stung by angry bees and felled perhaps by an ancient falling redwood tree, if not struck by lightning produced by the most sudden thunderstorm experienced in those parts in fifty years.

These are only a bland sampling of nature's capabilities for self-expression. If sufficiently provoked, nature may smite you with hurricanes, tornadoes, blizzards, drought, 600 inches of rain, a plague of locusts, a depredation of fire ants, an onset of neuralgia, a stampede of tomato worms and a storm of politicians while depositing your car in the Land of Oz and your summer house in the Gulf Stream.

I shall stay out of sight, thanks, and leave the loving to you. If you promise not to mention that I am here, I shall not point out that yours is a highly unnatural love.

On Top in Wampum

We vacationed on historic Wampum Island. Everybody felt superior.

The people who live year-round on the island felt superior to the summer visitors. The people who were born on the island felt

On Top in Wampum

superior to the people who were not born on the island, even though they lived year-round on the island.

The summer people who owned houses felt superior to the summer people who rented houses, and the summer people who rented for the entire season felt superior to the people who rented only for the month.

The people who rented for the month felt superior to the people who rented for two weeks. The people who rented for two weeks felt superior to the people who rented space in rooming houses.

Everybody felt superior to the people who came by boat in the morning and left by boat in the afternoon. These people were called "the day trippers." The day trippers felt superior to the people who had to stay back in the city.

All day they would throng the streets of Wampumburg, the island's only town, blockading traffic and feeling superior about being there, and everyone else would come out of doors and drive into Wampumburg to feel so superior to the day trippers that they forgot how inferior they were to so many other persons on the island.

Even within the well-defined class groupings there were subtle variations in superiority feelings. Among people who lived year-round on Wampum, for example, those who could move out of Wampumburg for the summer and take a cottage in Squatting Wampum, a small village over the horizon, felt superior to those who stayed in Wampumburg all summer.

Among summer people who owned houses, people who owned houses on the water felt superior to people who owned houses off the water.

People who had private beaches felt superior to people who had to go to public beaches.

Some people arrived on immense sailboats and tied up in the marina. They felt superior to the people who arrived on immense powerboats and tied up alongside them. People in immense powerboats felt superior to people in small sailboats while people in small sailboats felt superior to people in small powerboats.

People who had confirmed ferry reservations for their cars felt superior to people who did not. People who had confirmed seats on the airline felt superior to people who had confirmed car reservations on the ferry.

People who had private planes felt superior to people who had to use the airline, and people who had private jet planes felt superior to people who had private propeller planes.

The eating competition was intense. Those who could afford to dine at the Wampum Plenty Swordfish House felt superior to those who had to eat at the Surf'n'Turf Beach Shack. In the home-kitchen division, people who had found fresh corn and tomatoes felt superior to those who had had to settle for canned peas and frozen asparagus.

People who had tans felt superior to people who had sunburns, and people with sunburns felt superior to people with sallow skin. Men in this year's madras felt superior to men in last year's blazer. Women with expensive backhands felt superior to women with ludicrous lobs.

One could go on, but it would only make life on Wampum seem unpleasant, which it was not. In fact, it was socially sound. One night, for example, the Wampum Electric Company experienced a power failure which blacked out much of the island for most of the night, and there was no looting.

Everyone was having too good a time feeling superior to yield to the lust for such base pleasures as trashing the Wampumburg Oilskin Shoppe. In a society where everyone has somebody to feel superior to, the citizenry has too much stake in the status quo to risk destroying it on a casual rampage.

Red Meat Decadence

Nobody who remembers the Depression of the 1930's will be impressed by the heroism of boycotting meat for a single week.

Red Meat Decadence

During all the years of that era there must have been one or two pieces of beef, a pan-fried steak somewhere in 1934 or 1935 surely, but if so it left no imprint in history.

Canned salmon, on the other hand, remains vivid in memory over almost forty years. It must have been ridiculously cheap then —ten or eleven cents for a big can. It now costs ten times as much, as does chipped beef, which was another staple of Depression diet.

With chipped-beef gravy one night and fried salmon cakes another, we were eating fairly well, the meat boycotters might say. We certainly thought so. We did not feel deprived on the third night when the main course was macaroni and cheese.

Chicken was the luxury meal at our house, as in a great many American households of the time, and this treat was invariably served on Sunday. Sunday was the day for noble dining in America, and most of us who were children then probably grew up believing that when some fancy writer referred to "a Lucullan feast," he was talking about chicken, mashed potatoes, gravy and peas.

The chicken was always either fried or roasted. Fried was best. Roasted meant it was going to be leathery, and the elders at the table who remembered the glorious eating of the 1920's would make jokes about its being rooster.

Looking back, one realizes that they may not have been joking, that the leathery fowl really may have been roosters, but there was so much joking at that table—joking with gaiety in it and not the embittered undercurrent that distinguishes the humor of our present age—so much joking that my memory of the period hears laughter everywhere.

That is a mystery still. It was such a bad time. What were they laughing about? They had one foot in the serene stability of the Edwardian age and the other in the mess of 1914–1929. They had been badly wrenched out of one time into another, but with nothing really damaged much. Perhaps their survival had left them permanently delighted.

Our children will probably not, at ages forty and fifty, hear us laughing in their memories. Oh, we are a glum bunch! Where did it come from, that glumness of ours that already echoes from our children's music and in the mission of moral uplift to which so many have dedicated themselves?

Those are deep questions, and on the theory that a deep question deserves a frivolous answer, I would suggest that the gloom we exude comes not from our Depression childhoods, but from our turning in early adulthood into a generation of beef-eaters.

This beef madness began during World War II when richly fatted beef was force-fed into every American warrior. Meat twenty-one meals a week was the formula for beating the Axis, although the men who really did the job, of course, were living on good old Depression foods, like Spam, while they were at work.

After the war there was no tapering off. We had become a nation of beef-a-holics. By the 1950's the smell of barbecued beef hung like smog over 100,000 American suburbs. A social crisis was no longer your relief check's failure to arrive before the rent was due, but the arrival of a steak cooked medium rare when you had ordered it rare.

This was not a crisis met with a gay smile on the lips, and a joke. Tension prevailed over the table. One was aware that his manhood had been challenged by the chef. Did one dare to threaten nuclear retaliation by demanding to see the manager? Would one lose face if . . .

One sweated.

One? We all sweated. It was the age of sweating. When people were relaxed, which was rare, they acknowledged it by saying, "No sweat." And beef and all those other meats every day of the year—they kept us sweating, and grim.

Nowadays if you want to hear laughter, you must think of macaroni and cheese and listen very carefully, and it may—just may, mind you—come dimly through the beef-clotted memory.

Jolly Old Capital Losses

Internal Revenue eve is always a joyous time at our house. Grandmother always comes over early in the day to take charge of the kitchen, and soon the air is rich with the good smell of roasting checkbook and Grandmother's delicious minced pay voucher.

Mother will have been up since dawn scrubbing and polishing J. K. Lasser's tax guide, and the children stand around with saucers as big as eyes watching Uncle Charlie put up the tax tree.

Later in the evening everybody will pitch in and trim it with gifts for the Voice of America, the Pentagon and CIA, the Department of Agriculture, the elevator operator of the Washington Monument and all those other wonderful people who do so much for us, not only on April 15, but 365 days a year.

In the fireplace we have a blazing copy of the tax code and stockings are hung by the chimney with care in hope that H. and R. Block soon will be there.

With the fall of dusk the children put "Hail to the Chief" on the record player, and then "I'm Dreaming of a White Taxmas." Brimming cups are lifted to the old deductions that are no longer with us, and we all speculate warmly about which people will receive our very own share of the tax to be offered on the morrow.

"Gosh, Dad," one of the children will say, "do you think your payment might wind up buying some of the jet fuel needed to fly Henry Kissinger to confer with President Ford on vacation?"

I allow as how I wouldn't be a bit surprised and point out that, with all the tax I will be contributing to our country, I might be personally responsible for getting Mr. Kissinger's plane all the way from Harper's Ferry to Hagerstown, Maryland. Thoughts like that make you feel good about paying taxes.

Grandfather, of course, always tries to spoil the mood. "Bah, humbug!" he will say. "Your share will be used to print thirty-five pages of the *Congressional Record.* You might as well throw the money to the winds."

But the magic of the night cannot be so easily ruined for the children. "Tell us the story of the first loophole," they cry.

This is the cue for Uncle Charlie to perform, and everyone falls silent as he retells the ancient tale of three wise tax lawyers who saw a brilliant star in the east one night.

"Setting out in limousines from their homes in Georgetown," he says, "they traveled eastward for many miles until they reached a great domed building called the Capitol of the United States.

"There the three wise tax lawyers found the Senate Finance Committee sitting in a bare committee room, and they said, 'Lo, we have seen the strange star that burns in the eastern sky and have traveled these many miles from Georgetown to learn what miracle has been wrought.' "

The children always interrupt at that point. "Tell about the gold, frankincense and myrrh, Uncle Charlie," they always say.

"And the three wise tax lawyers said, 'We bear gifts of gold, frankincense and myrrh.' Whereupon the Senate Finance Committee said, 'We don't care about the frankincense and myrrh, but if you leave the gold with our reelection-campaign-fund managers outside the door, unto you a tax loophole shall be born.'

"Then they went outside and left the gold, and on their return they found a newborn loophole. It was wrapped in swaddling language so dense that none but a wise tax lawyer could discover it. Thus were the first men excused from the heavy burden of paying taxes."

One of the younger children always says, "But didn't those first men excused from paying taxes feel cheated of the right to transport Mr. Kissinger from Harper's Ferry to Hagerstown or contribute thirty-five pages of the *Congressional Record* to the country?"

"Of course, they were cheated," I always explain, "but the rest of us were enriched and made happier, for you see, it meant that the rest of us could pay more to make up for the shortfall. In that way, every Internal Revenue eve we have the joy of knowing that we can fly Mr. Kissinger a little farther or provide a few pages more of the *Congressional Record* than would have been possible before the first loophole. In this way, our joy on this beautiful night is increased, for we are more precious to our country."

"Bah," Grandfather always says at this point, "and humbug."

Benighted Nations

Russia is terrible. It snows and snows and snows. If you look out the window and say, "It snows too much," a Government machine reports you to the police and they lock you in a madhouse to have your brain altered. Russia is terrible.

India is not much fun. It is exceedingly hot and rains at odd times. When you say, "India should get a new Government that will do something about this heat," the police come in the night and take you away. India is not much fun.

Northern Ireland is extremely unpleasant. When you go out for a beer they blast you into many separate pieces with high explosives and answer your children's complaints by saying you died for the cause. Yes, an extremely unpleasant place.

Lebanon is simply intolerable. If you take a walk into town, either Moslems or Christians will shoot you down. Though its religious zeal is commendable, Lebanon is simply intolerable.

China is unspeakable. Everyone wears a quilt and behaves with suspicious sincerity. If you speak with wit or asperity, they ship you out to the country where commissars reeducate you in the evils of hilarity, the virtues of party regularity and the gravity of sex. China is unspeakable.

England is definitely flawed. You can't get there if there's fog. If you do, they fill you with tea and an overpowering sense of your educational inferiority. Though they don't shoot you, jail you or alter your brain, they soak you for weeks without end in the rain. Oh, England is definitely flawed.

Saudi Arabia simply won't do. If the Government catches you having a drink, there is no telling what it might do. And it is extremely dry there, too. Saudi Arabia simply won't do.

Uganda is barbarous. If they don't like your face, your thoughts or your creed, the Government seizes everything you own and ships you to England without a raincoat, although sometimes it offers to shoot you. Bah to you, Uganda. Bah.

France is out of the question. They charge almost as much as Internal Revenue, and if you despair they say they don't care and ask why you don't refuse to pay taxes as they do. What is worse, they say it in French. France is out of the question.

South America is almost acceptable, but only if you have no objection to being kidnapped by guerrillas, although in Chile the Government might extract your fingernails slowly, which hardly seems almost acceptable unless you are not finicky about things like hands.

Bangladesh is not everyone's cup of tea. If the typhoon isn't drowning you, you are either starving to death or being suddenly murdered for not being on the right side of the latest Government upheaval. Even for tastes that are medieval, Bangladesh is not everyone's cup of tea.

Switzerland is much too clean. They rise at dawn every day and polish their money and, because they have so much of it, hardly ever finish before sundown. At sundown they take in the sidewalks to keep them from getting dirty during the night. Afterwards, there is nothing to do but join the rest of the country in taking a bath. On Mondays, they wash their paper money, and on Tuesdays, iron it. Switzerland is much too clean.

Italy is extremely risky. They send the Mafia to cut off your ear and hold you for absurdly high ransom, or alternatively, they haul you off to Pisa or Lucca for a festival and make you dance some tarantella with a lovely young creature whose inamorato will amost surely take it amiss and disfigure your nose with his fist. Italy is extremely risky.

Germany is nothing to cheer. They stuff you with sauerkraut and float you in beer and fit you in ridiculous leather pants and cry, "Ach, if only you could have been here in the old days," and cry in their beer for the day when Americans were as rich as they and brought more money than they do today. Germany is nothing to cheer.

The world as a whole is not worth a visit. They shoot you, or starve you, cut off your ear, or bomb you. They disfigure your nose and jail you for drink, alter your brain if you say what you think; they rain on you, rob you, torture and mob you, and afterwards weep for the world that was. The world is not what it was. It probably never was. As a whole, not worth a visit.

Batting .667

For a long time I used to slip into my graveside face whenever one of those earnest clods with the sociological cast of mind asked if I was aware that one of every three marriages ended in divorce. They enjoy spoiling your day, people like that, and the sooner you give up and look miserable, the faster they will move on to the next victim.

And anyhow, it sounds like a powerful statistic. One of every three. This figure is usually summoned to clinch an argument that doomsday is upon us in one form or another. Old values dying, family obsolete, relationships between men and women destroying both parties, immorality rampant, permissiveness spreading its evil blight, Communism resurgent, kids don't believe in anything anymore—that sort of argument. The grist of television specials and magazine padding. "Is Motherhood All Washed Up?"

In fact, the proposition that the present divorce rate means the game is up for America makes very little sense. What we have here is another instance of statistics misinterpreted by killjoys.

Any sensible person with no ax to grind would give a different reading. Looking at the divorce figures, he would point out that a couple married today have two chances out of three of staying married.

In racetrack terms, marriage is practically a sure thing. In baseball terms, marriage is batting .667, and not even Ted Williams did that well.

When we think about it calmly, it seems surprising that so many marriages endure, for it is not easy to stay married these days. It is all very well for Grandfather to go on about how people in his time really meant it when they said "till death us do part." Maybe they did and maybe they didn't, but if they didn't there wasn't much they could do about it.

The social stigma then attached to divorce tended to confine its relieving delights to millionaires, the sort of people who married stage performers, and similar minor species with a contempt for mass opinion.

It was also physically difficult to get divorced. Real people in Grandfather's time simply did not go to Nevada. Most of them, if pressed, would have confessed that they did not really believe Nevada existed. Real people got into the Ford and drove into town and drank a Coke and saw a movie, which may have been silent and may have been shown in a tent and may have had a fellow in it who'd gone all the way up there to New York or even Chicago, to which places real people did not go either, any more than real people went to Nevada.

So people went onward into the outermost limits of marriage, even when it was actually the inner circle of hell for them.

Nowadays, it has become almost as hard to stay married as it was, in Grandfather's time, to get divorced. Popular magazine articles marinate the senses in literature about the mechanics of seducing other women's husbands and what to wear during the divorce. Many of the old state divorce laws have been rewritten so that one need no longer submit to clownish humiliation to satisfy the statute. Everybody travels everywhere, and often takes advantage of the divorce to vacation in some exotic climate, or vice versa.

Batting .667

Often, of course, the law still allows the wife in the case such money exactions that the husband spends the rest of his days in burlap suits, but if the women's liberation movement succeeds even this final deterrent may soon be dissolved. For now, the divorce pauper is a familiar and fashionable man about town. You see him everywhere, bright-eyed and amusing, entertaining mixed audiences with tales of his court-ordered penury.

Divorce has come a long way since Grandfather's time. It is not only accessible to the masses, but also socially acceptable, and, in some circles, even fashionable. Who has not been present at a large party when it was discovered that one of the couples present had been married ten or fifteen years? Who has not noticed curious glances aimed at this odd couple? In the embarrassment of their strange singularity, such couples must feel themselves socially backward. Not quite like wearers of white socks perhaps, but odd. Distinctly odd.

It would be oversimplifying matters to assert that divorce has now become easier than marriage, but if the trend toward universal birth control continues, with a more intense development of the teeny-weeny little nuclear family, the conventional decision to submit to marriage's discipline "for the sake of the children" will surely become less persuasive.

Marriage is hard, at least according to all the testimony of the poets and philosophers. It has endured probably because it created the family, which has until now been the absolutely essential survival instrument. Nowadays, people seem to be shifting their ultimate loyalty from the family to the state. If Big Brother replaces Mom and Dad, and Alfa Romeo replaces the kids, then logically divorce ought to replace marriage.

People are not logical. That's what's wrong with them. Or, maybe, what's right with them. In any case, the cheering statistic is that as between marriage and divorce, it's still marriage, two to one. Therefore, what? Why, obviously—old values still thriving, family still vital, relationships between men and women still sound, morality on the increase, permissiveness on the run, Communism . . .

Too Cool for Comfort

President Nixon worried too much about coolness. He seemed to believe that coolness was a good quality. He talked about having it himself in large quantity.

"The tougher things get, the cooler I get," he once told a national television audience, sounding like an overheated volcano. After his 1972 election victory he spoke in the same spirit to a newspaper interviewer.

He did not spend valuable time watching television, as Lyndon Johnson had done, he said. It tempted men to hot, hyperthyroid views of the world, which he could not allow to distort his own cool, calm deliberations about the world as it really was.

When the White House people discussed President Nixon in public, they often emphasized his coolness. He was frequently described in moments when decisions were being made as "the coolest man in the room."

This was surely the sycophantic praise of courtiers eager to please their principal by telling the world what they know he likes to hear, even if it isn't so. Successful presidential hangers-on almost always have a nasty talent for striking the delusionary note that will ingratiate them with their bosses.

The fact, of course, is that President Nixon had a very short fuse. When the spark hit the powder he went sky high.

In his earlier political career he used to acknowledge that he had a hot temper, that he occasionally "blew his stack," as he used to put it. The stories of the legendary stack-blowing in Caracas after he escaped from the famous mobbing in 1958 are part of the lore of men who have followed him over the long haul.

The question, however, is not whether he was cool, but why it seemed to matter so much to him. We have had two unashamedly hot-tempered Presidents in recent times—Truman and

Too Cool for Comfort

Eisenhower—and we don't seem to have held it a weakness in them.

Coolness is an idea whose time seemed to come in the Kennedy era. It had something to do with shorter answers in presidential press conferences, with narrow lapels and a good fit through the waist, with an occasional crackle of dry wit and—

But all that is silly, of course. Meaningless, imprecise. It doesn't get to the essence of the famous Kennedy style. But what does? In politics, the Kennedy style pledged us to go anywhere, pay any price, bear any burden. It made us adventurers on a new frontier. Was this coolness? Surely not. Surely it was hot and hyperthyroid.

Still, the idea of coolness fetched the Kennedy people. It must have sounded good, being called cool. There was a great deal of talk and writing in the early 1960's about the coolness of it all, even during the 1962 missile showdown when the White House bet Khrushchev he wouldn't dare put up the hottest war ever held.

Afterwards, the memoirs agreed that when things were at their hottest, President Kennedy was the coolest man in the room.

When Lyndon Johnson ran in 1964 he exploited the notion that Barry Goldwater was dangerously hot-tempered. Whose finger did we want in position to "mash that button"? he used to ask. Cool Lyndon's or hot Barry's? As we now know, between speeches about the danger of hot Barry mashing the button, cool Lyndon was already quietly embarking on the most disastrous American war since 1861.

And then we had President Nixon insisting that he was the coolest of them all. He had what it takes, he told us. Coolness.

Somebody in the White House could have struck a small blow for reason by telling the President the truth. "Mr. President," he might have said, "you are kidding yourself about being cool. You are not cool. You have a short temper, and it gets you into trouble sometimes.

"The beauty part, however, is that you don't have to worry about not being cool, because there have been several uncool Presidents who were just fine with the American people."

We all know that nobody in the White House would dare tell a President he isn't cool, and we know why. It is because they all believe it.

Little Red Riding Hood Revisited

In an effort to make the classics accessible to contemporary readers, I am translating them into the modern American language. Here is the translation of *Little Red Riding Hood:*

Once upon a point in time, a small person named Little Red Riding Hood initiated plans for the preparation, delivery and transportation of foodstuffs to her grandmother, a senior citizen residing at a place of residence in a wooded area of indeterminate dimension.

In the process of implementing this program, her incursion into the area was in mid-transportation process when it attained interface with an alleged perpetrator. This individual, a wolf, made inquiry as to the whereabouts of Little Red Riding Hood's goal, as well as inferring that he was desirous of ascertaining the contents of Little Red Riding Hood's foodstuffs basket, and all that.

"It would be inappropriate to lie to me," the wolf said, displaying his huge jaw capability. Sensing that he was a mass of repressed hostility intertwined with acute alienation, she indicated.

"I see you indicating," the wolf said, "but what I don't see is whatever it is you're indicating at, you dig?"

Little Red Riding Hood indicated more fully, making one thing perfectly clear—to wit, that it was to her grandmother's residence and with a consignment of foodstuffs that her mission consisted of taking her to and with.

At this point in time the wolf moderated his rhetoric and proceeded to grandmother's residence. The elderly person was then subjected to the disadvantages of total consumption and transferred to residence in the perpetrator's stomach.

Little Red Riding Hood Revisited

"That will raise the old woman's consciousness," the wolf said to himself. He was not a bad wolf, but only a victim of an oppressive society, a society that not only denied wolves' rights, but actually boasted of its capacity for keeping the wolf from the door. An interior malaise made itself manifest inside the wolf.

"Is that the national malaise I sense within my digestive tract?" wondered the wolf. "Or is it the old person seeking to retaliate for her consumption by telling wolf jokes to my duodenum?" It was time to make a judgment. The time was now, the hour had struck, the body lupine cried out for decision. The wolf was up to the challenge. He took two stomach powders right away and got into bed.

The wolf had adopted the abdominal distress recovery posture when Little Red Riding Hood achieved his presence.

"Grandmother," she said, "your ocular implements are of an extraordinary order of magnitude."

"The purpose of this enlarged viewing capability," said the wolf, "is to enable your image to register a more precise impression upon my sight systems."

"In reference to your ears," said Little Red Riding Hood, "it is noted with the deepest respect that far from being underprivileged, their elongation and enlargement appear to qualify you for unparalleled distinction."

"I hear you loud and clear, kid," said the wolf, "but what about these new choppers?"

"If it is not inappropriate," said Little Red Riding Hood, "it might be observed that with your new miracle masticating products you may even be able to chew taffy again."

This observation was followed by the adoption of an aggressive posture on the part of the wolf and the assertion that it was also possible for him, due to the high efficiency ratio of his jaw, to consume little persons, plus, as he stated, his firm determination to do so at once without delay and with all due process and propriety, notwithstanding the fact that the ingestion of one entire grandmother had already provided twice his daily recommended cholesterol intake.

There ensued flight by Little Red Riding Hood accompanied by pursuit in respect to the wolf and a subsequent intervention on the part of a third party, heretofore unnoted in the record.

Due to the firmness of the intervention, the wolf's stomach underwent ax-assisted aperture with the result that Little Red Riding Hood's grandmother was enabled to be removed with only minor discomfort.

The wolf's indigestion was immediately alleviated with such effectiveness that he signed a contract with the intervening third party to perform with grandmother in a television commercial demonstrating the swiftness of this dramatic relief for stomach discontent.

"I'm going to be on television," cried grandmother.

And they all joined her happily in crying, "What a phenomena!"

Verb (U.S.): Go-go

The important thing in America is to go.

It doesn't matter where you go, but it is better if you go a long distance.

It is particularly good if you go but don't know where you're going. Guitar players will write songs about you, and there will be a general feeling in the country that you are a poet.

Young people should go at least three times in the summer and once during each of the other three seasons, preferably in Volkswagen buses with curtains on the windows, in airplanes or by hitchhiking.

Singles should go in sports cars. So should couples who are living together but not married, unless they wear jeans or overalls, in which case they should go in Volkswagen buses with curtains in the windows.

Married people with children should go in station wagons.

Verb (U.S.): Go-go

Businessmen and politicians should go in airplanes and never check their luggage.

Cowards should go in trains and ships.

People who like to feel cuddled deep in the center of a great cone of noise should go on motorcycles and wear sunglasses.

Rich people who start drinking before lunch and have skin that looks as if it might be on loan from an alligator suitcase should go in their private boats.

Presidents of the United States should go in personal four-engine jets, yachts, helicopters, limousines and golf carts. When they get there, they should issue a press release.

To go is not only an infinitive, but also the most American act it is possible to perform. Nothing is more American than a good go. Going is the one thing which, if subtracted from American life, would leave America stranger and more repugnant to Americans than the subtraction of any other one thing—be it democracy, salesmanship, consumption, violence, optimism, bribery, capitalism or hamburger.

Going is the only thing an American can do without making a lot of other Americans angry.

Columbus was a go-er.

So were Lewis and Clarke.

Thomas Wolfe, hearing those train whistles in the night, made the whole South want to go, and Woody Guthrie would go out to Oregon and write a song about it faster than a pioneer would go to Louisiana with his banjo on his knee.

Jack Kerouac loved to go.

"Go west," said Greeley. Go-getters with plenty of get-up and go got up and went for the pure love of going and getting, and because it was the one thing every American approved of, because every American, looking at go-getters getting up and going, felt wonderful about being part of a country that was on the go.

What explains the visceral appeal of those two savage guttural vowel noises, go-go? It is because the old-timers who did the first big go across the Atlantic were followed by the middle-timers who did the long go across the country who were followed by the

[91]

good-timers nodding in ecstasies of sensuous surrender to Henry's seductive Fords, and we still feel all those memories in our blood. Hit the drum, burp the electric guitar, start the hips jiggling, pectorals rippling, shout, "Go-go!" and, man . . . !

Get out the car. Down to the airport. Up on the motorbike. Untie the boat. Blood humming those go-go songs. By the time I get to Phoenix you'll be leaving on a jet plane to get your kicks on Route 66 and fly me to the moon so we can shuffle off to Buffalo on the Chattanooga Choo-Choo.

Go-go, go-go. Don't ask where. Buy the insurance. Collision, personal liability, life, mutilation, luggage theft, loss of a leg, loss of an arm, loss of a tire.

When you go-go, you go because you think there has to be something better up ahead, just has to be more fun in the next town, but all the same you wouldn't dare bet against having a disaster on the way there.

The kind of insurance you need they don't sell. This is insurance against the ultimate disaster, which is that (1) not only is there not going to be more fun in the next town, or any other town; nor (2) is there going to be anything better anywhere along the 75,000 go-go miles you intend to traverse in the next two weeks; but also (3) there is not even going to be any next town, not anything whatsoever up ahead.

The probabilities of these disasters are rising, as more and more of the places up ahead become identical to the place we thought we just left behind, as the next town turns out to be just another interchange on the interstate.

I do not think this will stop Americans from going for another generation or two. For that long, motion alone may satisfy the go-go need in the blood. And in the meantime, somebody might invent an economical, styrene, easy-to-install new place that can be taken out of the car trunk and erected at officially approved sites after every 500 miles of going.

The last important human activity not subject to taxation is sex. Why this curious exemption? When we are compelled to pay taxes for food, clothing and shelter, does it make any sense to leave sex tax-free like municipal bonds?   **—A Chaste Deduction**

Elections are probably the most dangerous part of democracy. I say "probably," because a very strong case can also be made for the jury system, which puts a person's fate in the hands of twelve people anxious to be shed of a nuisance in time to get home before dinner.
—Yes No Other

The odd thing is not that we are in the business of overthrowing other peoples' governments, but that we can still be surprised when somebody reminds us of it. In Asia, Latin America, Africa, the Mediterranean and the Middle East we have been propping up and knocking down governments more or less openly for the past twenty-five years.

It is an established policy. Everybody knows it. It is supposed to be done covertly, which is only sensible if you hope to succeed since publicity in matters of this sort can only make the natives resentful and defeat the project. Imagine the chauvinistic rallying around President Nixon that would have occurred if Canada, say, had announced that her agents were going to destabilize United States society so that discontented Americans could heave the Nixon Administration out of office.
—Our Uncle Is Now Dorian Sam

Like American beers, presidential candidates these days are all pretty much the same—heavily watered for blandness, and too much gas.
—The Boys in the Ads

[93]

They Don't Make That Anymore

I needed something they didn't make anymore. It was a hinge of the type called a 2 1/2-inch parliament butt.

I suspected they didn't make it anymore. Once they find out they are making something you might need one of these days, they immediately call the factory and tell them not to make it anymore.

The hardware salesman looked grave when shown the broken 2 1/2-inch parliament butt which I wanted to replace. "They don't make that anymore," he said.

Was there something similar that they did still make?

"How about a 3-inch parliament butt?" he suggested.

If it could be fitted onto an interior window shutter with very thin wood where the screws went, I said, I would take it. I took it. At home, the screws turned out to be too broad. They split the wood. Removing the shutter, I went to a mill for a replacement.

The salesman examined my shutter with contempt. "They don't make that anymore," he said. He sold me a complete set of the very latest shutters. They were so heavy that they pulled out of the screw holes while being installed, fell outward and shattered the window frame.

The lumber-company salesman looked at my shattered window with absolute delight. "And you want a replacement for this window? You must be kidding."

"I assume they don't make it anymore."

He smiled in triumph and sold me the new window they were making that very day, which was so big that the old window space had to be enlarged to receive it. While cutting open the house with a power saw, I accidentally sawed through a supporting

They Don't Make That Anymore

beam, and a large part of the second floor fell into the dining room.

"I need a jack strong enough to raise my second floor out of the dining room without, at the same time, sending my dining room crashing into the cellar," I told the salesman of construction equipment.

"I know exactly what you want," he said. "It's the lightweight second-floor elevating jack, Model 1322, but I got bad news for you, pal. They don't make it anymore."

There was nothing to do but buy a brand-new second floor, so I had a second-floor salesman come look at my old one. He said they didn't make that kind anymore, and sold me the very latest thing instead.

With a little help from the neighbors, I almost got it into place, but it was so much heavier than the old second floor that when the weight began to settle it pulled the roof down through the attic, which collapsed the attic floor, which fell onto the dining room, the living room, the kitchen and the television set.

When the family arrived home they were not amused. "What's been going on here?" they asked.

I told them I was replacing the broken 2 1/2-inch parliament butt on the dining-room-window shutter and had run into complications. They said I had better do something about the house right away as there was likely to be rain.

"Relax," I said, "they probably don't make rain anymore."

The house salesman I saw about replacing the house said they didn't make houses like mine anymore, and showed me a mobile home which they were making that week.

When I loaded the family aboard to set out upon the mobile life, the children, who were vast adolescents, said it was too small and refused to go. There was no time to argue and we had to leave them behind, but I told my wife not to worry because we would get some replacements.

"They don't make that kind anymore," she said.

After driving for several years, my wife turned off the television set one day and said mobile living was all right, but it would be better if there were some places to be driving to.

"They don't make them anymore," I told her.

One day as the house was driving along a highway by an ocean, a hinge on the refrigerator door broke. "Let's drive to a hardware store and replace that hinge," she said.

I ordered her to get out of the house, aimed it at the ocean and jumped free as it went down for the third time. "Why did you drown the house?" asked my wife as I came ashore.

"A magnificent gesture," I declared.

"They don't make them anymore," she said.

The Aged, Shopping
[1974]

Old people at the supermarket make you feel what's the use.

Staring at 90-cent peanut butter. Taking down an orange, looking for its price, putting it back.

Old turn-of-the-century babies with 1965 dollars, who remember Teddy bears, Teddy himself, Woodrow Wilson, Kaiser Bill, Arrow collar man, flaming youth, wandering among $7 ribs, pausing at sugar that is 60 cents a pound and rising.

They shop like sappers going through a mine field, like Onassis looking at new corporations for sale.

Old people dress up to go to the supermarket, but their money becomes shabbier every day, and how do you put a gloss on those old 1965 dollars they dig out of their purses for the checkout clerk?

It is sad watching them fumble through antique old dollars, and hearing the clerk call for more.

"These ancient dollars, madam, have been heavily discounted since you were last in circulation and are quite worthless except in great bulk."

Clerks do not utter this advice aloud to old people. It is simply implied thunderously by everybody in the country and every

The Aged, Shopping

mouthful of food in the supermarket. Old people have a way of laboriously counting their change at the cash register and trying to engage the clerk in sociable conversation, as though asserting a bit too defensively their right to be there despite their shabby old out-of-date dollars.

Maybe only because they have no place to arrive at in a hurry to pick up a batch of the new 1974 90-cent-peanut-butter dollars.

Do old people at the supermarket care about Henry Kissinger's latest flight for peace? Does it matter to them that Republicans and Democrats are quarreling about whether the Democrats have a mandate?

And the latest economic program for ending inflation by 1977, is it of any interest to them at all?

Do they think of President Ford's meetings with Soviet leaders as news?

Perhaps so. News nowadays is largely an entertainment of flying professors, pointless quarreling among telegenic careerists, posturing theorists and presidential travelogues, and old people rely heavily on television for entertainment.

Perhaps they would turn it off if the news switched from entertainment to reality and dealt with the pain of not being able to afford an orange or the embarrassment of delaying the checkout line to take back the crackers 1965 dollars can no longer buy.

Old people at the supermarket make you wonder about all those middle-aged people you see jogging the streets to preserve their vascular systems for another fifty years.

And about all the people of all ages all over the country who are eating less, drinking less, smoking less, driving safer and in general looking for a death-proof safety suit to get them over the peak years and down into the valley of old age fit to enjoy the fruits of their abstention and labor.

Will anyone care when they get there?

Will they be able to afford an orange?

And if not, will professors quit flying for peace, politicians cease thumping their clavicles, theorists stop forecasting millennia for the next generation and Presidents forgo red-carpet arrivals at distant airports long enough to say, "Hey, old people in this country still have a hell of a problem: let's close the circus long enough to do something about it"?

Old people at the supermarket are being crushed and nobody is even screaming.

Old people at the supermarket make you feel what's the use.

Anti-Anglo-Saxonism

The Supreme Court recently declared seven ancient Anglo-Saxon words unfit for general broadcast on radio and television. All seven refer to bodily wastes or sex. What was found offensive was not the subject matter they dealt with, but the use of Anglo-Saxon vocabulary to discuss it.

All seven words have long-winded Latinate synonyms which are commonly used without producing a blush outside the most sheltered backwaters of society. Anyone who undertook court action against a broadcaster for saying "micturition" or "defecation" into a microphone would doubtless be dismissed as a crank or a fool.

But let the same subject be broached in one-syllable Anglo-Saxon words and the Supreme Court assembles to ponder the implications for the future of the Republic. Very few persons, one suspects, would be much offended if, on tuning in their home tubes, they were to hear someone refer to "sexual intercourse," "practitioner of fellatio," "female reproductive canal," "incestuous male issue" or "female mammary glands."

In fact, these phrases seem to be bandied about on television almost as freely as "Get some right away" and "Get him down to the morgue," though, admittedly, usually by goateed men or granny-glassed women.

Something about the Anglo-Saxon tongue has the power to make us see red. Or, in the case of the seven unspeakable words, blue. This may go back as far as the Norman invasion of England when the conquerors from France tried to destroy Saxon culture, and in the process succeeded in stigmatizing the Saxons as crude barbarians. Part of the conquerors' policy was to impose Norman French as the language of civilization.

To this day, most people labor under the notion that the Saxons were little more than savages, though in fact their civilization was in most respects more advanced than the French. In any case, the Normans won the propaganda war. One result is that when English-speakers today try to sound civilized, they shun the Anglo-Saxon word as nasty and barbaric.

Here the Supreme Court has simply recognized a social reality bred into the marrow of English-speakers. When we recoil from Anglo-Saxon terms for mundane bodily functions, we are probably responding instinctively to 900 years of conditioning to the idea that Anglo-Saxon was the tongue of savages and Latin-root speech the voice of civilized humanity.

The effort to restore dignity to the simpler beauty of Anglo-Saxon has produced a gallery of martyrs, ranging from James Joyce to Lenny Bruce, and has placed innumerable judges in the ridiculous position of having to find legal justification for keeping in step with rapidly shifting definitions of good taste.

It is not only among the seven unspeakable words, however, that the war against Anglo-Saxon is waged. Ironically, at a time when Latin is no longer taught in American schools and is thought to be dead at last, Latinate English seems to be on the verge of smothering American usage.

As in the case of "micturition," "defecation" and "incestuous male issue," the use of Latin is commonly adopted to take people's minds off what is being said. People who transpose these mind-dulling Latinisms into plain Anglo-Saxon English are often accused of being "shrill" and "emotional," of using "loaded words."

During the Vietnam war, "bombing" was turned into "interdiction." Those who pointed out that it was, nevertheless, bombing and that people were being killed were said to be unduly emotional and urged to Latinize their thinking. Admittedly, there were "casualties," as there would be in any "program of pacification."

In general, Government justifications for the war were issued in Latin. People against the war were Latinized into "dissidents" with their own connivance. A "dissident" was far less likely to disturb his neighbor than a "war hater." When "dissidents" wanted to set public teeth on edge, however, they shouted in Anglo-Saxon. ("Stop the killing!") The American minority who still liked to communicate talked in Saxonic monosyllables—of "hawks" and "doves."

General Curtis LeMay even performed the commendable feat of condensing the Latin "nuclear" into a sharp-edged new Anglo-Saxon word, "nuke." ("Nuke 'em.") After that, LeMay was persona non grata in the Government, which was smart enough to realize that if people began to understand what the Government was up to, it would be in deep trouble.

It is not only Government that prefers to cloud men's minds with Latin narcosis, however. Even violent Government haters have fallen into the vice. Among angry gun toters who want to build a better world, for example, it has become the fashion to "execute" helpless captives. The theory, I suppose, is that it would seem shrill if you said they had been "murdered."

It is a rare subject nowadays that can make our blood run cold; but when it comes to sounds, we are all very delicate.

The Cheap Blue Yonder

I wanted an airline ticket.

"First-class with frills?" asked the clerk. "It is our most expensive flight."

"What do I get for my money?"

The Cheap Blue Yonder

"A comfortable seat, a genuine airline meal, two free drinks, wine with your meal, a movie, a headset shaped like a stethoscope, a free life insurance policy, a set of aluminum ware and your own personal in-flight magazine which you are encouraged to take with you when you deplane," said the clerk.

"Will there be a qualified pilot at the controls?"

"Two qualified pilots, a flight engineer, six flight attendants, emergency oxygen equipment and a small cake of soap in the lavatory."

The clerk quoted a price. It was staggering.

"Could I see something a little more reasonable?"

"How about coach with one frill? You get a seat with inadequate knee room, a genuine airline sandwich and a headset shaped like a stethoscope with which to listen to your choice of eight channels of stereo music."

"What's the frill?"

"The pilot walks through the cabin and asks if you are enjoying your flight."

At the price, it didn't seem like much.

"Perhaps you want our forget-the-frills flight," said the clerk. "It's considerably cheaper, but you do not get the genuine airline sandwich and the pilot does not make a personal appearance."

"Do I get the headset shaped like a stethoscope?"

"Yes," said the clerk, "but only one of the earplugs is in working order."

Was there something even cheaper?

"How about our miser's-delight service?" asked the clerk.

"Now you're talking," I said.

"Passengers are required to bring their own folding chairs, seat belts, emergency oxygen equipment and a small cake of soap to qualify for use of the lavatory. There is no genuine airline food of any variety and passengers are not permitted to bring their own food. Any passenger caught eating smuggled food is taken to the pilot's cabin and force-fed a three-course genuine airline meal."

I said I'd take it.

"Impossible," said the clerk. "Our miser's-delight service is completely booked through the rest of this year. May I suggest a real bargain?"

"Name it," I said.

"Our shanghai service."

"I don't want to go to Shanghai."

"You don't understand," said the clerk. "You give me your destination and return home. When enough other travelers to fill a plane to your destination have submitted their names, we send out a truck with a crew and round all of you up—we 'shanghai' you, as it were—haul you to the airport and put you aboard."

"I could spend days sitting home waiting. Suppose I was out when the truck came to collect me?"

"Then you would have to pay a penalty," said the clerk. "The truck crew is under orders to track down any passenger not in waiting process at his residence and thrash him within an inch of his life."

Wasn't there something equally cheap but a little friendlier?

"Ah," said the clerk. "We have just the thing. Our cheapskate's party flight."

"I like it already," I said.

"Under the regulations which enable us to offer this incredibly low fare," said the clerk, "you are required to walk to the airport. On arrival, all passengers must assist our loading crews in unloading baggage from one of our overseas flights."

"So where's the party?"

"In the hangar. After offloading baggage you proceed to the hangar where our maintenance crew is readying your plane for its flight. There you join the maintenance men in cocktails and replacing faulty engine parts, rebuilding the radio equipment and patching holes in the fuselage."

"Holes in the fuselage?"

"Only by using our equipment to its maximum capacity are we enabled to offer this fantastically low fare."

I hoped the pilots would not be joining passengers and maintenance men in cocktails as we readied our plane for flight.

"Pilot," said the clerk. "On the cheapskate's party flight, you get only one pilot, but he does not take cocktails during the plane-preparation process. When airborne, however, he joins the passengers in the cabin for martinis, and as the flight proceeds, for fine whiskeys and cognac, all of which, of course, the passengers are required to supply."

I asked why didn't they require the passengers to fly the plane.

"In fact," said the clerk, "this often turns out to be necessary."

I said I'd take the bus.

The clerk said not to do anything brash. "We'll come up with an even cheaper plan you can't resist before you get to the bus station."

They probably will.

Most Wanted List

Here is the latest Wanted list of the most despicable people in the United States today:

Elizabeth (Betty the Breadbasket) Goolarik: Wanted in thirteen states on charges of being overweight in a public place, and ten counts of failure to look like a bone sack when dressed for dancing. Goolarik was last seen in Peru, Indiana, washing down chicken tetrazzini, mashed potatoes, gravy, an ear of corn and a slice of pecan pie with a high-calorie cola drink. Goolarik is easily recognized by a coating of flesh, which she wears attached to her bone structure, and by her inability to swoon when the waiter suggests a chocolate parfait. Should be approached with care, as she is skilled with fork, spoon and knife and has, in several cases, lured pursuers into joining her in an order of spaghetti with chicken livers.

Ernest (Mister Clean) Cloxbury: A three-time loser, Cloxbury has been convicted of sexual inhibition, repressing a minor and wearing pajamas in bed. He is wanted by sociologists in California and New York on charges of monogamous heterosexuality and hiding a copy of *Forever Amber* in the laundry hamper during visits from his grandmother. Cloxbury can be identified by his refusal to undress until the lights are out.

Alphonse (Wheels) Caramba: This insatiable gasoline guzzler strikes without warning, pulling his car into filling stations, aiming a wad of $20 bills and ordering attendants to "fill her up." He has bought eighty gallons in four cities within the past month. In his wake he has left scores of small economy cars so desperately scarred by contact with the voracious appetite of Caramba's powerful car that they are ashamed to resume normal gasoline consumption. Caramba is known to fear that he may be mobbed and beaten by jealous small-car owners and is said to carry two loaded gasoline containers at all times. Use extreme caution.

Gertrude (Butts) Blitzer: Blitzer has committed barefaced cigarette smoking in restaurants, parlors, lobbies, taxicabs and lounges of six states, as well as several airplanes. She is identifiable by cigarette holes in her skirt and ashes in her coffee. She carries a lighter and a spare pack and will smoke without warning.

Andrew Upchurch: Known among social enforcers as "Hah-Hah," Upchurch has cut a swath of terror from Milwaukee to Bridgeport by bursting into dying dinner parties and telling ethnic jokes. In Ashtabula, while hitchhiking with a prominent Democrat, he got off a Pakistani joke, a Canadian joke and a Swedish joke before being stopped by a state-patrol roadblock. By that time it was too late to save the driver, who is still in coma, and Upchurch blasted his way out with three rapid-fire Hindu jokes that have left the Ohio State Police deeply offended.

B. B. (The Oinker) Burns: Sought in thirty-nine states and Canada for ruthless male chauvinism, Burns was last seen in San Francisco opening a door for a woman. Her condition is still critical. Lucinda Burns, his wife, is serving a ten-year sentence in the campaign speeches of Bella Abzug after being convicted of doing the dishwashing. Burns is thought to be eating off dirty plates and may be desperate enough to get off a hail of mother-in-law jokes unless taken by surprise.

Casper Haspell: The most notorious do-gooder and bleeding heart on the continent, Haspell has committed a vile series of good-doings that have made his name repugnant to politicians, editorialists and policemen from coast to coast. Convicted of attempting to commit do-goodism in the Congress, he escaped by shocking authorities with a free lunch. "There is no such thing as a free lunch!" they cried in amazement, as Haspell climbed unnoticed over the top line. He has since been convicted in absentia of not being a bottom-line man. People in trouble should be particularly on guard, as Haspell is a seasoned do-gooder whose bleeding heart may leave unsightly splotches on unpayable bills without warning.

Elvin (The Juice) Broomster: Sometimes called the most revolting beast in America, Broomster is guilty of at least 15,000 recorded acts of materialism, ranging from getting his suit pressed once a month to shunning the Bicentennial Celebration fireworks of 1976 because he couldn't see how it was going to improve his earning power. Broomster was last seen having his house rewired to accommodate eighteen new electric appliances. Unmarried, he is said to be looking for an electrician who will wire an accommodating woman so he can be the first man in his neighborhood with an electric wife.

A Golden Moment

This space is yielded today to Mr. O.W. of Bath, Indiana, who has sent us his theory of the present inflation explosion. Leading economists have dismissed Mr. O.W.'s explanation, and only, Mr. O.W. believes, because he is not an economist, but a trombone player.

"They cannot stand having a horn player make monkeys of them," Mr. O.W. writes, "and, so, suppress my theory." However that may be, Mr. O.W. makes sense about inflation.

"A few years ago," he writes, "it was impossible to get a taxicab in New York City. This was because cab fares were so low that maybe 3 or 4 million New Yorkers could afford to pay them. As a result, all the cabs were constantly filled and the curbs were lined with New Yorkers who wanted cabs but couldn't get them.

"This was an illogical situation, for the taxicab is the rich man's transportation, and rich men were being kept from their natural mode of transport by people who should have been riding buses and subways.

"Some people got together. I don't know who they were. Rich men, probably. The kind of men who were meant to ride taxicabs. They must have said, 'This is silly. What is the point of being rich if we have to stand on the curb getting rained on because all the taxicabs are taken by the bus-and-subway classes?'

"Whatever they said, the result was a boost in the price of a cab ride. The fare increase again separated the taxi riders from the bus-and-subway people, and nowadays, if you are well heeled, there is no trouble getting a cab in New York.

"I go on at length about this because it is a small but classic illustration of inflation (the rise in the cab fare) being caused by the natural distaste of rich people for standing on curbs being jostled by multitudes.

"When 3 or 4 million New Yorkers could afford taxis, it meant that 3 or 4 million New Yorkers were, in a sense, rich. And the nub of the whole thing, of course, is that when everybody is rich, being rich is no longer very satisfying.

"The natural economic correction is inflation. Prices increase

A Golden Moment

until only a limited number of people can pay them and, for these survivors—the rich—being rich means something once again.

"In New York in the old days the well-to-do stood on the curb in the rush hour and reflected bitterly on the uselessness of their wealth. No longer. Inflation has restored the point of the system. Being rich means being able to get a taxicab.

"When the present inflation explosion began, the entire country had reached the stage of New York before the boost in taxi fares. Half the people in America had begun living the way rich people live.

"Two and three cars. A boat. A second house at the ocean, the lake, the mountains, Porterhouse steak every night. The best Bordeaux. Fine woolens from Britain, perfume from Paris, shoes from Italy. Vacations in Jamaica. Skiing in Switzerland, flying back and forth to Europe, California, Florida, Maine.

"It was an unnatural situation. With half the population living the rich life, a lot of satisfaction went out of being rich. It was like the old days when you couldn't get a cab in Manhattan.

"Now the hotels in Jamaica were all booked solid for the winter. You couldn't get a lobster because 60 million other rich people had bought them all up. And what was the point of your fine woolens from Britain when the butcher was wearing a cashmere apron, or the shoes from Italy when the office boy was wearing exact duplicates?

"When being rich ceases being satisfying, the natural economic correction—inflation—naturally takes place. This is now happening. Millions of Americans are being priced out of competition for the good life. When the process is finished, being rich will mean something once again.

"Once we understand this natural tendency of inflation to occur whenever too many people start living like the rich, the solution would be easy. This would be a series of Government-sponsored lectures explaining to the multitudes that even a few years of living like the rich is better than an uninterrupted lifetime of subway riding."

Talking Clothes

As Americans lose the ability to speak coherently to each other in words, they speak increasingly in clothing, jewelry, gimcracks and hair. Just the other night I met a woman whose finger told me she was divorced. The finger bore the latest thing in talking jewelry—a divorce ring. A divorce ring looks like a wedding band with a crack in it and costs between $300 and $350.

An expensive way, you may say, of notifying strangers that you have been in and out of marriage, and so it is, but in the age of talking costumes it is a commonplace sum to pay for the pleasure of avoiding conversation.

In Henry James's day, this woman and I might have had a subtle conversational encounter from which I might have ingeniously extracted her story. These days it is no longer necessary. Her Florentine purse instantly told me everything I needed to know of her reckless disregard for money, which had doubtless led to the divorce. Moreover, my Brooks Brothers suit and my naked ring finger told her everything she needed to know about me; to wit, that I was not an adventurer, that I was married and that I was devious.

All this was announced by the suit, which said, "Married, not adventuresome," and the absence of a wedding ring on my marital-status communication finger, which said, "He is trying to conceal his married state." After my dreary old button-down collar had assured her that I had no eye whatever for chic, we moved apart, having communicated everything without having spoken a word.

Life is full of these mute exchanges nowadays. In certain homosexual circles, I understand, *aficionados* of the sadomasochistic endeavor communicate absolutely everything about their personality quirks by the manner in which they wear leather and metal.

Talking Clothes

A can opener worn on the left hip signals a taste for plum brandy; a leather eye patch draped over the Adam's apple, a liking for old W. C. Fields films; and so on.

In New York at least, males of the moneyed class announce their wealth through their shoes. On meeting a New York man, one instantly looks at his feet for the buckles of Gucci, which declare: "Rich." This is to prevent possible confusion created by the fact that rich New York men now commonly dress above the ankle like sheepherders.

The battered jeans, sweaters and fur-lined suede say, "Don't care about the worthless material things of life." The Gucci sandals immediately correct any possible misapprehension by declaring, "But don't get me wrong, Buster; I can afford it all if I want it."

Psychologists have long held that dress is a way of telling people in fast shorthand what you want them to think of you, and of course, what you want people to think of you is often misleading, if not false. Most of us, in fact, do not have much idea who we are most of the time, but we solve the problem by slipping into false identities which can be slapped together with costume and jewelry.

The conventional rebel costumes of the 1960's—jeans, granny dresses, wire-rim specs, bushels of hair, etc.—became such a universal uniform that the more timid citizenry felt itself in the grip of an army of occupation, although, in fact, as we now know, all those young soldiers of protest were just as puzzled about who they were as the rest of us.

I bring this up because of a personal oddity lately noticed. Struggle though I do to avoid talking clothes, I have lately found myself buying neckties that say, "Countess Mara," "Christian Dior" or something similarly commercial in large lettering. I don't really want to buy these ties, but cannot stop myself, any more than I can stop myself from wearing them.

I frankly admit to not knowing who I am. This is why I refuse to buy clothes that will tell people who I want them to think I am.

It seems frighteningly possible, however, that if one is not consciously dressing in talking clothes, then one's subconscious may take charge in an effort to tell him who he really wants to be.

If so, these neckties can mean but one thing. I want to be a billboard. I believe this makes me what the politicians would call "a great American," depressing though it seems.

Turning Back to the Campus

Rob Bascomburger is not your ordinary overeducated, overtrained college boy writing sniveling letters to the editor and complaining to Government charity officials because he cannot find a job. Rob is the kind of young man who does something about it, as his letter here illustrates:

I am writing to solicit your support for an entirely new kind of American institution. I propose to call it uncollege. Its tasks will be diseducation and detraining. The need for such an institution is desperate. Its contributions to American life will be immense. Please bear with me while I outline the case.

I have been out of college for more than a year now and am still unemployed. I am informed that my jobless condition results from a miscalculation as to the requirements of the contemporary work force which were made at the time I undertook my education.

At that time, the projections foresaw the need for a much larger force of highly educated, highly trained workers than the economy, in fact, now requires. Having become highly trained and highly educated, I now find myself, along with hundreds of thousands of other young persons, economically superfluous. All of us with our overeducated, overtrained mentalities have become surplus people and, therefore, disposable.

When applying for work which requires little training and less education, I am repeatedly rejected on the ground that overeducation and overtraining disqualify me for the job. Personnel scientists have apparently learned that such people adjust poorly to jobs that do not fulfill their expectations and give them outlets for their skills. One gathers that such persons are potentially dangerous malcontents likely to sow unrest, if not revolution, among the less educated and less highly trained workers.

Whatever the explanation, many of us remain "unemployable." Thus we swell the unemployment figures and place a financial drain on the rest of the work force. The solution should be obvious, but until now no one has undertaken to provide it.

It is to establish the uncollege.

I am persuaded that within months of its opening, the first uncollege could have an enrollment of 30,000 college graduates eagerly seeking to have the defects of their college educations corrected.

At uncollege, these wretched graduates would undergo four years of diseducation. At the end of that period, if they had successfully disachieved down to the high school level, they would be awarded certificates attesting to their fitness to enter the labor force.

Highly trained graduate students, of course, would be required to undergo three additional years of detraining after passing their rigorous four years of diseducation. A certificate of detraining would, of course, be far more difficult to obtain than a simple diseducation diploma. Candidates might, for example, have to be able to demonstrate an inability to do simple sums at a cash register like their working comrades who are already in the labor force.

How, you will ask, can such an ambitious undertaking be established? At first blush, the costs would seem prohibitive. We shall need a large faculty highly trained in detraining and diseducating. These would not be called professors, but "stupidifiers." We would need extensive plans to give the destudent body every opportunity to master woolgathering, repetitive error, clock-watching, time killing, indifference, incompetence, passivity and the hundreds of other valuable nonskills essential to rescue them from the ranks of the unemployable.

Can you doubt that the parents of America, who have already shown their eagerness to mortgage their lives to put their children through college so that they might become employable, will gladly accept more financial chains if they can save their young from the unemployability which college has inflicted upon them?

If parents balk at making a second trip to bankruptcy, we can bring the powerful force of guilt to bear on their bank accounts. Was it not the parents' sin of pride which led them to render their children unemployable by lavishing expensive college educations upon them? Do these parents not now owe it to their children to atone for their sins by shelling out?

Frankly, I believe we can get in on the ground floor of the mint if we move quickly. This is why I am offering you this splendid opportunity to invest now in the American bonanza of the future —uncollege. Remember, a little learning may be a dangerous thing, but a lot of learning ain't what makes the world go round no more.

Yours for enterprise,
Rob Bascomburger

Stomach-Bulge Defense

The difference between barbarity now and in other times is that now everybody sees it on television.

Massacres, assassinations, bombings and even genocide used to be conducted in comparative privacy. Those who had witnessed or survived them came back and told about them through the soft filters of time, memory, distance and words.

It was hard to believe that such things really happened. It is easy to disbelieve mere witnesses and survivors when they tell things we would rather not believe. They were too close to events, one could object. They were overwrought, inclined to exaggerate, given to lapses into bad taste, apt to overdramatize for effect.

Stomach-Bulge Defense

So the world seemed a better place then. It wasn't, of course. It was only more conveniently remote from common experience. Now that television sits in the living-room corner ready to show us the absolute worst at the touch of a switch, we have to construct other defenses.

In Baltimore, watching the late news the other night, I saw what might be called "the bulging-stomach defense." The man reading the news began by warning that we were about to see some film we might think offensive for the children to witness and advised us to clear them out of the room, a piece of advice that was probably as well intended as it was calculated to make every child in Baltimore battle for his right to view.

Then we saw scenes of horror from Vietnam. Some people who had been in an open boat for several days fleeing from the enemy had arrived at a besieged port. The boat was filled with dead children, whom we saw briefly, open-eyed. Bodies wrapped in shrouds. An apparently legless woman being carried ashore. Mothers weeping in agony.

Some of the children who died in the flight had been buried at sea, said the reporter. It was harrowing stuff. We could imagine those burials.

Then a handsome young woman appeared on the screen. She had just purchased a superior brand of panty hose. They performed wonders for her figure, she said. They even suppressed her stomach bulge.

The picture shifted. Another handsome young woman. This one had made a study of headache nostrums. She discussed them briefly and recommended a particular brand.

Memory blurs at this point but I know the news went on as it does every night. Someone may have discussed the hazard of dying battery and told us how to avert it. No doubt a mother of thirty-two instructed her daughter of twenty-eight, and all the rest of us, which brand of tomato paste was most powerful at holding a marriage intact. I don't know, but these are the kind of things commonly used in bulging-stomach defense.

What is happening here is a destruction of value differences. At one instant, we are dwelling on two minutes of horror for humanity in Vietnam. Then come two minutes of the nightmares of living-room America—stomach bulge, headache, dead battery, third-rate spaghetti.

The next moment—at least in Baltimore on this night—we went to Cambodia to watch Lon Nol say his farewells to his country before embarking on exile. It threatened for an instant to become touching.

We had a brief glimpse of Lon Nol, who had never been much more than a printed name which spelled the same backwards, looking taller than we had thought, and human. He walked as a man in pain. For the fraction of a second, as the reporter said this was surely the last time he would ever see his country, Lon Nol seemed to be starting to cry, but we could not be sure, for the picture ended abruptly.

Cloudy weather was shown on a blackboard. It was approaching the Tennessee Valley. A number of women at a Baltimore shopping center had been fooled on camera—it was April Fool's Day—by a silver dollar which the television station had glued to a sidewalk. They took it like good sports when they discovered the joke.

And so on. Everything had been reduced to the same value. Despair in Vietnam is grave, but so is bulging stomach. Lon Nol may have cause to weep, but people can still smile on April Fool's Day in Baltimore. And yes, once again tomorrow there will be some weather.

The grossest barbarities, to be sure, stick in the mind. Those dead children with open eyes. Later we will use them as false evidence to persuade ourselves that the world has never been so depraved as now, refusing to believe that the world's depravity is immemorial and different now only by being available for immediate inspection in the living room.

Mostly, however, we remain as sheltered as ever from this timeless unpleasantness, lapped in the horror box's constant assurance that our daily fears, whether failed spaghetti or stomach bulge, are not to be sneezed at either.

[114]

In 1959 the old propeller-driven Lockheed Constellation in which President Eisenhower used to travel the country was displaced by the new jet-powered Air Force One, and the age of the worldwide presidential air circus was born. It was yet another triumph for technology in its struggle to expand man's scope for inconsequentiality.
—**Presidential Catnip**

I heard of a man and woman recently who had fallen in love. "Hopelessly in love" was the woman's antique phrase for it. I hadn't realized people still did that sort of thing jointly. Nowadays the fashion is to fall in love with yourself, and falling in love with a second party seems to be generally regarded as bad form.
—**Meaningful Relationships**

Maybe Washington really is another country. Certainly nobody living in the United States could have dreamed up the suggestion, which came out of Washington the other day, that filling stations be allowed to charge for washing your windshield, checking tire pressures and performing similar small services.

In the United States, filling stations have not performed services of this sort since 1973. Most motorists pulling up to a gas pump these days would no sooner think of asking to have their tires checked than they would dream of asking the attendant to clip their toenails.

You can't even get a free road map anymore. Certain generous filling stations will let you look at the house road map, but if you are lost in hostile territory nowadays you stay lost until you get pulled over for a traffic violation, which gives you a chance to ask directions from the judge.
—**Farewell My Heroes**

Strange Feet

The world is as follows:

Upon removing his shoes at bedtime, P. B. Sykes observes that the feet inside his socks are not his feet, but quite obviously someone else's feet. His wife, noting an unusual expression on his face, inquires if something is wrong. "No," says Sykes, quickly dousing the light.

Sykes firmly believes that terrible things, like finding another person's feet attached to your ankles without even a seam showing, can happen only to other people. Not to P. B. Sykes. So long as he does not tell anyone, the event may yet choose not to happen—or, more precisely, to unhappen—to him. So he does not tell Mrs. Sykes. By morning, he believes, the alien feet may have vanished as mysteriously as they have come, and his dear familiar old feet may be back where they belong.

Next morning finds the strange feet still there. "How's everything, P.B.?" a dozen people ask him before lunch. To each, Sykes replies, "Fine."

He telephones a doctor. A receptionist says the next available appointment is three months distant. Sykes says he has an emergency. "What seems to be the trouble?" asks the woman. Sykes cannot tell her the truth, for he is certain she is incapable of believing that feet can be switched, like umbrellas traded in a restaurant mixup, and will think him mad and dispatch him to psychiatry.

She is insisting, in fact, that she be lied to. "Chest pains." "Ah, agony in my appendix." Any of a hundred such lies would satisfy her insistence that life never be inexplicable, unorthodox, interesting.

Sykes does not lie, for he knows that even should he break through to the doctor the truth would be ill-received. "Wrong feet, eh, Sykes? Well, well, one man's feet will do as well as another, I suppose. Here, take two of these every four hours and get out of the office more, get off for a good long vacation somewhere, plenty of golf and salt water. . . ."

Strange feet can be lived with. Perhaps Sykes's problem is not as rare as one might think. Are there others in the same pickle? He will write to the press and perhaps uncover thousands of persons with a wrong-feet condition. Perhaps there is a club, regular mixer dances, group cruises.

"Dear Editor: I was shocked the other night to discover that I had someone else's feet on," he begins.

His letter draws only one reply. "Dear Editor," it begins. "Your correspondent Sykes may have been amused to discover that he was wearing another man's feet, but except in the most barbarous English usage, he could not possibly have been shocked. I would concede that he might have been shocked if the two feet in question had not matched, although purists, I believe, will agree that he would merely have been disturbed by this discovery. For my part, sir, I am alarmed at the decline of the language which is so depressingly illustrated by the prose of this curiously footed Sykes."

Sykes runs a classified ad requesting anyone with information about an accidental mixup of feet to address him at a postal box. In response, he receives three obscene letters and an advertising flyer for 8-mm movies smuggled out of Mexico.

The Government cannot communicate with Sykes about his problem. Since there is no program for the relief, rehabilitation, subsidy, preservation, licensing, suppression or inspection of persons lucklessly left with other people's feet, a Federal telephone explains, Sykes cannot be put into a computer, and since he cannot be put into a computer it is impossible for the Government to communicate with him.

Intoxicated at a party one night, Sykes reveals his secret to a beautiful woman. She is an editor with a great publishing house and immediately signs Sykes to a three-book contract. *Feet, Son of Feet* and *Strange Are the Toes.*

Sykes's feet become the biggest attraction on television talk shows. After each appearance, thousands of cranks swamp network switchboards with calls to say that Sykes is wearing their long-lost feet.

Robert Redford and Dustin Hoffman star in the filmed story of Sykes's life, with a special cameo appearance by Sykes's wrong feet. The feet become so swollen with their success that they ache eight hours a day to remind Sykes what a failure the rest of him is.

Sykes becomes such a gigantic international celebrity that he is signed to star in a television commercial for corn plasters. At the studio, he meets Aleksandr Solzhenitsyn, who is making a television commercial for a new Russian dressing in an aerosol can.

That is what the world is like.

Spaced In

We have just moved to New York, and outside the window at this very moment a man is parking a twenty-foot car in a nineteen-foot space. He has been working at it for ten minutes. It is a classic illustration of the New York temperament. If this man were a San Franciscan, he would give up and go play tennis. If a Washingtonian, he would already have a reserved parking space. Getting a reserved parking space is what Washington is all about. When it comes to parking, the true Washingtonian makes Machiavelli look like Anne of Green Gables.

The New Yorker, however, has to fit life into spaces too small for it. What he calls home would look like a couple of closets to most Americans, yet the New Yorker manages not only to live there but also to grow trees and cockroaches right on the premises.

A window affording a view of the sky is something to boast about. Getting a seat on the subway is an exciting start to his day.

Spaced In

On such a day, he suspects, the gods may even favor him with a lunch table expansive enough to contain not only his pastrami but also a dish of pickles and a glass for the cream soda.

The sight of a nineteen-foot parking space makes him giddy with delight. The average $250,000 town house is only seventeen feet wide. Is it a wonder that a nineteen-foot parking space looks to him like a berth fit for the QE2?

So he backs in with his twenty-foot car, nudges the car parked behind him, calls on his horsepower and applies brute force to the car behind. Would he really be so unfeeling toward another car's gearbox? Not unless he had to. He pulls out, cuts his wheels, goes into reverse, steps on the gas.

The machine behind, locked in parking gear, shudders under the impact, leaps back a few inches. He cuts his wheels, attacks the car in the front position.

First he nudges it around the bumper with the soft nuzzling of a tentative seducer. The front car declines to yield. He goes into reverse. Bashes rear bumper against rear car. Rear car shudders, leaps. Then—gear in forward position—slam on the gas—bang the front car. Everything vibrates. Back he goes—bang—into the rear car. Forward—boom—into the front.

This goes on daily outside this window. Shattered pieces of red taillight covers regularly litter the gutter. Whatever ruin occurs to internal automotive organs will become manifest only later when thousands of rush-hour motorists sit cursing another breakdown on the East Side Drive.

Once in a while the owner of one of the parked cars under assault will arrive during the brutality and take exception to the violence. This raises the prospect of combat. Eagerness for combat is another New York characteristic. This is only natural. When you are trying to live a twenty-foot life in a nineteen-foot space, you have to be ready to fight for every millimeter.

Although the papers regularly report homicides committed during parking quarrels, I have never seen one end in bloodletting outside the window here. Occasionally there will be a stream of vile language and threats to commit horrors, but so far the police have always arrived in the nick of time.

The most dangerous crises arise when two parkers simultaneously spot a nineteen-foot space and simultaneously start to pull into it. This leaves one car with its front end sticking out and the other with rear end blocking traffic. These impasses produce passions out of Italian opera. Threats, oaths, cries of hatred, tears, pledges to exact vengeance and screams of dismay from other cars jammed behind the blockade.

Trying to fit life into spaces too small for it takes a toll on civilization. Blood pressure among New Yorkers is probably always high. One goes through life most days with temperature just one degree below the boiling point. It takes very little to push it into the danger zone.

New Yorkers instinctively realize this about each other, and, recognizing the danger, try to avoid encroaching on each other's limited life space.

This may be why New Yorkers instinctively avoid making eye contact with each other in crowded places, why they "look right through you," as dismayed visitors often complain. They are not looking right through you at all; they are discreetly avoiding an intrusion into your space. They sense the danger in a place where a one-degree temperature rise can mean an explosion.

A man newly arrived in town tells of parking his van at the curb in Greenwich Village one night, returning next morning and finding a message on the windshield. It said, "If this truck is parked here again it will be destroyed." He never parked it there again. He suspected the threat was probably bluster, but on the other hand this being New York . . .

Uplift Through Shot and Shell
[1975]

The average person rarely meets any terrorists, except those connected with the Government, and so, in our ignorance of them, we tend to think of them as bestial and inhuman. This probably does them a cruel injustice.

It is true that terrorism requires its practitioners to be unpleasant, even murderous, to other people. But their motives are invariably kind, humane and even high-minded. Indeed, few forms of human behavior more adequately express the quintessence of *Homo sapiens* than a terror bombing, for it satisfies the human urge to be beastly to one's fellow man, woman and child and justifies the cruelty on the ground that it will make the world a better place.

The terrorist is a believer in uplift. He believes in the perfectibility of man and is prepared to kill you in order to improve the world for you.

Most of us, of course, have a horror of sudden and premature dispatch to the beyond, even for the sake of improving the planet, and for this reason we tend to disapprove of small-scale terrorism. This distaste is intensified by the fact that the noble cause for which we are to be dispatched often seems less than vital to us.

In fact, there is such a variety of terrorists at work these days in such a variety of good causes that it is altogether possible to be hied rapidly to the grave without even being aware of the good cause you died to promote.

If you travel to Northern Ireland you will probably know that the high-minded cause for which you are bombed at your beer is either independence from British rule or continuance of British rule, but if you cross to London the ground is trickier.

Not long ago terrorists in a passing car pumped bullets into a West End hotel, and since there had been a spate of bombings there in the cause of a better Ireland, you would naturally have assumed, had you been shot there, that it was to improve life on the Emerald Isle. In this you would have been wrong.

The police deduced that since there was a Jewish gathering in progress at the hotel, the real point of the mayhem was to promote justice for the displaced Arabs of Palestine. Thus, in your last millisecond on earth, it is entirely possible these days to be cruelly deceived about which great cause you are nobly serving by passage to the other side.

"I am crossing for old Ireland," you might sensibly conclude, having considered the terrain, when in fact, all unbeknownst, you are actually improving the Middle East, striking a blow for oppressed peoples of Argentina, helping to end warfare in Vietnam or—who knows?—helping stop cruelty to animals in Sarawak.

When one is compelled to part with life for high-minded causes one likes to know what the cause is. It is highly unsatisfying to cross the chasm for uplift without even knowing what will be uplifted as a result.

Governments, which are far and away the most vigorous practitioners of terrorism, understand this human quirk. When they make war they first saturate you with official announcements explaining that you are to be killed for freedom, or for liberation from the coils of imperialistic capitalism, or for something equally improving, and then they saturate you with bullets, fire and bombs.

All through history, people have tolerated terrorism when its purpose has been adequately explained to them, and most people probably approve it. Probably one of the chief reasons for American resistance to the Vietnam war was the Government's failure to come up with an explanation of which great humanitarian purpose was being promoted by the bloodshed.

Government terror is not limited to the use of bombs and guns. In places like Chile, it embraces torture to create a society purified by release from Communism. In the Soviet Union, it includes imprisonment in insane asylums to create a world where all people can approach nearer to Paradise.

In the United States, keeper of police files on citizen activities, tapper of telephones, opener of mail, one is never aware whether Big Brother Sam is watching or not, but is nevertheless aware that if one's name is on file at the FBI, or the phone is tapped, or the mail is being steamed open at the post office, it is for a wonderful cause—the preservation of individual freedom.

Government defense of these practices is the same as the small-bore terrorist's defense of dynamiting helpless people at the lunch counter. The cause is too noble to be lost through squeamishness. What neither government nor unofficial terrorist ever concedes is that terror, besides being so good for humanity, also fulfills some dark human yearning to give one's fellow man the works.

Letter from Washington
[1976]

I have been in Washington a few hours, and phone an old friend. He is one of the relics. We both remember Washington when men of the future, which turned out to be Vietnam, jumped into Bobby Kennedy's swimming pool.

"Why Washington in January?" my friend asks.

"To take the pulse of the city."

He is mildly convulsed. It reminds him of a Marx Brothers scene: Groucho holding Harpo's wrist at the pulse, staring at his watch, then looking straight at the camera, saying, "Either this man is dead or my watch has stopped."

A very Washington reaction this winter, I find, as my stay lengthens. Nothing that is happening seems to be meant seriously.

There are these people, very important people, going through motions. It is ritualistic. I, of course, know all those motions. Once I lived here, had even been a low-grade "insider," the kind of piffle obsessionist who knows who will be appointed Ambassador to Malagasy before it is published, who discourses at dinner on "the President's thinking."

It being January, the President makes a turgid speech written by a committee. "The State of the Union." Congress interrupts with regular tedium-charged bursts of applause. Democrats "react" with mimeographed denunciation, Republicans with praise. The notorious Budget is revealed. Media giants analyze, commentate, disclose significance.

This year, however, the motions seem emptier than usual. This time everyone seems to realize that it is just . . . *motions.* The performers seem like mechanical figures in a grotesque clockwork machine. The machine whirs, cogs engage, doors flap open, men adorned in quaint politicians' suits pop out to perform the immemorial movements and the villagers go through the ancient dispute about whether their beloved contraption needs major repair or merely fresh grease.

One wonders whether President, Congress, President's men and would-be Presidents would have troubled going through with it had there been no press or, more urgently, no television willing to connive in the pretense that something is happening. After the State of the Union speech, a mouse at whose delivery the White House had labored for weeks, I ask one of President Ford's men if it was not mostly a media event, a nonhappening staged because reporters would pretend it was a happening. "It's all a media event," he replies. "If the media weren't so ready to be used, it would be a very small splash."

With so much credulity to be exploited for political gold, the performers may safely commit absurdities to distract attention from the shortage of substance. Thus we have the spectacle of the Tory Ford exhorting the populace to march in the spirit of Tom Paine, a revolutionary so offensive to established order that he had to flee Europe for America to avoid being hanged by men of Mr. Ford's political philosophy.

In Washington, almost everybody of importance, man and woman, has run out of imagination. Wit's end seems not far off. All that remains to talk about is how the money is dwindling away and whether the next bank-loan payment can be met. The business of the Republic has become a glum quibble among bookkeepers. We are in the hands of men who make no music and have no dream.

At a certain time in the sixties, I had begun to feel a chill between me and my old pal, the Government.

This is not so easy to explain without sounding naive, but I grew up in the Roosevelt age when most people—though certainly not many rich men—looked on the Government as a friend. It had always seemed to be on my side in life, and during World War II we pitched in and worked together, and afterward, through Truman and Eisenhower, we developed a relationship of mutual respect. At this particular time in the sixties, it occurred to me that the Government was no longer my friend and, indeed, that it regarded me as little more than a nuisance, someone to be tolerated with barely veiled contempt and, when I annoyed it, to be thrown out of the office by receptionists.

I do not mean to personalize this. It wasn't only I who had been left behind by this immensely successful new Supergovernment. It was all of us. And I don't mean "the people." I mean the persons of America, the ornery, difficult, fascinating 200 million individuals who were the United States of America.

It seemed to me that the Government had no use any longer for us persons. It was deferential enough to "the people," to be sure, and was constantly pushing us around for the good of "the people." The Government had become something like the fellow you knew in high school who grew up to be the most important man in television; you might get a Christmas card from him now and then, but you wouldn't dream of burdening him with twenty minutes of your anguish, pain and dreams. The Government's energy was too valuable to be spent on persons; it had to be husbanded for "the people."

Some blood connection between Washington and the country had been snapped. It was suddenly easy for Washington to talk about pain and death because they had been reduced to statistics. War was glossed over in terms of "body count" and "megadeaths." Old age was a percentage point, unemployment a manageable figure in the economic forecast. The Government not only was in the death-dispensing business on the grand scale, it was also dealing with humans as though they had no humanity.

Eventually I left Washington and almost immediately felt in touch with life again. I think of this as I return now in deep winter, the Potomac sliding under the wing of the airplane, ice floes visible at the big curve by Watergate and, on the ground, a merciless wind out of the Arctic.

There is an old horror story entitled *Donovan's Brain,* in which this poor devil has his brain removed from his body and kept alive in a cupboard to do nothing but think about its predicament. Gradually, the brain acquires nasty powers to control events outside, events with which it has lost all physical connection. The brain exerts pure mental power undiluted by connection with human reality.

Washington, it seems to me, has become like Donovan's brain and the rest of us like Donovan's disconnected body. On instinct and reflex, we may twitch and convulse, but Washington sits in its brainpan solution in the cupboard, severed from any feel of the struggle and the pain.

The politicians of Washington complain that the people have become cynical about Government and lost their faith in Washington. This is a typically disconnected Washington view of reality, with the common flaw that it assumes "the people" is human. The real case seems somewhat different. The persons of America, it seems more likely, don't much believe the Government is capable of realizing there are persons out there. When Washington looks at you in this epoch, it seems to see only a statistic.

There are signs of decay in Washington that could be mustered for yet another essay on a city demoralized, disheartened and dispirited in the ruin of Watergate. The old hands sit around, romantically hoisting the brandy to the good old days, which turned out to be such rotten old days, and moping that it's all over and nothing remains but lunkheads and midgets. Thus the special joy with which they joke about President Ford as a punchy heavyweight stumbling over dogs and bumping his head on the icebox.

Tales of human inferiority are conversational staples. President Kennedy's sex life is exhumed over the dinner table. What a fall is there from Camelot! Someone has heard that Jackie has dropped the Kennedy from her name in business usage, now calling herself Jacqueline Bouvier Onassis. Someone else says Mrs. Kennedy smiles too much. The Democratic leadership of the House is described in Laurel-and-Hardy terms. At dinner, a local lady famed for knowing all and telling it acerbically recites tales of the Democratic eminence whose gizzard has been so long marinated in alcohol that he regularly finishes public banquets snoring face-down in his plate. When an evening with someone from the White House reaches the convivial stage at which confidences can be exchanged, the invariable question is, "Is Ford as dumb as everybody says he is?" (Invariable answer: No.)

Ruin and despair in Washington can be overdone, however, and Watergate, after all, is some two years past, which is an eternity in the Washington measure of time. In fact, I saw very little ruin in Washington. The machinery which makes the place so fierce seems remarkably intact and all ready to roar again once we return to normal Government. Normal Government is what is in ruin at present. Given an unelected President of conservative Republican mind and a Democratic Congress distinguished only by poor leadership, lack of organization and total absence of any political philosophy, it would be unreasonable to expect anything more than caretaker Government, and caretaker Government is what we have.

Are the media the Frankenstein monster of our time? Occasionally, someone among them seems to sense the worst. During an insensate descent of Washington reporters on Iowa in late January, Jack Germond of *The Washington Star* seemed to be writing dangerously close to the edge of reality. The reporters had decided that the outcome of an arcane caucus process among Democrats would have fateful results on the distant presidential elections, and Iowans, seeing the reporters descend, decided to take it as seriously as the media. Is the press here because of these caucuses, asked Germond, or are the caucuses being held because the press is here?

Well, of course, Ford has been on television; the Democrats get equal time. The Democrats have no program either. Actually, the Democrats may not even be a party anymore. I tend to the theory that they are just a memory. But never mind. They want a crack at afflicting prime-time America, too. So we have Senator Edmund Muskie for forty minutes right after dinner.

Muskie makes a basic mistake. He thinks people listen to television. People do not listen to television. They look at television. I had to cover the first Nixon-Kennedy TV debate in 1960 and, so, didn't have time to look at it. I had to listen to it. If you listened to it, Nixon won. Not by much, but he had the edge. Most Americans watched it on television. They didn't listen. They looked. And Nixon lost by a knockout.

Muskie had a great television moment in 1970. He came on television and spoke calmly. He came on immediately after everybody had looked at Nixon out West carrying on like a speed freak. And then they saw Muskie talking calmly. Ask anybody who thought it was a great speech what Muskie said. Nobody can tell you. But everybody remembers what he looked like. Calm. Rational.

So here is Muskie six years later doing a Nixon 1960. He is reading a speech as though folks out there are going to be listening. I am sitting in an elegant Georgetown house in company with two senior Democratic Senators, and I am looking at the two Senators. They are not smiling with that sappy faraway look Democrats get when they look at old films of Franklin Roosevelt. They are frowning ever so slightly.

There are other Democratic biggies present. Eight of them have drifted to a back room and the food before Muskie even begins. Afterward I go to visit a Republican. He loves Muskie's speech. "The Republicans should have paid for his television time," he says.

I go to the White House and watch the reporters bait Ron Nessen as though he were Ron Ziegler declaring yesterday's White House statements "inoperative." Again there is the sense of people going through motions. Having been sandbagged once at the White House press office by the lamentable Ziegler, the reporters seem fated to go on and on performing their role as testy watchdogs of presidential cover-up.

There is some empty fencing over a forthcoming presidential

medical examination. Will the doctor disclose everything, Ron? Nessen's reply that the doctor has "professional reservations" about going totally public, what with the doctor-patient relationship, draws crisp reminders that this doctor is now on the public payroll. Public obligations! Is he aware of that, Ron?

Nessen says everything will be told. (It always is after these physicals, and the President is invariably pronounced in tip-top condition; it is apparently the world's healthiest job.)

I go to the Capitol in search of Congress and find only policemen. The place is swarming with them. They are on steps, in doorways, outside elevators, patrolling corridors, behind the bust of Aysh-Ke-Bah-Ke-Ko-Zhay ("A Chippewa Chief") and the statue of Will Rogers. I roam through acres of cops, and at the House of Representatives, I am forced to pass through a metal detector before they let me enter the press gallery.

At the public galleries, some 200 tourists are emptying pocket and purse of keys, coins, souvenirs. This is only a mite of the total-security orgy which is placing a blockade of guns between Government and the governed. And is it not necessary? In the past few years, the Capitol has been bombed, maniacs have attacked over the White House lawn and sundry deranged persons have been aiming guns at President Ford. Eventually, I am told, bulletproof glass walls may be installed between the congressional galleries and the Senate and House, and Congress will become known as the men in the glass booths.

The effect of it, finally, is to heighten the sense of disconnection between the Government and us. So many police hips bulging with firepower, so many cool appraising police eyes, give one the impression of being looked upon as a menace, of being not quite safe. One hesitates about striding right through doors and gates. There is a sense of lost freedom.

Under the surface of police which Congress presents to the public, the one grim issue tormenting Congress is the rise of police power and what to do about it. Restraints on the FBI? Shall the CIA's secret international police operations be curtailed? Does national security mean that the President must have no constraints placed on his extensive powers to police international affairs?

The Senate's Church Committee and the House's Pike Committee are grappling unhappily with these weighty questions, and the Congress is watching them with increasing unhappiness. Press leaks of garish deadly goings-on in the CIA and lawbreaking in the FBI have apparently surfeited the public with illustrations of what these agencies should not be doing—namely, breaking the law. But there is little discussion of what they should be doing.

This has given defenders of secret centralized executive power an opening to charge that Church and Pike threaten to destroy vital parts of the national security machinery. No Congressman can live long with the imputation that he is damaging the national security and, not surprisingly, Congress's interest in any kind of tighter controls on the executive seems to be waning.

At the end of the month, in fact, the House voted to forbid publication of the Pike Committee's CIA report until the President (meaning, of course, the CIA) had removed material he considered damaging to national security. This was an extraordinary retreat for a Congress which had come to Washington a year ago declaring, in Congressman Brademas's words, that it was going to run the Government. Now it was making the President its own censor.

Most of the report's juicier tidbits, of course, had already been published in press leaks, which made the House vote doubly interesting. What alarmed the House was not the publication of the secrets, but the possibility that Congress could be blamed for spilling them. It did not want to assume public accountability for intervening in CIA affairs. The best guessers I could find believe that after the investigations and the uproar subside, Congress will leave all the old machinery intact.

Which brings us to the ultimate question of the imperial Presidency. Is it really dead, as the conventional wisdom proclaimed when Nixon was routed back to California? Morris Udall, the

Letter from Washington

House Democrat, who understands power in Washington, says that it is. Henry Kissinger constantly laments that it is, and considering how brusquely Congress has undone so many of his international ventures this past year, he would seem to know what he is talking about.

I was not persuaded during my call on Washington. I saw a Congress that no longer trusted Kissinger making it clear they didn't trust him. I saw a President with no mandate to govern being treated like a President with no mandate to govern.

But the imperial Presidency seems intact. Congress has passed no significant law to dismantle any of the powers built into the Presidency under Roosevelt, Truman, Eisenhower, Kennedy, Johnson and Nixon. Press and television still focus most of their light on the White House and ignore Congress. And, most important, all thought and discussion center on the monumental question of who the next President, the genuine, elected President, will be.

After so much devastation, one thinks, something basic should have changed, and yet very little has. Although Watergate has ruined men, the apparatus of the Superpresidency (along with the machinery of normal Government) is still there, and public expectations of the office still seem to make Americans hunger for an ideal man to fill it, which, finally, is what makes our Caesars fatten.

Most Americans still seem to be dreaming of the perfect President, that amalgam of Washington, Jefferson, Lincoln and Roosevelt who will one day appear out of the tube to save us. One might have thought that after so much catastrophe from greatness, we would be delighted finally to settle for a competent second-rater who would tell us that while Government may be a grimy business, somebody has to do it, and there is no reason why it cannot at least be done with honor.

It is hard to foresee such a man prevailing in Washington anymore. There is still too much hunger for charisma and grandeur to match that marble whiteness.

Francs and Beans

As chance would have it, the very evening in 1975 Craig Claiborne ate his historic $4,000 dinner for two with thirty-one dishes and nine wines in Paris, a Lucullan repast for one was prepared and consumed in New York by this correspondent, no slouch himself when it comes to titillating the palate.

Mr. Claiborne won his meal in a television fund-raising auction and had it professionally prepared. Mine was created from spur-of-the-moment inspiration, necessitated when I discovered a note on the stove saying, "Am eating out with Dora and Imogene—make dinner for yourself." It was from the person who regularly does the cooking at my house and, though disconcerted at first, I quickly rose to the challenge.

The meal opened with a 1975 Diet Pepsi served in a disposable bottle. Although its bouquet was negligible, its distinct metallic aftertaste evoked memories of tin cans one had licked experimentally in the first flush of childhood's curiosity.

To create the balance of tastes so cherished by the epicurean palate, I followed with a *pâté de fruites de nuts of Georgia,* prepared according to my own recipe. A half-inch layer of creamy-style peanut butter is troweled onto a graham cracker, then half a banana is crudely diced and pressed firmly into the peanut butter and cemented in place as it were by a second graham cracker.

The accompanying drink was cold milk served in a wide-brimmed jelly glass. This is essential to proper consumption of the pâté, since the entire confection must be dipped into the milk to soften it for eating. In making the presentation to the mouth, one must beware lest the milk-soaked portion of the sandwich fall onto the necktie. Thus, seasoned gourmandisers follow the old maxim of the Breton chefs and "bring the mouth to the jelly glass."

Francs and Beans

At this point in the meal, the stomach was ready for serious eating, and I prepared beans with bacon grease, a dish I perfected in 1937 while developing my *cuisine du depression.*

The dish is started by placing a pan over a very high flame until it becomes dangerously hot. A can of Heinz's pork and beans is then emptied into the pan and allowed to char until it reaches the consistency of hardening concrete. Three strips of bacon are fried to crisps, and when the beans have formed huge dense clots firmly welded to the pan, the bacon grease is poured in and stirred vigorously with a large screwdriver.

This not only adds flavor but also loosens some of the beans from the side of the pan. Leaving the flame high, I stirred in a three-day-old spaghetti sauce found in the refrigerator, added a sprinkle of chili powder, a large dollop of Major Grey's chutney and a tablespoon of bicarbonate of soda to make the whole dish rise.

Beans with bacon grease is always eaten from the pan with a tablespoon while standing over the kitchen sink. The pan must be thrown away immediately. The correct drink with this dish is a straight shot of room-temperature gin. I had a Gilbey's 1975, which was superb.

For the meat course, I had fried bologna *à la Nutley, Nouveau Jersey.* Six slices of A & P bologna were placed in an ungreased frying pan over maximum heat and held down by a long fork until the entire house filled with smoke. The bologna was turned, fried the same length of time on the other side, then served on air-filled white bread with thick lashings of mayonnaise.

The correct drink for fried bologna *à la Nutley, Nouveau Jersey* is a 1927 Nehi Cola, but since my cellar, alas, had none, I had to make do with a second shot of Gilbey's 1975.

The cheese course was deliciously simple—a single slice of Kraft's individually wrapped yellow sandwich cheese, which was flavored by vigorous rubbing over the bottom of the frying pan to soak up the rich bologna juices. Wine being absolutely *de rigueur* with cheese, I chose a 1974 Muscatel, flavored with a maraschino cherry, and afterwards cleared my palate with three pickled martini onions.

It was time for the fruit. I chose a Del Monte tinned pear, which, regrettably, slipped from the spoon and fell on the floor, necessitating its being blotted with a paper towel to remove cat hairs. To compensate for the resulting loss of pear syrup, I dipped it lightly in hot dog relish which created a unique flavor.

With the pear I drank two shots of Gilbey's 1975 and one shot of Wolfschmidt vodka (nonvintage), the Gilbey's having been exhausted.

At last it was time for the dish the entire meal had been building toward—dessert. With a paring knife, I ripped into a fresh package of Oreos, produced a bowl of My-T-Fine chocolate pudding which had been coagulating in the refrigerator for days and, using a potato masher, crushed a dozen Oreos into the pudding. It was immense.

Between mouthfuls, I sipped a tall, bubbling tumbler of cool Bromo-Seltzer, and finished with six ounces of Maalox. It couldn't have been better.

The Evil of Work

I read in the papers recently that there are 500 million marginal people on the earth. These are people the world can't use. There is no economic need for them—no jobs, not enough natural resources, not enough arable land, not enough food. Socially and economically, they are useless, if not worse, since they cause political upheaval, high taxes and slums.

It must be very dispiriting to be one of the world's marginal people. Knowing that the blue-chip people wish you would just disappear cannot help self-esteem, and living in the margin must be cheerless and demeaning.

Even at its best, as in the United States where old people in the margin dine on pet foods and marginal mothers are tyrannized by welfare bureaucrats, the sustenance offered by a robust state is poisoned by the bile of the benefactors. Uselessness and idleness stand high on the American tables of cardinal sin. Helplessness is a condition not lightly forgiven, and charity's reward is a tax deduction.

Yet even in America, marginal people seem to be an economic necessity, since Government efforts to control inflation invariably come down to policies that put more people out of work, that shove more people into the margin in order to stabilize the price of milk.

And afterwards, what? Shall we go on, old-style, abusing them as idlers, welfare bums, failures, shameful takers of Government handouts, life's losers, people who have let the country down?

These traditional views rest on the notion that work is good and that people who work are, therefore, good too, and ought not to be burdened with the support of people who don't work (bad).

Surely, however, this traditional view fails to recognize economic reality. If more people must go into the margin to halt inflation, then the people who go are doing a great service to the state.

The Government should point out that these are people who have made great sacrifices to enlist in the war on inflation. They should be honored, not reviled. Service in the margin, like service in Vietnam a few years ago, may be an honor largely confined to the luckless, but we can at least refrain from treating it with scorn.

We might go further toward a truly sensible policy. At present the ranks of marginal people are filled by a sort of draft process; this is, nobody asks you if you care to become marginal, you are simply plucked out of your life's work one day and pressed into the margin.

Would it not be sound to follow the military's example by abolishing the draft and switching to a volunteer margin? Vigorous recruitment programs might persuade workers in secure jobs to leave them for service against inflation in the margin. All those who now complain about having to work hard to support the idlers in the margin should be easy targets for recruitment, persuaded as they appear to be of the pleasures of idleness and the burdensome nature of work.

I am not naive. I realize that there is a serious obstacle to recruitment. This is the national faith in what President Nixon used to call "the work ethic," a conviction that working is ethical and not working isn't.

The Government can change this with its propaganda machinery. What, after all, is so ethical about work when the country is crying out for unemployment to save its economy from being inflated into an uneconomy?

If the country needs fewer workers, not more, it has every reason to preach the nobility of the nonwork ethic. Uncle Sam needs idlers. That should be its slogan.

Once we have lured into the margin all the additional people necessary to save the dollar, what would we do with them? Give them a distinctive lapel button they could be proud of, I suppose, and unemployment compensation until the crisis passes, and then, when enough time has gone by, go back to wishing they would disappear, like all old heroes.

Do Not Go Gentle

It speaks eloquently of the general public squalor into which the Republic is settling that there is scarcely a man left in the country who would not feel demeaned, humiliated or insulted if someone called him a gentleman. Indeed, the word is so rarely used these days that its sound has archaic overtones conjuring up memories of high-button shoes, horse collars and embroidered samplers over the velveteen settee.

In politics today it would be far more damaging to call a man

Do Not Go Gentle

a gentleman than to call him a thief, a rogue, a pimp, a boor, a loudmouth, an imbecile, an unprincipled lout or an unmitigated swine, for in this catalogue we recognize the heroic figures of the late twentieth century, whereas in the gentleman we detect a suspicious alien, somewhat like the notorious Outside Agitator whom we distrust simply because he is not one of us.

This is not to say that an occasional gentleman does not slip past us now and then and turn up in political office. There was one in the House of Representatives briefly in the late 1950's. I forbear to identify him by name since I hear he is running once again for office and have no wish to destroy him by exposure. When he was in the House it did not take long for his fellow citizens to smell him out and replace him with someone more apt for mail fraud, pillaging the Treasury and suborning juries, but I believe he has since changed his ways, taken to gratifying the public taste for oleaginous hypocrisy and, so, gained a reputation as a formidable political philosopher.

It is misleading, however, to dwell on the absence of gentlemen in the nation's capital. Nowadays, New York has even fewer than Washington, where I can count seven for certain. Admittedly, three of them are in retirement and a fourth is a scholar, and hence easily able to indulge an eccentric taste. In New York, however, it is hard to count beyond four gentlemen without resorting to statues and transient sea captains. I will not get into the matter of Southern California or the new South beyond saying that they are in the vanguard of the present trend.

Is it not curious that while men have been escaping the onerous social claims made upon them by the gentleman, women have had so little success at escaping the burden put upon them by lady-hood? Try as they will to convert "lady" into an insult, the feminists have had scant success, and this, I believe, is because they have failed to absorb the lesson of the American male's escape from the gentleman.

The feminists appear to believe that a woman can quit being a lady by performing acts of loud public negation, by announcing her resignation, as it were. To treat a woman "like a lady," the feminists maintain, is to oppress her, the theory being that the lady is a constraining social concept, a kind of cage for womanhood, created to stop women from flying.

And yet, although pronouncements are issued against ladyhood and women announce their resignations, the thing persists. The facile explanation is that too many reactionary sisters enjoy oppression and, hence, continue cultivating the abomination. In view of the ease with which men put the gentleman behind them, this strikes me as doubtful.

The gentleman, of course, was a social concept that oppressed men. As long as you were expected at least to try to be a gentleman, you could not come to the table in shirt-sleeves, much less in your undershirt. Nor could you commit family, social or public betrayals and continue to be regarded as a well-adjusted and representative man of the era. Unnatural constraints on male freedoms were extensive. One was forbidden barbarous discourse, coarse exclamations of contempt or ignorance, gross lies and, in general, everything that was rude and uncivilized.

In shucking off what now seem like oppressive constraints, men did not bother issuing pronouncements, publishing tracts or rebuking women as chauvinist beasts for calling them gentlemen. The gentleman was a creation of men to establish minimal standards of decency in relations among men. When men quit being interested, the gentleman's time had passed.

Women can abandon the archaic lady in the same manner. By simply and quietly quitting. Perhaps then we could get them interested in becoming gentlemen, and the Republic might elevate itself a bit.

Saturday morning we woke up to distressing news. The President, said the papers, wanted to rally public opinion. Rallying public opinion on a weekend in June is almost unheard of. It made you wonder if the President had a firm grip on the calendar. June is for leaving people alone so they can fish, get married, graduate the children, wax the car, watch baseball and make the seasonal switch to gin and tonic.

—This Is Not the Season to Stage a Rally

Shocking though it may seem, the Soviet Union and the United States now have enough salt to ruin every bowl of soup on earth at least thirty-six times. It is this grim statistic with its nasty implications for the palate of mankind that has led to the salt talks between Moscow and Washington.

—Saline Solution

Listening to the economics wizards talk about the recession, you get the feeling that things are going to get better as soon as they get worse.

—So Glad to Be Recessed

The Portrait of a Lady deals with a woman who doesn't know what to do about a failing marriage because she doesn't have access to a newspaper that carries the Ann Landers column. How lucky we are that journalism has left Henry James in the dust.

—How to Read Your Newspaper

Few persons of modest attainment hesitate these days about telling you how good they are. Turn on the electronics, open a paper, walk into an office—it doesn't matter—in a few minutes on comes some character to thump his chest and treat you like a full-length mirror.

—Meatballs for Caviar

The Injustice Department

Here is an alarming little news story. It is about eight men who went to Florida in 1972 with a mind to stage some sort of protest against the Vietnam war.

It was not an illogical place for protest. Both Democrats and Republicans held their conventions that summer in Miami Beach, largely because Miami Beach is an artificial city cut off from the world by a natural moat, and this moat mentality arose mainly from a sense among men who ran the country that they had behaved so badly about the war that sensible persons might be tempted to make an embarrassing scene about it.

Politicians dislike scenes in election years. They want to hear their excellence praised before the multitude, and this was the game plan in Miami Beach, at least for the Republicans. From inside the moat they filled the television screens of six continents with self-praise of a density and volume that would have made a Pharaoh blush.

All that is politics, and perfectly all right, the politician's trade being, on occasion, to fool all of the people some of the time, but only for their own good, mind you, only for their own good. The eight men in this alarming news story were in politics, too, the politician's trade being, on other occasions, to make life embarrassing for politicians they disagree with.

Very quickly, however, they ceased being in politics and became in jail. The Justice Department had them indicted on charges of conspiring to do violence within the moat, which they never reached, of course, on account of their major problem with the law.

They were tried in Gainesville. After deliberating briefly, a jury found them not guilty. This was fourteen months after their arrest and five weeks of trial.

The Injustice Department

Lovers of American law customarily give themselves airs at this stage of this repetitious story, for, they say, it proves that the American legal system manages finally to service justice. And yet, very little justice was done in this case, or in many others like it which have ended in acquittals for persons charged with political crimes in the past decade.

This alarming little news story, for example. It states that the eight men who wanted to protest the war at Miami Beach have bills of about $150,000 as a result. Being tried by Uncle Sam is an expensive luxury.

In fact, Uncle Sam is something like the man in the cigar commercial who keeps threatening that he is going to get you. When Uncle Sam sets out to get you, he is going to get you. He doesn't know how. Maybe by putting you in prison, maybe by letting you escape prison and merely driving you into bankruptcy. But he is going to get you.

The financial drain of being tried by the Government is only part of the grand disaster. What of the fact that the eight men were deprived of their right to make their protest?

How about being required to spend fourteen months of their lives preoccupied with lawyers and absorbed with the threat of imprisonment? Who among us could afford to be distracted from his normal work for more than a year while the Government attempts to put us away?

Whether defendants in such cases are convicted or not probably makes small difference to the Government. The punishment for being indicted is severe enough to make a man swear off disagreements with reigning politicians for the rest of his life, which is really what governments want.

The Nixon Administration's use of these indictments to preoccupy, harass and bankrupt opponents of the Vietnam war was part of a general policy of injustice pursued by the Justice Department to compel people to quit complaining about Vietnam and love the war.

The remedy seems obvious enough. If the Justice Department is going to function as an Injustice Department, then the Government ought to provide a comparable source of wealth and power for the aid of persons whom the Government sets out to get.

The legal costs of being a defendant ought to be paid in full by the Government if it fails to get you. Why should an innocent person have to go into bankruptcy because the Attorney General doesn't like his looks? Travel costs should be paid, too. Hotel bills and bail fees, compensation for time missed from the job and compensatory damages for worry and fretting and time lost from active opposition to the Government.

Why not, in fact, permit the bringing of extremely expensive, time-consuming indictments against any Attorney General who has you indicted for a political crime and can't make it stick? With a clear understanding, of course, that he has to pay all his legal costs out of his own bank balance, even if a jury clears him.

If the Government can't get you fair and square, it ought to have to think twice before it tries.

Policeman Explosion

City policemen help children cross the street, give you parking tickets, solve homicides, settle family quarrels, deliver babies in taxicabs, write down the names of people who have been robbed, talk the deranged out of jumping from high buildings, take drunks home safely and park in no-parking zones without getting ticketed. They are named Captain O'Malley and Officer Mosconi.

State troopers wear puttees and big pistols, make U turns across median strips of superhighways and chauffeur politicians at ninety-five miles an hour. They are extremely neat. With their well-cared-for fingernails, they keep alert for messy-looking people in unkempt cars, whom they nudge to the side of the road and sniff for the telltale aroma of marijuana smoke while examining their driver's licenses, registration, taillights and tire tread.

Vice-squad policemen wear old clothes and hate to see people having a good time at the horse parlor, out of wedlock or in the movies.

The fire-department police keep an eye on your housekeeping and investigate you for accumulations of oily rags around the furnace and rusting bolts on your fire escape.

The alcohol police sit in liquor-store parking lots until you come out with a bottle of gin, then follow you across the state line, where they seize your gin and automobile for importing out-of-state alcohol without paying the sales tax.

The credit-bureau police watch your bank account, keep records on how rapidly you pay your bills and slander you throughout the business community as a deadbeat if you make them cross.

The smoke police stand in grocery stores and elevators and take you to jail if you light a cigarette.

Military policemen wait until you have signed a contract to fight for your country and then hover over you on weekends to make sure you do not have a good time or a loose necktie.

The nicest policemen are the Capitol policemen in Washington. They wear baggy pants and big pistols, but do not know how to shoot anyone and are not encouraged to learn, since they would almost certainly hit a Congressman. Their task is to awaken and reprimand visitors who sleep in the Senate gallery.

White House policemen live in small boxes on the White House grounds, keep their gold braid beautifully polished and arrest maniacs who attack the White House by automobile.

The Executive Protective Service policemen sit in beautiful blue cars outside embassies and keep city policemen from ticketing diplomats' illegally parked cars.

The Secret Service policemen wear business suits over their guns, seize counterfeit dollar bills and try to keep armed people at a safe distance from Presidents.

The policemen of the FBI used to send threatening anonymous letters to people they want to scare out of town, make harassing telephone calls in the night, keep secret dossiers on Congressmen, tap your telephone and make tape recordings of the sexual activities of prominent persons whose peccadilloes they believe might amuse the President. They don't do that anymore, at least for the moment.

The Army's policemen accumulate files on people whose views do not accord with Henry Kissinger's and store them on computer tape.

Narcotics policemen ingratiate themselves with your children, and then ask them where they can buy some pills, and then send the children to prison for telling them. Sometimes they surround your house in the night, knock down the doors, kick you in the shins and point guns at your wife because they meant to raid a house on the far side of town but read the address wrong.

Immigration policemen track down people without a visa, uproot them from their neighborhoods and export them overseas, sometimes to unspeakable fates.

The Internal Revenue police rummage through your bank records, pass your tax return around among politicians, investigate the sexual and drinking habits of political candidates, seize your property if they think you are a suspicious customer and tie you up in court for two or three years if they don't like the way you have deciphered the tax law.

The Federal airplane policemen inspect your laundry, frisk you for weapons and keep a hard eye on you if you make jokes about air travel being dangerous.

The Central Intelligence Agency policemen steam your mail open, copy it and store it in file cabinets. They also burglarize your house, tap your telephone and watch to find out whom you talk to if you leave the country.

The policemen who police the CIA policemen watch them like hawks day and night to find out if they are really enemy spies.

Company policemen keep you from entering your place of business if you forget your company identification badge.

Would it not be comforting to be a policeman? There is an excellent chance, of course, that you are. These days, who isn't?

Secrets, Anyone?
[1976]

State Department fellow calls up. He's got some classified documents he wants to leak. Says America ought to know about this. It's red-hot stuff. Will I meet him, take the documents, splash them in the papers?

"You think I got a sponge in my head?" I hang up sweating. Suppose the phone is tapped? It rings again. I tear it out of the wall and put it in the trash.

Little while later, a knock at the door. Who could it be? The FBI? Bozo the Congress on one of its $350,000 stamp-out-these-unpatriotic-leaks investigations?

"Who's there?"

"A State Department fellow. Open up and get your red-hot leaked classified documents."

I put the chain on the door, then nail up a two-by-four to brace it against bodily assault, go back into the living room. He's standing there smiling. "Came in the back window while my stooge faked you out at the door," he says.

I ask does he want to ruin me in the news game. Doesn't he know I can be wiped out if I start reporting things the Government doesn't want people to know? I am scared. Scared of being investigated by Bozo the Congress. Scared the President will sic the FBI onto my bank accounts and love life. Scared Henry Kissinger will tell the world I'm the mug who is destroying America's standing in the world. Scared that the CBS affiliates will phone my boss and ask him to fire me.

"What kind of news hawk are you?" he demands.

"A chicken news hawk," I tell him.

He lays a paper on me. "A subpoena?" I ask. "Read it," he says. I read it. It says Henry Kissinger is strongly in favor of the American home.

He hands me another. It says Henry Kissinger has taken the position that the American mother is the greatest mother on earth.

Another. It says Henry Kissinger loves the American flag.

"If you have any journalistic courage, you will expose Kissinger's secret views for what they are," he says, "and let the chips fall where they may."

It is breathtaking. I am almost tempted. "You're giving me— me, a small-bore print writer—the chance to reveal that Henry Kissinger is in favor of home, flag and mother?"

"Do you have the courage to do it?"

Yes, I am almost tempted. But I remember the fate of Daniel Schorr, who revealed that what the papers said Bozo the Congress had found out about the CIA was actually what Bozo the Congress had found out about the CIA. I don't want to be put out of work like Schorr. I don't want to be investigated for revealing to the public what the public already knows.

And I think of this brave State Department fellow, who is willing to risk his career so America can know what kind of man Henry Kissinger really is. Do I have the right to help him destroy himself?

I stall. "Do you have any other red-hot documents?" He draws the blinds. Perspiring heavily, he produces a sheaf of papers. Classified records of Kissinger's diplomatic conversations with foreign statesmen! I recoil.

"But—but—" I can't even speak.

"I know what you're going to say," he murmurs. "These papers reveal that Henry Kissinger is absolutely brilliant."

"Dynamite!" I gasp. "Kissinger will be furious."

"He will be thunderstruck," says the State Department fellow.

I agree to sleep on the proposition. "But what about you?" I ask as he leaves. "You know, of course, that Bozo the Congress will ferret you out as the leaker."

He smiles the smile of a man who knows a thing or two.

"I don't think we will have much trouble out of old Bozo with this sort of thing," says he.

"You mean it's too hot for them to touch?"

"Let us just say that Bozo the Congress isn't going to risk having the President take away its clown suit," he says.

I am really moved by this guy's courage. I tell him I know it will be very bad for him when Kissinger finally tracks him down as the leaker who exposed Kissinger's brilliance and love of home, flag and mother.

"Yes, terrible," says the State Department fellow. He shudders.

"What will Kissinger do?"

"He will call me into his office and threaten that if I ever do it again he will send a note home to my mother."

I am unable to subject the poor devil to this kind of treatment. After he is gone, I put the secret papers in the fire.

A week passes and he phones in a rage. "Are you ever going to print those secret documents," he demands, "or are you trying to get me fired?"

After the Flood

The news that the entire United States Senate has undergone sex-change surgery has apparently shocked no one. Few persons seem even mildly interested. The news has been so grotesque for so long that people are surprised by nothing anymore.

In fact, we may have arrived at a stage where news no longer exists, which is to say, a condition in which the astounding occurs with such regularity that it is no more interesting than a bologna-and-cheese sandwich at the desk.

Newspaper people date this development from the Watergate period when the incredible became as routine as the weather forecast. This was followed by the CIA revelations, which put the public to sleep with sensational news breaks. Then came the disclosure that Internal Revenue agents had been getting drunk with Government girls in motels to train themselves not to give away secrets under the influence of booze and sexual temptation, which was considered such a dull story that the papers scarely played it at all.

Vice President Rockefeller's resignation and subsequent flight to Japan, which had asked him to take over the country and become Emperor, left most of the nation bored despite the splashy headlines.

I was in an Irish pub on 57th Street the night Rockefeller arrived in Tokyo and a colleague in gin said to the bartender, "It's always the same old news, Pat. Would you mind switching over to the Yankee game?"

The fall of China produced even less visible interest. "Well," I said to a cabdriver that afternoon, "China has fallen."

"What hasn't?" replied the cabbie.

That was the day it finally occurred to me that the entire country had simply had too much news, but it still seemed possible that something might happen so outlandish, so absurd, so improbable that vast numbers of Americans would still read three or four paragraphs about it and possibly even discuss it at dinner.

And so, when the papers disclosed that President Ford had had Ronald Reagan crated in a box and shipped to Senator Goldwater as a birthday present, I went back to my Irish pub to see how the customers were taking it.

"One fellow did mention it to me," Pat reported, "but all he said was, 'It's still business as usual in Washington, I see.' "

Around the newspaper office where I work it was a bad time. "Isn't there any news at all?" the managing editor asked one night when the presses were rusting silently.

"Just the usual," said the assistant managing editor: "Mother shoots seventy-three motorists on New Jersey Turnpike. One hundred largest corporations indicted in church poor-box thefts. Queen Elizabeth kidnapped by terrorists. Castro explodes first atom bomb."

"Stop!" cried the managing editor. "You're putting me to sleep."

That was the night it started raining, you may recall. The interesting thing about the rain was that it fell all over the world, which was reported in the newspapers, which was probably why nobody thought the rain was particularly interesting.

The rain lasted forty days and forty nights, but long before the fortieth day the Secret Service had built an ark, put the President aboard and launched it on the Potomac.

When the rain stopped, the ark was gone. "What do you think of the ark's loss?" I asked a sandwich cutter on Ninth Avenue. "I don't follow the arks, myself," he said. "I'm a Mets fan."

It was obvious that the world had had more news than it could handle. On the day the papers finally reported the ark had been found on Mt. Everest and that the President had entered an ashram in the Himalayas American newspaper sales dropped to an all-time low. At the pub, Pat explained, "There's never any news anymore."

"No, Pat," I said. "There's too much news."

"It's one and the same thing," he replied, turning on the television. "Will you look at the Yankee game or watch the film clips of the House of Representatives being buried earlier today in a volcanic eruption?"

"The Yankees, Pat. I'm tired of humdrum."

The Easy Way

When Presidents talk about getting on with the great tasks confronting America, it seems to be only foreign policy and war-making readiness that they have in mind.

These are big tasks, all right. But are they really the great tasks? Surely they are the routine tasks every Administration has had to see to since we became a superpower. It is the fate of superpowers to be the object of envy and dislike. Avoiding the bellicosity that results naturally from this condition is an inevitable task of their rulers, as is their duty to deal effectively with war when it cannot be helped.

The great tasks, however, have to do with perfecting the nation, and they are rarely, if ever, either exciting to read about in the newspapers or satisfying to the governing class's appetite for drama and game play.

It is easy to see why Presidents since F.D.R. have preferred to dwell upon war and peace. They are, after all, grave themes. They are glamorous, exciting, dramatic themes. Men who deal in them seem more glamorous, exciting, dramatic than men who deal in, say, problems of agricultural production.

There are uniforms, flags, international travel with red carpets and reviewing the troops and toasting the mysterious Chinese. There are heavy bombardment, Paris peace talks, spies, beautiful maps on the wall with brightly colored pins in them, lovely headlines, brilliant audiences, heartbreakingly clean visits to the cemetery on bright patriotic days, occasionally moving speeches followed by taps.

Most important of all perhaps, they also present governing men with relatively simple problems. A President may enjoy an occasional success at peace or war, but at the really great tasks he can expect only despair.

We have been told constantly how complex and difficult the disarmament negotiations with the Soviet Union have been, yet Presidents have had a mild success in them. By contrast, they have had no success at all in disarming dangerous Americans.

This is odd, for the question how heavily armed our households and pedestrians should be is surely pertinent to the truly great task of perfecting the nation. Shall we be a people as fully armed as we are now?

Merely raising this question makes politicians shudder, for hunters and sportsmen—a large part of us—are so fearful of statist limitations on their liberties that they may turn against any politician who is hesitant about total personal armament for everybody.

Not surprisingly, Presidents prefer to talk disarmament with Russians.

The Easy Way

There is the question of how America should smell.

At the end of each summer several million Americans returning from rustic vacations discover, after living on genuine air for a few weeks, that their hometowns and highways smell of the sewer.

Smell has become a highly emotional issue in politics. If you bring it up, a lot of people call you an ecology freak, with that mean inflection they used to get in their voices when they called somebody who disagreed with them a Communist.

Well, and why shouldn't a lot of people? If you make your living in certain ways you have to leave some garbage behind, and garbage usually smells bad. But you're doing your best, aren't you? Making a product people need. Why should you be the one they pick on to pay the bill because of a lot of ecology freaks?

Not surprisingly, politicians are not going to say you should be. Especially if, instead, they can be on television from the Paris peace talks telling you how they, with their tremendous dedication to the country and its great tasks and their matchless grasp of the hideous complexities of the Paris peace talks, are trying to bring you—you!—a generation of peace.

It is a lot easier to get a generation of peace than it is to get the country smelling halfway presentable again.

Nevertheless, stopping the country from smelling bad is a very great task, for a generation of peace is worth a good bit less if it has to be spent in a stench.

It may be worth nothing at all, if your luck is poor, in a land where armed maniacs may gun you down for stepping on their corns in crowded buses.

So there are a lot of great tasks. Maybe the greatest of all is to decide where America is going, so we will know whether a generation of peace is worth looking forward to.

School vs. Education

By the age of six the average child will have completed the basic American education and be ready to enter school. If the child has been attentive in these pre-school years, he or she will already have mastered many skills.

From television, the child will have learned how to pick a lock, commit a fairly elaborate bank holdup, prevent wetness all day long, get the laundry twice as white and kill people with a variety of sophisticated armaments.

From watching his parents, the child, in many cases, will already know how to smoke, how much soda to mix with whiskey, what kind of language to use when angry and how to violate the speed laws without being caught.

At this point, the child is ready for the second stage of education, which occurs in school. There, a variety of lessons may be learned in the very first days.

The teacher may illustrate the economic importance of belonging to a strong union by closing down the school before the child arrives. Fathers and mothers may demonstrate to the child the social cohesion that can be built on shared hatred by demonstrating their dislike for children whose pigmentation displeases them. In the latter event, the child may receive visual instruction in techniques of stoning buses, cracking skulls with a nightstick and subduing mobs with tear gas. Formal education has begun.

During formal education, the child learns that life is for testing. This stage lasts twelve years, a period during which the child learns that success comes from telling testers what they want to hear.

Early in this stage, the child learns that he is either dumb or smart. If the teacher puts intelligent demands upon the child, the child learns he is smart. If the teacher expects little of the child, the child learns he is dumb and soon quits bothering to tell the testers what they want to hear.

At this point, education becomes more subtle. The child taught by school that he is dumb observes that neither he, she, nor any of the many children who are even dumber, ever fails to be promoted to the next grade. From this, the child learns that while everybody talks a lot about the virtue of being smart, there is very little incentive to stop being dumb.

What is the point of school, besides attendance? the child wonders. As the end of the first formal stage of education approaches, school answers this question. The point is to equip the child to enter college.

Children who have been taught they are smart have no difficulty. They have been happily telling testers what they want to hear for twelve years. Being artists at telling testers what they want to hear, they are admitted to college joyously, where they promptly learn that they are the hope of America.

Children whose education has been limited to adjusting themselves to their schools' low estimates of them are admitted to less joyous colleges which, in some cases, may teach them to read.

At this stage of education, a fresh question arises for everyone. If the point of lower education was to get into college, what is the point of college? The answer is soon learned. The point of college is to prepare the student—no longer a child now—to get into graduate school. In college, the student learns that it is no longer enough simply to tell the testers what they want to hear. Many are tested for graduate school; few are admitted.

Those excluded may be denied valuable certificates to prosper in medicine, at the bar, in the corporate boardroom. The student learns that the race is to the cunning and often, alas, to the unprincipled.

Thus, the student learns the importance of destroying competitors and emerges richly prepared to play his role in the great simmering melodrama of American life.

Afterward, the former student's destiny fulfilled, his life rich with Oriental carpets, rare porcelain and full bank accounts, he may one day find himself with the leisure and the inclination to open a book with a curious mind, and start to become educated.

Magazine Rack

I read *The National Enquirer* when I want to feel exhilarated about life's possibilities. It tells me of a world where miracles still occur. In the world of *The National Enquirer,* UFOs flash over the Bermuda Triangle, cancer cures are imminent, ancient film stars at last find love that is for keeps. Reached on The Other Side by spiritualists, Clark Gable urges America to keep its chin up. Of all possible worlds, I like the world of *The National Enquirer* best.

Not that the world of *People* isn't a pretty gosh-darn wonderful place, too. Life may not be very exhilarating in the world of *People,* but it is beautiful. There I meet Prince Charles, who has no problems, and Erica Jong, who has fame, beauty and success. And J. Paul Getty, the richest man in the world! I learn that Catherine Deneuve is beautiful and Liza Minnelli is talented and Mikhail Baryshnikov is happy. What a sweet world. It is what the world of F. Scott Fitzgerald would have been if Fitzgerald had been ghostwritten by Dr. Norman Vincent Peale.

Sometimes, of course, I sneak into the world of *Playboy* for a wallow in hedonism. In the world of *Playboy,* Ernest Hemingway wears a silk union suit in a sleeping bag at a Holiday Inn. It is a world in which Henry VIII is played by John Travolta and Oedipus tears out his eyes because the tone arm on his record changer is not properly balanced.

So much less fearsome than the world of *Esquire,* where Dante Gabriel Rossetti always seems to be jogging with Muhammad Ali while Norman Mailer is on a pub crawl with Vergil.

After so much rich masculinity, one needs repose. There are

several possible worlds for this. The world of *Foreign Affairs,* for example, where the Harvard faculty assembles to administer a high colonic to Anwar Sadat. Or the world of *U.S. News & World Report* where deep slumber can be enjoyed in the complete text of Ronald Reagan's declaration of faith in the American marketplace.

I tread cautiously whenever I stumble into the world of *Ms.* As I tiptoe about, looking for an exit, I hear Mark Antony declaring over the corpse of Brutus, "This was a person." In my panic I will take any exit at all. Once, I dashed out of the world of *Ms.* and found myself right in the middle of the world of *Psychology Today* —a convention of embalmers arguing how to proceed with Mickey Mouse's synapses.

Another time, I stumbled into the world of *The New York Review of Books.* Basil Rathbone and Errol Flynn were dueling for Olivia de Havilland. Rathbone won, provoking Olivia to a brilliant denunciation of his footwork, which so enraged Rathbone that he promptly rowed back to his ship and composed a 12,000-word rebuttal of Olivia's criticism, in the course of which he revealed that as a student at Smith she had ranked only ninety-seventh in épée and seventy-third in saber, and furthermore had taken a morally weak position on William Howard Taft's 1908 campaign.

Whenever I need a complete change of worlds, as I did then, I run to the newsstand for *Cosmopolitan.* What a flattering world it is for a man. Not a man in the place, and all these women sitting around studying techniques for trapping one. I always consult my horoscope there because I know that in the world of *Cosmopolitan* it will declare me a first-rate subject for love in the coming month. The women giggle when they see me and try to lure me with frozen-food dinners by candlelight and with artfully constructed foundation garments, but I pay them no heed, for I know they only wish to practice their lessons in how to steal a husband on a working girl's budget.

How do I know such things? Because I spend part of every week in the world of *New York* magazine, a world that trains you for survival. As a regular denizen of the world of *New York* magazine, I can instantly identify the owners of the ten most expensive brass beds in Manhattan and tell you which new cheeses are chic. There I have learned how to exude power through my necktie and how to buy a subway token. I know the fifteen best places for rape in the Wall Street district and how to come in from the rain.

This is different from the world of *The New York Times,* where life seems so gravely beset by imminent catastrophe that it is useless to study survival. The only hope in the world of *The New York Times* is Professor Kissinger, who is constantly taking me aside at 35,000 feet for private assurances that things are not as desperate as the riots at the last airport might suggest. I tire of these constant reassurances. They are, after all, only reminders that the world will continue to be a place where no miracles are possible.

So I whoop with glee when a new edition of *The National Enquirer* hits the newsstands and step into the world where Gable can cheer me up from The Other Side.

Right? Wrong!

Not long ago I was right about something. I knew it for an absolute fact, an indisputable certainty. It was a rare moment. Like most people, I am almost always wrong about whatever the business at hand may be, and for an instant it was exhilarating to sense that I was the only person in a room full of people who was absolutely right.

In fact, it was not a moment for exultation. It was a moment of extreme peril. There are few things more dangerous to social or political success than being right. Persons who are truly lucky never find themselves suffering from this affliction. One of the most successful politicians in recent times has been wrong on

Right? Wrong!

absolutely everything for the past twenty-five years and has been regularly rewarded with reelection by vast majorities.

This is not surprising. Most people are wrong most of the time. It is the human condition. Their hearts go out to a man who is so thoroughly one of them that his only superiority consists in an ability to be wrong even more consistently than they. "Good old Bill!" they say. "He's my kind of guy."

By contrast, there used to be a man in the United States Senate who was right about everything. In ten years of watching him perform, I never saw an occasion on which he was not utterly, breathtakingly right. He clearly saw distant dangers to the country and how they could be avoided. He knew precisely what was ailing the economy and how it could be healed. He even knew what was wrong with the Senate and forcefully explained how it could be corrected. What's more, he never flinched from giving the Senate an irrefutable argument illustrating how right he was.

Time and time again, this poor, afflicted wretch saw his small efforts to improve man's lot gleefully voted down by majorities of ninety to one. It is a hard fate to be right. It is a curse to be right and not be able to keep it a secret.

The more clever politicians are very good about handling themselves when right, as they occasionally are. They sense that to be right is to be in danger, to court dislike and possibly unemployment. They handle their rightness like herpetologists nursing a king cobra, all too aware that we who are wrong strike with sharp fangs unless carefully jollied.

In business and social life, the person who is unashamedly right is an intolerable lout to be disposed of by transfer to the Samoan branch office or struck from the guest list as a boor. In politics, he is often punished by dis-election.

Politicians have met this problem with characteristic elasticity. Their trick is to avoid being right at the wrong time. One of the most fatal judgments one politician can deliver against another is: "He was right too soon."

Wayne Morse and Ernest Gruening were "right too soon" when they cast the only two Senate votes against Lyndon Johnson's full-scale entry into the Vietnam war. The fact that great numbers of politicians eventually found the war to be disastrous did not much reduce the feeling among Washington types that people who came out against it "too soon" were, if not wrong, at least too insensitive to the nuances of timing about rightness to be fully skilled in the governmental art.

Everett Dirksen stated the politician's philosophy of being right when he finally switched his position on civil rights and declared, one hundred years after the Emancipation Proclamation, that fair treatment for black people was "an idea whose time has come."

This is another way of saying that it is wrong to be right until the multitudes are so busy being wrong about something else— the Vietnam war, in this case—that they no longer much care.

It isn't particularly surprising that we don't want politicians being right soon enough about a-borning disasters to save us from the worst. Nor is it surprising that politicians oblige us.

The thing I was absolutely right about not long ago was the population of the United States in 1920. Everybody else in the room was wrong by at least 10 million people. I could have pulled down the almanac and proved that I was the only soul there who knew what he was talking about and sent them away feeling stupid. I didn't. There were people there whose guest lists I didn't want to be stricken from. Later, one or two will get the population figure right, but I shall not remind them that I had it right all along. I don't want to be stigmatized as one of those kooks who are always right too soon.

New York WASP

In New York everyone belongs to a minority group. This gives you pride in your roots and encourages you to feel everybody else is picking on you, which is one of the basic pleasures of the New York experience.

New York WASP

My group is called "the WASPs," which is an acronymic word standing for "white Anglo-Saxon Protestants." I did not want to join the WASPs but I was press-ganged into it. The reason I didn't want to join was that the WASPs are the only minority who cannot have any fun.

All the other minorities are entitled to make a mess of Central Park once a year or paralyze traffic by marching on Fifth Avenue. They also enjoy the right to hold noisy demonstrations and tell all the best ethnic jokes.

All the WASPs can tell are Harvard jokes. This is because all WASPs are supposed to have gone to Yale, or at least Princeton, or to act as if they had, even if they haven't. Instead of marching down Fifth Avenue or eating wonderful old WASP food in an annual Central Park WASP Festival, WASPs have to sit around dim, musty clubs reading the *Yale Alumni Bulletin* and talking about their ancestors.

I have never liked clubs since I was sneered at in one in Baltimore many years ago for wearing a green double-breasted suit with a red stripe and unmatching two-tone shoes.

Talking about ancestors, however, is very enjoyable. Upon first coming to New York, I used to do it frequently among friends like Fried, Ciccelo, Moynihan and Leventhal. When they reminisced about ancestors who had been beaten by Cossacks, tortured by Fascists and shot by the Black and Tans, I told them about my great-great aunt who had been fatally gnawed by a bear.

This did not please Fried, Ciccelo, Moynihan or Leventhal. It was bad form for a WASP to have an ancestor with nutrient appeal to bears. WASP ancestors were supposed to spend their time knitting samplers, extolling the virtues of sexual repression and Brooks Brothers stylings.

Friends who belonged to other minorities seemed to think it was cheating for a WASP to talk of interesting ancestors. It was useless to protest that I did not want to be a WASP and, in fact, didn't even qualify since my normal hue was closer to gray than white. Efforts to escape destiny with a frail joke about my grayness —"I'm a GASP, not a WASP"—cut no ice. In New York one had to belong to a minority, and the only one I came close to fitting was the WASPs.

There was no escaping. My wife, who is pink and Celtic, was allowed to join the Women, a group which qualifies as a minority in New York, although they are in the numerical majority. This means she does not have to wear tweeds or pinstripes all winter, the way I do, and can talk about being oppressed whenever the mood is upon her and be sure of a sympathetic audience.

If she wants to reciprocate our friends' invitations to knishes, pigs' trotters or canelloni by inviting them to corned beef and cabbage, they respect her for loyalty to her edible roots. But if I invite them for a feast remembered from my own tradition—heaping platters of boiled kale and chitterlings, say—they regard me as a traitor to WASPism. WASPs are not allowed to like interesting food.

This seemed like tyranny at first. One began to feel paranoiac, persecuted. Why should I be forced to wear tweeds and pinstripes? To sit in clubs, which I hated, reading alumni bulletins which made me weep with boredom? If others could serve ravioli and blintzes to applause, why did chitterlings on my table merit nothing but contempt? Why did I have to have a great-great aunt who knitted samplers instead of getting gnawed by a bear?

The worst part was the sexual repression that one was supposed to exhibit on all possible occasions. No, on second thought, it wasn't the sexual repression. It was the inability to have a mother like everybody else.

Members of all the other minority groups had mothers who had driven them, smothered them with love, worried about them, cherished ridiculous hopes for them, trained them in guilt and tyrannized them in emotional family relationships. In short, they had mothers.

As a WASP, I was not permitted a mother. Attempts to prove that I had one were met with knowing glances passed surreptitiously among my listeners. What does a WASP know about mothers? An old lady wearing tweeds and pinstripes and telling Harvard jokes—call that a mother?

WASPs don't have mothers. They have old ladies sitting in dim, musty clubs reading the *Vassar Alumnae Bulletin.*

Who Wouldn't Love New York?

Things to do on Saturday in New York:

1. Put on five suits of clothes and walk crosstown talking out loud to yourself in Esperanto.

2. Put on a pair of brushed suede trousers and get a $35 haircut.

3. Burn down a building in the Bronx.

4. Get together with two other women on 12th Street and argue about who has the best Cuisinart.

5. Get rained on for twenty minutes while waiting for a bus on York Avenue.

6. Diet until you look like you are made of sticks. Then put on an elegant fur coat and find a girl in an elegant fur coat who also looks like she is made of sticks. Go together to a pet shop and buy a dog that looks like it is made of sticks and then all three of you take a walk in the East Sixties.

7. Wait for the telephone to ring and then don't answer it. Afterward, hide under the bed until your neighborhood burglar arrives for your television set. Introduce yourself.

8. Buy some antiques and frozen bagels.

9. Argue with your wife, husband or lover about whose turn it is to go outside to find out whether the sun is shining.

10. Get together with several people from the Upper West Side and display the keenness of your sensibility by deploring the banality of Italian opera, contemporary architecture and *The New York Review of Books.*

11. Get stuck for two hours in an elevator with somebody holding advanced views on calendar reform.

12. Telephone several acquaintances and ask if they have heard

of any interesting new liberation movements worth joining. If they haven't, ask if they have heard of any interesting new opinions worth declaring truculently to liven up dull parties.

13. Go to Ninth Avenue and look at the groceries. Go to Eighth Avenue and look at the pimps. Go to Seventh Avenue and smell the grease. Go to Sixth Avenue and cringe under the architecture.

14. Think of the futility of life. Then ponder the certainty of doom. Reflect at length on the fact that nothing good has ever happened to you and that nothing ever will. Think on the certainty of rising taxes, deteriorating arteries, dandruff and disappointment in love. Then take a ride on the subway.

15. Meet with some really decent people in Central Park and have a really serious talk about ecology, good writing and social injustice.

16. Get into your own head, or into art or leather.

17. Buy the loudest transistor radio in midtown, tune in a rock station, turn it to maximum volume and carry it around the streets so everybody can admire your taste in music.

18. Discover an incredibly fantastic new restaurant in the Village that nobody has ever heard of and which would be ruined if everybody did. Then telephone several people and feel superior by not telling them about it.

19. Write a letter to the editor denouncing Senator Proxmire, deploring the middle class's persecution by the poor or demanding to know why the editor permits so much unmitigated trash to be published in his newspaper.

20. Get a job in a snooty delicatessen or a snooty Italian boutique on Fifth Avenue and assure customers that you do not regard them as people of sufficient quality to deserve your lox or Florentine toothpicks.

21. Stand in a Third Avenue movie line for an hour and have a really deep talk about cinema and existentialism while eating a pretzel.

22. Buy a house on Sutton Place and lie in bed until 3 P.M. thinking how rich you are, yet unloved for all your wealth. Tele-

phone an old school friend out in Brooklyn and tell him how you have envied his poverty since discovering that money can't buy happiness. Afterward book a Concorde flight to Paris for Sunday brunch.

23. Have a friend over for lunch and make her respect you by explaining the correlation between the Manichean heresy and hot pastrami.

24. Walk around the East Side until you see Jackie Onassis, Greta Garbo and Woody Allen or develop blisters. If unsuccessful on all four counts, buy some blisters on Madison Avenue so you will have something to talk about Saturday night.

Lobster Unlimited

Mouths watering for lobster, we came to Maine. "Got any lobster?" we asked the man at the pound. He said one thing he sure had was lobster. He picked two lobsters from a tank and held them out. They seemed much too small to make a meal for two people who had their mouths set for a real lobster dinner.

"We'd like something bigger." He returned to the tank, brought out two bigger lobsters and said, "These'll run about two pounds apiece. Don't often get 'em that big anymore these days."

The man obviously didn't know the appetite he was dealing with. One had to speak to him tartly. "Perhaps I have not made myself sufficiently clear. We are not looking for canapé spread. We are looking for lobster."

He gave us a hooded glance. "Two-pounders ain't enough?" he inquired. "How about a nice three-pounder?"

"Lobster, man! We want lobster, not bird food."

He smiled. "Well," he said, "I might just be able to give you what you're looking for."

It was our turn to smile. He called to a young man. "Bring out Old Sam," he said. The young man looked at us, then looked at his employer, then shrugged. After a considerable wait, he returned from a back room with a reasonably large lobster.

"This is Old Sam," said the lobsterman. "He'll run about seven pounds."

We were still not sure. "Do you think he'll make a full meal?"

The lobsterman looked us both squarely in the eyes. Not a muscle twitched in his face. "There's a lot of good eatin' on that lobster," he said.

We took it. Old Sam was put in a paper bag and driven home. We put on a pot of water. As it started to boil, Old Sam began to shake the paper bag, indicating an unhappiness with the proceedings. We ripped the bag and he came out thrashing. At the pound he had not looked like much, but on the kitchen table he had claws the size of Muhammad Ali's fists. We recoiled.

"Pick him up and drop him in the pot," each of us said instantly to the other. But Old Sam was touchy. As the cook's hand reached toward his carapace, he countered with a left hook and crossed with his right, nearly amputating an index finger. The two of us glared uneasily at him and he glared right back, and then it became apparent that even after we captured him there was going to be trouble, since the boiling pot was not big enough to contain half of him.

We decided to try it anyhow. We couldn't just let him push us around and take over the house. While one of us distracted him in the front, the other sneaked up behind him, grabbed his tail, swung him through the air and dropped him into the pot.

Boiling water splashed over stove and floor. Old Sam's tail rested momentarily in the steam, but his claws hung over the edge and he stared at us with an expression of absolute disenchantment, before hoisting himself over the side of the ineffectual pot and diving to the safety of the floor.

One of us screamed as he moved in for the attack, and two local men who happened to be passing on the beach ran up to investigate. They immediately grasped the situation.

"It's those people that bought Old Sam this afternoon," one of them said.

"Might have known it," said the other. He produced fishing line, threw a lasso around the lobster, trussed him tightly and rolled him on his back.

"If you're of a mind to boil Old Sam," his companion suggested, "better get rid of that saucepan and fire up a washtub."

They graciously assisted in this operation, and when the tub was at a rolling boil and the lobster had been safely immersed, one of them asked, "What are you going to do with Old Sam when he's boiled?"

"Eat him, of course."

"Mind if we bring a few folks over to watch?"

We certainly did mind. Hospitality has its limits. They shrugged and left, full of winks and sly grins.

That was seven days ago, and Old Sam is still with us. After the first night's meal, there was lunch of cold lobster claw. The second night, it was lobster salad from the carapace meat. The next day, cold lobster tail with mayonnaise. Then lobster roll. Then lobster stew. Then sliced lobster.

Periodically, grinning children stick their heads in the window and ask, "Getting near the end of Old Sam yet?" In town, solicitous Maine folks ask us if it looks like Old Sam will last us another week. It does. There's a lot of good eatin' on that lobster, a seven-pound lobster being the marine equivalent to a 2,000-pound beef. Which gives rise to an idea. Maybe tonight, after everybody else has gone to bed, we'll sneak off to the highway and get a hamburger.

Grooving with Academe

For a long time I made commencement speeches. It started with high schools. One had sons, daughters. They went to high school, alas. Hawk-eyed principals desperate for someone—anyone—to harangue their steamy produce spotted me for an easy mark.

How could one resist making sons and daughters proud by a display of public prattling before their assembled schoolmates? More cunning parents resisted it easily. Wiser parents. Parents with no instinct for self-humiliation. Not me. I was easily dragooned. "Go forth, youth of America—." The snickering, I assumed, came from the soreheads, from the types awaiting Juvenile Court action for trafficking in hashish.

Word passed along the principals' grapevine. I was in great demand. "Go forth and light the light of wisdom, youth of America—." I was hooked. A certain college, whose scheduled Demosthenes had seen the light in the nick of time and fled to Samoa, sought me in desperation as a replacement.

It was irresistible. The academic robes, the academic procession, the academic drinking on commencement eve with the academic professors, the academic hangover next morning, the glorious June sunshine filtering through the academic elms—all were immensely satisfying. The young whom I had sent forth from high school four years earlier now sat sprawled before me like a sea of Supreme Court Justices, and I sent them forth again.

"Go forth, youth of America—." They were surlier now. As the 1960's crumbled into the 1970's, they were no longer agreeable about going forth. They were of a mind to stay behind and ignite the physics lab or blow up the commencement podium.

This was the period in which I began receiving honorary degrees. Any sensible person would have re-examined his position as soon as the first honorary degree was offered, but we are talking now about a fevered brain.

Was there something odd about an honorary degree being extended to a person who had been put out of college with a gentleman's C, and granted that release only because the professors feared that, if failed, he might return for one more year?

Was it curious that such a person, whose only notable achievements had been to acquire three cats and make a fool of himself on many public occasions, should be accorded the same recognition as Nobel Prize winners, donors of $25-million bequests and politicians who were, had been or were expected to be Presidents of the United States?

Grooving with Academe

A thoughtful person might have said yes—yes, there is something odd, something curious going on. He might have suspected that he was the token nonentity with which the student body was to be pacified. We speak, remember, of a time when the slightest provocation could turn an entire student body into sackers of Byzantium.

In this period, colleges far and wide desperately sought schlemiels who might keep the restless young amused by accepting their honorary degrees between the Nobelist in physics (nuclear, bad) and the politician who refused to support the Vietcong.

There has never been such a shower of honorary degrees upon life's fools. We would meet changing planes at O'Hare Airport and trade notes on honorary-degree conditions around the country and marvel that inconsequentiality was at last receiving its due.

I was oblivious to the reality at that time, of course, and so, when a college of splendid reputation in upstate New York asked me to make the commencement address and accept an honorary degree, I went. On the platform that day sat an unexpected, last minute guest. Ezra Pound. Mentor to T. S. Eliot, companion to Ernest Hemingway, poet extraordinary, a giant of twentieth-century letters. Ezra Pound. I was going to have to make a commencement speech at Ezra Pound.

I did it. "Go forth, Ezra Pound—." Ezra Pound sat through the whole thing. It may have been the most absurd moment in the history of commencements. I wanted to apologize, but Pound had taken a vow of silence and no conversation was possible, though I looked him in the eyes and thought they were saying, "Go forth —and follow my example."

At that moment I took a vow never to let another commencement speech pass my lips. I would have sworn, also, never to let another honorary degree fall upon me, but it wasn't necessary. The offers stopped coming in shortly afterwards, when the young had a change of heart and made peace with society. It was a happy development, not only because it meant that sanity was making a strong comeback, but also because it prevented me from beating Herbert Hoover's record for honorary degrees.

Hoover, who got eighty-nine, received more than anybody else *The Guinness Book of World Records* has been able to discover. If he had my experience afterwards, this means he was plagued by eighty-nine colleges to contribute to their building funds.

Hey, Ruble!

Leo Tolstoy is tired of writing for kopecks. He wants the big rubles.

"So you think you're ready for the big rubles, Leo," says his agent.

Leo Tolstoy says he wants it all. The 250,000-ruble advance. The 1,275,000-ruble paperback sale. The big movie deal. The television sale.

"Such talk is music to my heart," says his agent. "Go home and write me a few hundred words describing your novel."

Leo Tolstoy goes home and writes 250,000 words. His agent cannot wade through it. "Leo, Leo," he groans. "All this talk about Napoleon in somebody's parlor and I can't even keep the names straight. Go home and write letters to John Kenneth Galbraith and Norman Mailer and Philip Roth and ask them to give you some punchy sales lines for the jacket, and maybe I can find a sucker."

Leo Tolstoy writes letters of 100,000 words each to Galbraith, Mailer and Roth. They do not answer. Turgenev and Henry James, however, agree to send jacket blurbs on condition that Leo Tolstoy stop writing them 100,000-word letters.

Leo Tolstoy shows James's blurb to his agent. It says, "Leo Tolstoy has done it again!" Turgenev's says, "Couldn't put it down!"

"Leo," says the agent, "I will give it to you from the shoulder. James Turgenev does not sell books, but I will tell you what."

And he tells Leo Tolstoy to forget the book for the time being and write the condensation for *Reader's Digest.*

Hey, Ruble!

Leo Tolstoy writes the condensation. It runs to 575,000 words.

"Let's skip the condensation, Leo, and go right to the movie," says his agent. "Once you have written the movie, you can do the paperback novelization of the film and then work backward to the full novel."

At home, Leo Tolstoy writes a great movie. If filmed, it will run for thirty-seven hours, not including intermissions for meals. "Leo," says his agent, "nobody is going to buy a thirty-seven-hour movie, a 575,000-word condensation or a full-length novel that takes a 100,000-word letter to describe."

Leo Tolstoy is depressed. He sees the big rubles eluding him.

"However," says the agent, "if you write the sound-track music for the movie, it will create a terrific audience, which will then demand that the rest of the movie be made, which will make everybody want more and have the publishers begging you to write the full-length best-selling novel."

Leo Tolstoy goes home and sits down at the piano. After having a lot of fun learning to play "Chopsticks," he realizes he cannot write music.

"In that case, Leo," says his agent, "do the comic book first. Then we will hire a composer to write the music for the smash-hit film soon to be made on which the comic book is based, and point out that when the movie is finished it will be based on the full-length best-seller soon to be written."

Leo Tolstoy goes home and does the comic book. It is thicker than the Manhattan telephone directory and is very poorly drawn.

"Leo," says his agent, "I don't suppose you could make the bubble gum."

"Bubble gum?" says Leo Tolstoy.

"The 'War and Peace Bubble Gum,' " says his agent. "It would create a demand for the 'War and Peace Comic Book,' which would trigger demand for the 'War and Peace Sound-Track Record,' which would set up demand for the film, which would create demand for the condensation of the book on which the film is based, which will create demand for this best-seller you want to write."

Leo Tolstoy admits to an inadequacy. He cannot make bubble gum.

"Not to worry," says his agent. "We'll go all the way to the end and work backward. Go home and make me a 'War and Peace T-shirt.'"

Leo Tolstoy sits at home sewing. He sews for days. The T-shirt already covers fourteen acres. "Sometimes," thinks Leo Tolstoy, "literature doesn't seem to be my glass of tea." He toys with the idea of chucking it all and looking for the big rubles in the garment trade.

Lost Labor Love

Early in life, most of us probably observe an unhappy relationship between labor and wealth—to wit, the heavier the labor, the less the wealth.

The man doing heavy manual work makes less than the man who makes a machine work for him, and this man makes less than the man sitting at a desk. The really rich people, the kind of people who go around on yachts and collect old books and new wives, do no labor at all.

The economic reasons for dividing the money this way are clear enough. One, it has always been done that way; and two, it's too hard to change at this late date. But the puzzling question is why, since the money is parceled out on this principle, young people are constantly being pummeled to take up a life of labor.

In any sensible world, the young would be told they could labor if they wanted to, but warned that if they did so it would cost them.

Not here. In this country, labor is talked about as if it were something everybody ought to be dying for a chance to get into, like oceanfront real estate. We are forever haranguing each other about the nobility of labor, the dignity of labor, the rewards of labor, honest labor, decent labor and so forth, until all the starch is taken out of any potential upstarts who might be tempted to ask the sensible question, "How come, if labor is such a worthy way to spend your life, the pay isn't better?"

The answer they would get, of course, is, "Labor is its own reward."

I did not believe that, even when I was innocent. "I don't want the reward of labor," I would say. "I want wealth, yachts, old books, new wives." And I would say, "Look at J. Paul Getty; he toils not, neither does he spin, yet his is the wealth of Croesus. I want to be a nontoiler like Getty and have the reward of cash."

At first, people dealt with me patiently, and by people I mean statesmen who were wise beyond my years and understood wherein lay happiness.

"What!" they would exclaim. "Poor deluded lad! Behold the digger in his ditch. Does he not partake richly of nobility and dignity? Is poor Getty recompensed for being denied all that by the cold assuagement of lucre?"

To me, that cold assuagement seemed adequate compensation for missing out on blisters, and I determined to sacrifice a life of work for the Calvary of great wealth. It was a dangerous decision, and quickly abandoned, for fierce politicians began going about the country suggesting that such behavior was unwholesome, cynical and possibly subversive.

In brief, I undertook the joys of labor, joined sundry unions which sent regular mailings extolling my dignity and proclaiming dues increases and cunningly sneaked a sinuous route from bearer of hundred-pound flour sacks (that's labor!) to journalist (that's labor?) while enlarging my wealth in proportion to the decrease in my labors.

I am still not near the yacht class, fortunately for dignity, but I do have a canoe and have lately begun acquiring mildewed Book-of-the-Month Club selections of the late 1930's at garage sales.

The unions' desire to keep us persuaded of the splendor of labor is understandable. If everybody decided to be rich instead of working, the unions would go out of business. Union officers work just as hard as the average middle-management executives and have canoes, too, and it is only natural that they not want their members to give up the nobility of labor for the cold assuagement of lucre.

What is baffling is the Government's attitude in all this. The Government cannot afford to have a country made up entirely of rich people, because rich people pay so little tax that the Government would quickly go bankrupt. This is why Government men always tell us that labor is man's noblest calling. Government needs labor to pay its upkeep.

It seems to me that Government could make a concession here. Its present tax system is rigged so salaried income, which is the kind of income labor gets, is taxed at higher rates than rich income.

It would be a simple matter to switch the loophole. Rich income would be taxed at the high rate salaried income now pays, and salaried workers would get the kind of loopholes the rich now have—which is to say, loopholes that make it certain that somebody else will have to do most of the taxpaying.

I don't expect the Government to leap at this sensible suggestion. I expect it to reply that the rewards of labor are so rich we should all be glad to pay double for them, and anyhow, hasn't Government already given us Labor Day?

No Noise Isn't Good Noise

In Manhattan where I live, the block just to the south of us is always being dynamited. Sometimes it happens two or three times during dinner. Then two or three weeks will pass without a single explosion.

At first I used to jump up from dinner and run out to see the damage, and, of course, there wasn't any. There wasn't even any curiosity among the street crowds. They were calmly buying magazines, waiting for buses, carrying home pastrami and doing all those normal New York things which New Yorkers go right on doing immediately after hearing the sound of an entire block blowing up. I quickly began to feel foolish.

Buildings were all intact, manhole covers all in place, glass unshattered. Inside our house, the explosion had sounded monstrous; outside, where it must have happened, all was serene. Inquiries were futile. "Explosion? No, I didn't hear no explosion."

And yet the sound of the dynamiting went on at irregular intervals. Sometimes it occurred at midnight, sometimes at breakfast. After a while I stopped hearing it. Oh, it still went on, all right, but I had begun to develop the New York ear. The New York ear is the opposite of the ear which afflicted the narrator of Edgar Allan Poe's "The Telltale Heart." This poor homicidal devil became so sensitive to noise that he began hearing the nonexistent heartbeat of the man he had murdered. The possessor of the New York ear becomes so insensitive to noise that he stops hearing whole blocks blowing up and maniacs screaming in his face.

I noticed the change one night during dinner when an out-of-town guest jumped from his chair during the soup and cried, "What in God's name was that?" I had noticed nothing unusual. True, an instant earlier there had been the sound of an entire city block blowing up just to the south of us, but it had made no more impression than the clatter of spoon against bowl.

I confess to having felt a brief twinge of contempt for the guest, to thinking, "These out-of-towners! How easily flustered they are! How poorly fitted to live in New York!"

By that time I had stopped hearing all manner of noises. The automobile burglar alarms, for example. Do they even exist outside New York? Perhaps I should explain. These are shrill screech emitters which can pierce solid granite for a distance of two blocks. In theory, they are activated when car thieves try to break in, filling the air with their maddened screeches, thus terrifying the felons into flight and summoning policemen. In practice, they go off regularly whenever they feel lonely, which is usually between 2 and 3 o'clock in the morning.

Since the screech may continue for an hour or two before the car owner or policemen find time to tend to it, I used to thrash angrily out of bed and pace the house cursing through the pre-dawn hours until my New York ear became fully developed. Now it is quite different. Not long ago, in fact, I awoke at 2:30 one morning terribly aware that something was dreadfully wrong. The automobile burglar screecher which normally goes off under our bedroom window at 2 A.M. was absolutely silent.

The insane cacophony of the 72nd Street fire engines, which always sound as if they have been summoned against the fire-bombing of the whole universe, was shrieking away at its normal decibellage, which lent an air of security to the night, but the silence of the car screecher was almost unbearable. Fortunately, just when it seemed I might never get back to sleep, the entire block just to the south of us was dynamited. It was more restful than a double sleeping pill.

A few weeks ago there was a fierce gun battle just at dinner in front of our house. I believe it was a gun battle, although it may have been Greeks setting off firecrackers. The Greeks were cele-brating their independence day that weekend. We had a guest from the suburbs who called it to our attention, but by that time we were too numb to the sounds of New York to be much interested, and did not go to the window.

"It is either Greeks setting off firecrackers or two motorists waging a gun battle over a parking place," I pointed out. "If the former, there will be nothing interesting to see; if the latter, it means we shall soon have the usual ambulance siren to soothe us during the dessert course."

Just the other morning, at precisely 4:15, I was awakened by an unusual sound in the street. It sounded like a tractor-trailer driving through a plate-glass window. I was ecstatic. New York had come up with a brand-new sound which had the power to stir me. I did not rise to investigate, but fell immediately back into sleep when once again came this extraordinary sound as of a giant plate-glass window being smashed by a great truck.

"What's that?" asked a sleepy child.

"Just a tractor-trailer driving through a plate-glass window," I murmured. "Oh," yawned the child, and we drifted off as the entire block just to the south of us blew to smithereens.

A Nice Place to Visit

Having heard that Toronto was becoming one of the continent's noblest cities, we flew from New York to investigate. New Yorkers jealous of their city's reputation and concerned about challenges to its stature have little to worry about.

After three days in residence, our delegation noted an absence of hysteria that was almost intolerable and took to consuming large portions of black coffee to maintain our normal state of irritability. The local people to whom we complained in hopes of provoking comfortably nasty confrontations declined to become bellicose. They would like to enjoy a gratifying big-city hysteria, they said, but believed it would seem ill-mannered in front of strangers.

Extensive field studies—our stay lasted four weeks—persuaded us that this failure reflects the survival in Toronto of an ancient pattern of social conduct called "courtesy."

"Courtesy" manifests itself in many quaint forms appalling to the New Yorker. Thus, for example, Yankee fans may be astonished to learn that at the Toronto baseball park it is considered bad form to heave rolls of toilet paper and beer cans at players on the field.

Official literature inside Toronto taxicabs includes a notification of the proper address to which riders may mail the authorities not only complaints but also compliments about the cabbie's behavior.

For a city that aspires to urban greatness, Toronto's entire taxi system has far to go. At present, it seems hopelessly bogged down in civilization. One day a member of our delegation listening to a radio conversation between a short-tempered cabbie and the dispatcher distinctly heard the dispatcher say, "As Shakespeare said, if music be the food of love, play on, give me excess of it."

This delegate became so unnerved by hearing Shakespeare quoted by a cab dispatcher that he fled immediately back to New York to have his nerves abraded and his spine rearranged in a real big-city taxi.

What was particularly distressing as the stay continued was the absence of shrieking police and fire sirens at 3 A.M.—or any other hour, for that matter. We spoke to the city authorities about this. What kind of city was it, we asked, that expected its citizens to sleep all night and rise refreshed in the morning? Where was the incentive to awaken gummy-eyed and exhausted, ready to scream at the first person one saw in the morning? How could Toronto possibly hope to maintain a robust urban divorce rate?

Our criticism went unheeded, such is the torpor with which Toronto pursues true urbanity. The fact appears to be that Toronto has very little grasp of what is required of a great city.

Consider the garbage picture. It seems never to have occurred to anybody in Toronto that garbage exists to be heaved into the streets. One can drive for miles without seeing so much as a banana peel in the gutter or a discarded newspaper whirling in the wind.

Nor has Toronto learned about dogs. A check with the authorities confirmed that, yes, there are indeed dogs resident in Toronto, but one would never realize it by walking the sidewalks. Our delegation was shocked by the presumption of a town's calling itself a city, much less a great city, when it obviously knows nothing of either garbage or dogs.

The subway, on which Toronto prides itself, was a laughable imitation of the real thing. The subway cars were not only spotlessly clean, but also fully illuminated. So were the stations.

Your Fare, Lady

To New Yorkers, it was embarrassing, and we hadn't the heart
to tell the subway authorities that they were light-years away from
greatness.

We did, however, tell them about spray paints and how effectively a few hundred children equipped with spray-paint cans
could at least give their subway the big-city look.

It seems doubtful they are ready to take such hints. There is a
disturbing distaste for vandalism in Toronto which will make it
hard for the city to enter wholeheartedly into the vigor of the late
twentieth century.

A board fence surrounding a huge excavation for a new high-
rise building in the downtown district offers depressing evidence
of Toronto's lack of big-city impulse. Embedded in the fence at
intervals of about fifty feet are loudspeakers that play recorded
music for passing pedestrians.

Not a single one of these loudspeakers has been mutilated.
What's worse, not a single one has been stolen.

It was good to get back to the Big Apple. My coat pocket was
bulging with candy wrappers from Toronto and—such is the
lingering power of Toronto—it took me two or three hours back
in New York before it seemed natural again to toss them into the
street.

Your Fare, Lady

It seems to me you can't go more than five minutes with the TV
set this year without seeing somebody eat something absolutely
awful. Or somebody, usually a woman, getting ready to serve
something to eat that is absolutely awful. I wonder if we have
passed through some kind of cultural watershed here.

The big thing on television used to be headache. Every five
minutes they would stop the entertainment, and on would come
somebody with a headache, and then—bingo!—the headache

would be miraculously cured. For twenty years at least, headache was the king of television.

I haven't clocked a typical evening on the tube this year, but my impression—and with television, impressions are all that count—my impression is that the preparation and eating of absolutely awful food is beating headache by at least two to one. Not surprisingly, upset stomach and indigestion are also doing very well. My observations suggest that indigestion is neck-and-neck with headache while upset stomach is closing fast on hard-to-remove stains, in terms of time on tube.

I said that the food on television was absolutely awful, and that's not fair, of course, because I haven't eaten any of it, and don't plan to as long as I have the strength to resist force-feeding. The point is that the idea of this TV food—the concept—is absolutely awful. Food should be grown, but this food being sold on the tube has not been grown; it has been manufactured.

It is hard to understand the men who eat this food, because they are always smiling after the first mouthful, or nuzzling their wives after finishing the thing off. There is one mildly rebellious male who, upon being served some factory-made chicken, asks whatever happened to real chicken.

He is quickly put in his place by chortling harridans who tell him the factory chicken is not only better than real chicken, but also much easier to cook. There are threatening overtones to this encounter which are reminiscent of Strindberg's man-woman hate scenes, but the male turns out to be a sniveler. He eats the phony chicken happily instead of throwing it at the television camera and announcing that he will get some real chicken and cook it himself.

What the feminists call sexism is superficially preserved in all these commercials, since they always cast the woman in the cook's role and make the husband the breadwinner home from his labor to play stern judge of the wife's cooking. This is only superficial, however. What is really going on here is something much trickier.

The point about this television food is that it requires no skill, little time and not much work to put it on the table. A typical teledrama, for instance, concerns two wives unboxing a spaghetti dinner. Both dinners come in boxes. Wife One opens her box and finds nothing but spaghetti. She is in trouble because she will have to add meat. Not Wife Two. Her spaghetti dinner (the sponsor's, naturally) comes with meat boxed in. Everything in one box.

She nips off camera for a second and—presto!—reappears with a steaming spaghetti dinner with meat. Wife One looks surly and defeated, and with good reason, for she will now have to go to the food locker and open another box—of factory-made hamburger, perhaps. Wife Two had to open only one box to make dinner. Poor Wife One has suffered the drudgery of opening two.

So while the commercials seem to cast women in the cook's role, in fact they do not. How can the women be cooks when there is no cooking going on?

Most of what passes for cooking with this television food is nothing but opening, thawing and heating. The real message of the factory-food commercials is not that woman's place is in the kitchen. It is that if a woman has a benighted husband who believes such archaic claptrap, she can fake the cooking effortlessly, thanks to factory-made food, have idle hours in which to do as she pleases and then reduce the poor dolt to eye-rolling delight in her skill in opening a box.

Can any woman long be happy with such a man? Not likely. These food commercials could bring back the headache.

Feline Lib

The cats wanted a conference. Here was a disagreeable development. It was bad enough having conferences with people. A conference is nothing but a committee of the upwardly mobile in search of a victim, and one of the chief reasons for keeping cats was that they hated committees.

I said I did not confer with cats. Grandmother, who had brought the message, looked pained. It was obvious she had made the mistake of conferring with them and they had taken the opportunity to warn her that she was not doing an adequate job and was likely to be replaced by younger blood unless she shaped up.

Don't worry," I told her. "They're not going to force you to take early retirement as long as I'm running things."

This improved her day somewhat, but not mine. The gall of it! The cats asking for a conference! I called a conference myself. Closed-door. Executive session. No cats admitted. Each member of the family had that hooded look of the seasoned conferee ready to buck the blame for failure to somebody else.

Yes, it was true. The cats had walked right in and spoken up. "The cats are talking?"

They were. They had been watching pet-food ads on television and had seen other cats talking. They had even seen a dog singing Italian opera. The scales had fallen from their eyes. The spirit of feline liberation was aflame under their fur.

Here was appalling news indeed. Cats had been tolerable as long as they kept their silence. Now, in addition to the noise of family, phonograph, television, radio and telephone, the household was going to have to live with the gabble of cats.

Firm action was demanded. What was needed at this critical juncture was not Dr. Spock but Spiro Agnew. He had always understood the evils of permissiveness, and permissiveness clearly was the issue at hand. Oh, I had seen enough pet-food commercials to see which way the wind was blowing.

With the decline in the birthrate, Americans had stopped having babies and started having pets. The grocery industry, facing bankruptcy in baby food, had tried to salvage itself with a flier in pet food. You couldn't watch the tube ten minutes anymore without seeing some pampered, insolent beast turn up its nose at the leftover cauliflower and go into a sulk from which it could be rescued only by the advertiser's gourmet pet food.

These four-legged gourmandisers not only spoke an insistent

brand of English, but also engaged in peculiarly arrogant acts of ingratitude by subtly tormenting their owners with suggestions that they were unworthy to practice the nutritional arts. The nation was raising a generation of spoiled animals. The infection had to be treated with powerful medicine. I agreed to see the cats, but only on condition that they not speak. One word out of either of them, I warned, and both would be put out of the house for a week to make do with the neighborhood garbage.

The spokesfeline was Alcibiades, a mangy gray specimen of femininity whom I had tolerated for ten years without once receiving the slightest token of affection, even though one year I had slipped her scraps from the Christmas dinner. Her colleague was a half-witted male, a black cat known simply as "the black cat." For years, he had lived under the illusion that he was a dog. He liked to retrieve thrown balls and lie panting by the hearth on winter nights.

Alcibiades bore a small placard which said, "Power to the Pets." The black cat was wrapped in demonstrator's ribbon, on which was written, "Dog Is Man's Best Baby Substitute."

Like the ruthless executive I am, I told them the facts of life. For years, they had idled uselessly around the house, doing nothing but shedding hair on the furniture. I had put up with that. A man can put up with a lot from any living organism that has the good grace to keep its lip buttoned. And what reward did I get? A demand for gourmet meals. Threats to verbalize. Did they think I wanted to listen to some mangy gray cat talking? First, it would be about food. Before long, it would be politics. Did they think I wanted to listen to an imbecilic black cat talk about the superiority of being a dog?

I let them make the choice. Long life on leftover cauliflower eaten in perpetual silence. Or the animal pound. They skulked out, knowing they had at last met a master. It made me feel dreadful. Could it be that I was incapable of love? Was it I who was the true beast?

At the supermarket, I spent a fortune on gourmet food, brought it home and begged forgiveness. Alcibiades refused. She said I had brought her an inferior brand. The black cat barked an aria from Italian opera. The telephone rang. It was for Alcibiades. The Maltese tomcat next door wanted to complain that his owners didn't understand him.

The Have-Nots

Every society needs a large supply of have-nots, and the American model is no exception. Being more egalitarian than most, however, it is developing a system under which duty in the have-not division can be rotated from generation to generation.

Young white men who nowadays find that they are the last to be hired do not understand the reasons for the change. Under the old order, young white men were always the first to be hired. Now, they complain, they are being discriminated against. They are correct.

And why not? If we are going to have an ample supply of have-nots, somebody simply must be discriminated against. Being discriminated against is unpleasant, but it is traditionally and respectably American. There have always been classes shouldering the harsh duty of being discriminated against. It is only fair that young white men—a class that has always escaped this duty—should now take up the burden for a while.

The theory underlying this change of discrimination victims is that since have-nots are here to stay, the have-not life can be made more palatable if the duty is rotated from time to time. Thus, black people, who have done long duty as have-nots, may draw strength to carry on from the expectation that their children will be given first crack at the good life even when there is an equally able white male applying for it.

The problem is how to make their children equally able. The solution is to discriminate in education. In the past, when white males were exclusively ticketed for the good life, it was arranged by discriminating against blacks at the schoolhouse, with the result that fancy employers could point out that they couldn't find any black people erudite enough for $30,000 jobs.

By discriminating against white male students, the country can get more blacks into the best schools and reduce the percentage of good-life competitors by creating more unqualified young white males.

Young white men nowadays often complain about the injustice of the new discrimination, which is frustrating their career ambitions and trapping them out on the economic margin occupied by the unemployable. Their plight is compounded by the feminist movement which, with Federal muscle behind it, encourages institutions also to mind their step before passing over female applicants.

Well, of course it's unfair to have to be so far superior to both female and black competition that you can't get ticketed into the have class without becoming the object of a Federal investigation. Even then, as many women and blacks can tell these embittered young men, you are likely to see the college or job of your choice go to a less qualified agent of a more favored class. The fact is that there is nothing new about the new discrimination, except the identity of the victimized class.

Women and blacks have absorbed a lesson that white males have yet to learn; to wit, that it is easier to make discrimination work for you than it is to eliminate it from American life. As groups, they have accepted discrimination as a reality and have applied political heat to make certain that if discrimination is to be the rule of the economy, it is at least going to work for them.

White males are still innocent on this point. As a class, they probably believe the myth handed down by generations of contented white forefathers that true merit will conquer all. To believe otherwise would confront them with the necessity of questioning the justice of the American system. And so it is more comfortable for them to complain that they are victims of an aberrational injustice inflicted upon them by noisy pressure groups than to admit that they have been politically outmaneuvered by people who understand the system better than they.

The question no one asks is why the country must have a large supply of people to be discriminated against. This takes us into dangerous water indeed, for when there are enough jobs to absorb a nation's talents and enough schools to fulfill people's desires for education, the need for discrimination withers away.

The country obviously does not provide enough jobs and schools. Some say it cannot afford to and that trying to do so would destroy a system which, after all, is working pretty well. If not, if have-nots in large supply are an economic necessity, then victims of discrimination are a vital part of the system, and the cunning will make sure that the duty of victimhood passes to somebody else.

Lunch of Champions

After becoming a success I was naturally plagued by interviewers. The envious young were the most annoying. They tried to pry out my secret so they could use it to replace me at the top of the ladder. "How did you become a success?" they inquired. I lied to them shamelessly. "Early to bed and early to rise," I always told them. "Plenty of hard work and exercise. Nine-tenths perspiration and one-tenth gastric distress."

Thus I cunningly misled them. The older interviewers, however, were full of sour envy and skilled at spoiling one's day. "Well," they would say, "now that you've lunched your way to the top, what do you do with your time?"

It was a hard question to answer, since at that time most of my energies were spent lunching. What, after all, is the point of being a success if one has to spend the day working? You can be a complete failure and spend the day working. I had not struggled all the way to the top so I could spend the rest of my life struggling. I lunched.

Lunch of Champions

Mornings were spent finding someone to lunch with, then in finding the perfect restaurant for lunching with this particular person, then in persuading the headwaiter to seat us at the perfect table for this particular kind of lunch. Evenings, I studied the works of the great lunchers on how to lunch right and read the latest fashion tips on what the most powerful lunchers in America were lunching on that season.

In my spare time, I kept an eye open for other successes who were lunching badly. Was Philips lunching with the wrong kind of people this spring? Had Sillman begun lunching in the wrong restaurants? Was Haddad still lunching on chef's salad and white wine now that all the great lunchers had begun lunching on poached peaches and mineral water?

Here was grist for murderous conversation at the Success Club. "They say Philips is not lunching well these days," someone would say. To which I could then reply, "But Haddad is no longer lunching with true power." And the question "Really?" could then be answered: "Yes, I saw him lunching just the other day on chef's salad instead of poached peaches." Thus was charted the rise and fall of great men.

The needling of interviewers, however, was relentless, and at length I decided to undertake other activities that would supply answers for "What do you do with your time?" A discreet study of other successes indicated that I needed a secretary. With a secretary, you could say, "Phone up Wilkins, Steadman, Borchert, Saks, Coleman, Lethbridge and Fried, and ask them to please hold the line." Then while all seven were holding dead telephones waiting to hear your voice, you could skim the telephone directory for nine or ten other people to be rung up and kept waiting.

Not wishing to squander good lunching money on secretaries, I practiced my falsetto and began placing the calls myself, posing as a Miss Bellamy. At one point I had eleven different people waiting simultaneously on the hold button, which I am told is not a record. Not surprisingly, many of these persons later phoned back to learn what I had to say to them, and since I had nothing to say to them, I began answering the phone with my Miss Bellamy falsetto and explaining that I was in conference and could not be interrupted.

My stock went up through the success community. Not only was I lunching like a champion, I was also conferring at a pace that left me totally inaccessible. The most eminent successes in town began phoning to lunch with me. Over the poached peaches they made my mouth water with tales of conferences they had held and people whose lives they had made miserable across the conference table.

Here was success with a purpose. I needed some people in my conferences, people who could be shown in no-nonsense terms what it meant to be in the same room with success, people who could be made to squirm under my successful glare, people, in short, whose agonies could be recounted to brighten the eating of the poached peaches and the drinking of the mineral water.

Since I had no people to make miserable, however, I would have to acquire some. For this purpose, I would need to acquire plant and staff, expand production, dicker with governments, hire lawyers, retain a real Miss Bellamy, rent a real conference room —in short, go back to work. I toyed with the notion no longer than twenty-two seconds, adopted my Miss Bellamy falsetto and made the perfect lunch engagement. "I came dangerously close to work today," I told my guest. "I'll pretend I never heard that," he replied.

We had the poached peaches and talked about the gross national product and the failure of socialism.

I am feeling well disposed to the Republican Party these days, which may indicate either an acute attack of euphoria or advanced arteriosclerosis, although I prefer to ascribe it to a sensible terror of having Washington occupied exclusively by Democrats.
—**Dumbness Idea**

When Americans reach the end of the economic line, they move in irresistible masses. Ask the Indians.
—**The Chillies Stir in the Ice Bowl**

Hype makes no critical judgments. The thing or person to be sold may be good quality or trash. Hype works on the theory that Americans will put their money where the noise is.
—**Meatballs for Caviar**

Millions of sensible people are too high-minded to concede that politics is almost always the choice of the lesser evil. "Tweedledum and Tweedledee," they say. "I will not vote." Having abstained, they are presented with a President who appoints the people who are going to rummage around in their lives for the next four years. Consider all the people who sat home in a stew in 1968 rather than vote for Hubert Humphrey. They showed Humphrey. Those people who taught Hubert Humphrey a lesson will still be enjoying the Nixon Supreme Court when Tricia and Julie begin to find silver threads among the gold and the black.
—**Ford without Flummery**

In a tight space, art's distortions get us fastest to the truth.
—**Conservative Chic**

The young cult of sociology, needing a language, invented one. There are many dead languages, but the sociologists' is the only language that was dead at birth.
—**Come Back, Dizzy**

Tomato Surprise

Several of us went to the country together one summer and grew tomato worms.

We were astounded, for we had not planned anything this ambitious at the start of our botanical work. None of us had much talent in the natural sciences, and if you had told us at the outset that we would discover the secret of growing tomato worms, it would have seemed as absurd as suggesting that we might discover a new planet.

Our project was quite modest. It called only for growing tomatoes. We bought six small plants from a farmer, placed them in the earth after the last frost date, placed a ridiculously large stake beside each plant, watered them occasionally and forgot about them.

After several weeks we noticed that the small plants had developed into a miniature dense green jungle of decidedly sinister appearance. We had not expected those small plants to burgeon so menacingly. They were at least five feet tall, extremely thick and shadowy and somehow seemed to defy human beings to come near them.

From time to time one heard the death struggles of birds and cats issuing from deep inside the foliage. As the summer sun burned down on this dark growth, however, delicate yellow blossoms developed small, green, wartlike excrescences which gradually became recognizable as developing tomatoes.

We assumed that the experiment was succeeding.

One sunny morning we awoke to an eerie spectacle. Overnight, the upper portion of what had been a leafy green jungle just the day before had been reduced to a stripped waste of leafless stalks. It was reminiscent of those photographs of old Civil War battlefields in which whole forests have been blasted to splinters by gunfire.

Tomato Surprise

This was, of course, the work of the tomato worm. Close inspection turned up a large crop of tomato worms. Some of us were angry until we saw the significance of what we had accomplished.

We had started with a bare patch of earth, and from it had created a fine, voracious crop of living organisms. Everyone could grow tomatoes, and did. How many people could grow tomato worms?

We are still uncertain how we did it, but we believe the secret is to start with tomato plants. Last year we had day lilies in that location and did not create a single tomato worm. Before that we had petunias and did not grow any tomato worms that year either.

If my theory is correct—that tomato worms cannot be grown without first growing tomatoes—the consequences for agriculture could be ponderous. Next year we could grow corn there and not have to worry about its being destroyed by tomato worms. By declining to grow tomatoes the American farmer would no longer have to dread the possibility of his crop being devastated by tomato worms.

This raises the question where the tomato worm lives when there are no tomatoes in its neighborhood. Does it lie in the earth for centuries waiting to be summoned to life in the sun the moment some passing gardener puts a tomato root into its bed?

Or do the tomato worms all congregate in some central location, like a union hiring hall, until they hear of tomatoes in the next county, and then crawl off to work? My own suspicion is that they spring from tomato seeds and grow right along with the tomatoes. Whatever the case, tomato worms apparently do not exist in active form until you put in tomatoes.

These days when all decent people want to live in brotherhood, or even wormhood, with nature, one feels compelled to find a purposeful role for his tomato worms.

We have tried turning ours loose on the crabgrass, but the tomato worms refuse to eat it. They lie there and sulk like spoiled children who refuse to eat their spinach. We tried placing a few on the dog to see if they would attack his fleas, but they seemed offended and rapidly dropped off and headed back toward the ruin of the tomato patch.

We want to live in harmony with nature, of course, and we are worried about what to do to make them happy once the last of the tomatoes has been eaten.

Great advances in knowledge almost always create problems like this. The invention of the car led rapidly to the traffic jam and the energy crisis. The discovery of how to grow tomato worms leads to bouts of despair about being hostile to nature because you cannot think of ways to keep the worms usefully employed.

Still, man is not stopped in his ceaseless forward progress. Next summer we will plant potatoes where the worms now thrive and with luck, we may discover how to grow potato bugs.

The Unipedal Mystery

Why does the washing machine take two socks and give back only one? Various theories have been advanced over the years, as, for example, that the washing machine eats one of the socks. Arlberg's brilliant monograph, "The Dynamics of Laundry," demolished this theory with laboratory evidence.

Postmortems on more than 1,200 washing machines which had expired suddenly during the rinse cycle showed no trace of socks in their digestive systems. Arlberg's investigations showed that the washing machine thrives almost entirely on a diet of crushed buttons, navel lint and small turtles left in the pants pockets of young boys.

After Arlberg the next important contribution was made by Klosson, under contract to the CIA. Richard Helms, then Director of Central Intelligence, had become alarmed by the mystery. On repeated occasions Mrs. Helms had loaded her machine with Helms's shirts, jeans, shorts and socks, and returned to find that though shirts, jeans and shorts were all present, one pair

The Unipedal Mystery

of Helms's socks had been reduced to one sock.

Naturally, Helms considered the possibility that an alien power was tapping his socks. He requested Klosson, Berkeley's distinguished Nobelist in laundry, to conduct a study at the Livermore Starch and Detergent Laboratory. Klosson was asked to answer two questions. No. 1: Had an enemy power developed a socknapping capability? No. 2: Was it possible to develop a washing machine that could filch one of Leonid Brezhnev's socks out of the Kremlin laundry and deliver it to the CIA for debriefing?

A brilliant theoretician, Klosson constructed a model laundry in a model Kremlin, placed one pair of a model Brezhnev's model socks in a model washing machine and conducted three months of sock games. His astonishing conclusion was that washing machines were developing human impulses.

Klosson theorized that washing machines were stealing the individual socks under the illusion that they were single-footed creatures, that they were unhappy with the monotonous lives they led, and that they were secretly storing up a supply of socks against the day when they could make a break for freedom and go into the world decently dressed.

To test the theory, Klosson proposed putting in a pair of shoes. If the washing machine took one of the shoes, he reasoned, scientists could verify his theory by monitoring the airport to see whether a renegade washing machine wearing a sock and a shoe boarded a flight for South America.

The $300-million appropriation to buy shoes for further research was abandoned when one of Klosson's young associates discovered most of the missing socks on the floor under the washing machine.

The young man turned out to be the brilliant Elmendorf, the father of gestalt laundry. The accidental discovery of those missing socks on the floor was ultimately to bring him fame and the Pulitzer Prize for Investigative Pre-Soaking, but not before his hands had crinkled into prune folds in the hot, sudsy pursuit of knowledge.

With the publication of "The Sock Dichotomy: Solecism, Solipsism, Paradigm and Epistemology" (written with the assistance of William F. Buckley, Jr.), Elmendorf advanced the argument that the American washing machine was developing delusions of grandiosity.

In a nutshell, Elmendorf's argument held that the washing machine had confused itself with the United States Government and had begun levying taxes for its services. By taking one sock of every two, Elmendorf contended, the washing machine was behaving as it conceived a Government should.

The sock revenue collected under the machine in Klosson's laboratory would eventually, he went on, be redistributed to people and institutions the washing machine liked. The oil industry would get a sock, two or three would go to the water softening cartel and the bulk of them would go to the Pentagon to improve the national sockurity.

Elmendorf was unable to verify his theory, due to an unfortunate onset of mental breakdown. It occurred one evening as he was dressing for a dinner at which he was to be introduced to the great Aptheker, the Viennese master of the spin cycle.

Noting that not a single pair of matched socks had come up from the laundry, Elmendorf went to the basement and searched under the washing machine for the missing mates. The floor was utterly bare. Elmendorf's theory, with all its years of work, was down the drain, leaving him nothing to do but become unhinged.

And so the mystery remains. Only the great Aptheker could possibly solve it, and he has no time, having dedicated the rest of his life to discovering whatever happened to tattletale gray.

The Unfairness of It All
[1977]

Just before the lights went out in New York the other evening President Carter gave us a disquisition on the innate unfairness of capitalism. The moneyed classes, he said, enjoyed many luxu-

The Unfairness of It All

ries unavailable to others, but this did not oblige the Government to provide matching luxury service to the impecunious.

He was explaining why he opposed Medicaid abortions for the poor, his point being that abortion was a luxurious form of birth control. Like Scotch salmon and summer houses on Long Island, he seemed to be saying, abortion might be one of the rights accruing to money, but the Government had no obligation to pay for it. It was one of those unfairnesses that are an unfortunate by-product of the system.

After this chilly exposition of the obvious, one wondered whether the poor folks would take their rotten luck like good sports. The answer came within a few hours when New York went dark and thousands of them started looting.

This is not to suggest that they needed Mr. Carter's lecture to learn that they had been living on the unfair side of the tracks, or even to persuade them that the Government was willing to let them grow old there. Very few probably even heeded the President's statement, if indeed they heard it.

Most probably did not even think in terms of fairness and unfairness, philosophical ideas which require a certain elegance of mind not usually found in the looting personality. The point is that while it is very sturdy of comfortable men to point out that life is unfair, the people it is unfair to are not apt to be morally or philosophically elevated by the announcement.

If you are going to preach that unfairness is inescapable for some, good sense suggests that you also accept the inevitability of beastly behavior by people who have to carry the burden. Unless you are a Dickens heroine, it becomes insufferable after a while constantly having all the unfairness left on your doorstep while the Mayfair swells are eating Scotch salmon, weekending in the Hamptons and enjoying exclusive membership in the Abortion Club.

You may not take to the streets with torch and shotgun, but you are likely to find your eyes going glassy when the professor, or the President, talks about social obligations. If the lights go out on a steamy summer night—well, life is unfair, isn't it? And how often does it provide a chance for a romp?

The trick in politics and government is to keep the lip buttoned about the unfairness of life while harping on the blessings that will soon descend equally upon all, thanks to the zeal and ingenuity of the governing class. Our recent Governments have decided against extending too much hope to life's losers, but until President Carter no one has deliberately rubbed their wretched noses in the inescapability of unfairness.

Under Presidents Nixon and Ford, economic policy required millions of them to remain unemployed as a defense against inflation. A floundering educational system helped train them for future uselessness, except as anti-inflation tools. Bankruptive welfare systems turned the malice of the taxpaying class upon them, and in Congress this was transmuted into a punitive hostility toward the cities, like New York, where they were herded away en masse but happily out of sight.

It was all very unfair, but, as everybody knew—the economists and the Congress and Presidents Nixon and Ford and the working class that was having trouble getting together beer money, what with all the taxes and having to feed the colleges to keep their children upwardly mobile—life was unfair, terribly unfair, and it didn't do any good to make promises you couldn't keep, even if you wanted to.

And, of course, life is unfair. There is no getting around it. It was unfair of those looters to behave as they did when the lights went out. Unfair to the merchants they destroyed. Unfair to New York City. Unfair to call attention to the grisly fact of what is out there behind the unemployment figures, the daily crime statistics, the welfare budget figures, the high school illiteracy scores, the illegitimate-birth statistics.

"Animals" and "scum," they were called by New Yorkers shocked by the unfairness of it all. Perhaps they are, although many of them seemed to be just children. In any case, they behaved badly. If you believe in President Carter's unfairness doctrine, you could hardly have expected much else.

Why Love Isn't What It Was

Sarah Seymour, sick with the dream of love, woke from a fevered sleep and found herself lifted in sinewy arms. The clink of armor and the distinctive aroma of Trojan after-shave lotion left no doubt that she was being kidnapped by Paris, son of Priam.

Out of her royal Greek bed he scooped the beautiful Sarah and sailed her over the Aegean to the topless towers of Ilium. Paris's love was Homeric, but the best was yet to come. "Dear Paris," she murmured on the dawn of the third day in Troy. "Silly, impetuous Paris. Mine is the face that will launch a thousand ships and topple the topless towers of Ilium."

"Don't give yourself airs," Paris advised.

"Soon will the angry Argive hurl his mighty fleet against Troy to avenge the ravishing of his royal queen," said Sarah. "Kingdoms will fall and men will die in multitudes because you and I, dear Paris, loved with a fever that scalded the wine-dark sea."

Patiently, Paris explained that this was unlikely. Neither the United States nor the Soviet Union, he pointed out, could tolerate a war between Greece and Troy. He was correct. The superpowers had the issue of Sarah's kidnapping placed on the agenda of the next session of the United Nations General Assembly, but it was quietly dropped after the CIA secretly provided Sarah's royal Argive husband with 30,000 brand-new Mark IV wooden horses and three new wives.

As the months passed, Sarah tired of life in a place where people spoke nothing but Trojan. Within the year, Paris was disappearing for days at a stretch and coming back with kidnapped queens from all over Asia Minor. "What has happened to love?" she sobbed aloud.

"You're snoring," said her husband, who was certainly not

Paris, nor even the irresistibly charming priest Abelard. She turned on her side and closed her eyes.

"Ma chérie," murmured the irresistible Abelard. *"Que je t'aime!"* How like Maurice Chevalier he sounded to Sarah.

"Wouldst thou love me, Abelard, though this violation of thy priestly vow require thy castration?" asked Sarah.

"Do not be silly, little one," he smiled. "That barbaric time is gone." He explained that the Church had been liberalized. If they married, he might have to abandon the collar, for he was cursed with a backward bishop, but that would not stop him from celebrating guitar masses. Their love could have a happy ending.

Sarah wept without understanding why. Perhaps it was because she did not want to spend the rest of her days with Maurice Chevalier doing liturgy on the guitar.

"Why don't you get up and watch the late, late movie?" her husband suggested.

"Romeo, Romeo, whatfor shall I do, Romeo?" Sarah asked the slender young Italian who lay unconscious by her bier. She wept with ecstasy at the spectacle of a young life surrendered so passionately on the mistaken assumption that she, divine Sarah, had taken a fatal draught.

Her tears were stanched by the arrival of an emergency ambulance crew, and Romeo woke from his doze. "I thought you fellows would never get here," he said. "Is this the woman who took the overdose?" asked a young doctor.

Romeo held her hand in the ambulance on the way to the hospital where Sarah's stomach was to be pumped. "In a few days when you're out of the hospital," he said, "we'll go home to Mama Montague and she'll fix you a nice plate of gnocchi, and afterward we'll have a lot of kids." Sarah screamed. She did not want her stomach pumped.

Her husband lumbered out of bed and went to get her a stomach alkalizer. Sarah was standing in a Russian railroad station savoring the last delicious moments of tragedy before throwing herself under the train wheels. When Count Vronsky heard the dreadful news, he would rue the loss of a love so constant that it preferred death to the humdrum boredom of bourgeois respectability. How delightful it would be to see Vronsky's face when he heard the dreadful news.

But where were the train wheels to end her tragic story?

"Where are all the trains?" she asked the insane monk Rasputin.

"Lady," said Rasputin, "there are only three trains a week these days. Everybody travels by airplane nowadays."

"Take this," said Sarah's husband, handing her a glass of water and a tablet. She sat up. Her husband turned on the television set and at 3:10 in the morning they watched the second half of an old movie about two people who fell in love, got married and lived happily ever after. "This is depressing," said Sarah.

"Frankly, my dear, I don't give a damn," said her husband, who then spoiled everything by not walking out forever.

Son of H-Bomb

Although I don't exactly love the H-bomb, it comes close to my idea of what a bomb should be. First, it fulfills the human need to have a bomb. Second, of all the bombs in circulation these days, it is the one you are least likely to be assaulted with.

In the more than thirty years since it became popular, it has never been used against anybody. A person could get fond of a bomb like that. There is no other bomb with a comparable safety record.

Twentieth-century humanity has many destinies, and while getting bombed is only one of them, it is also one of the more unpleasant. You can get firebombed, napalm-bombed, fragmentation-bombed or just plain old dynamite-bombed. You can get bombed in an Irish pub, a Manhattan office, a London restaurant or an Arab bazaar. You can get bombed by large governmental institutions which are bombing you to improve world society. You can get bombed by blithering maniacs. You can get bombed by patriotic heroes who are bombing you to fight injustices you have never heard of.

These possibilities leave me with mixed feelings about bombs. As a man of the twentieth century, I accept the need for bombs. There is something about them that fulfills people of our time and makes whole nations feel better. Show a nation that's got bombs a nation without bombs and right away the nation that has bombs wants to bomb the nation that hasn't. It's human nature, twentieth-century-style.

At the same time, I would prefer not to be bombed. The trick about bombs, it seems to me, is to satisfy the human craving for bombs while making sure that nobody is going to be bombed with them. This, of course, is what the H-bomb does and why it is the best of all possible bombs.

Now we have the neutron bomb, an offspring of the H-bomb, and a nasty little fellow it is, if my understanding is correct. The great charm of its sire is its ferocity. The H-bomb makes such a mess that nobody wants to clean up after it, and nobody, therefore, uses it.

The people who invent bombs, unhappy with such perfection, went back to the atom and came up with the neutron bomb. Their aim was a nuclear bomb that would leave less mess, the sort of bomb which, after being exploded, would leave the premises neat. If it was just a question of scrubbing down with extra-strength detergent to remove the after-bombing equivalent of waxy buildup on the linoleum, they reasoned, then the world could have a nuclear bomb it wouldn't mind using.

The neutron bomb is said to do this by killing only people—that's us, folks—with heavy doses of rapid-fade radiation while leaving the local property in reasonably good condition. I want to like this bomb as much as I like its progenitor, the H-bomb, but it isn't easy, and the Government's arguments about why I should are not persuasive.

The Government says it is really quite a decent bomb because it is only "tactical." If the Russian Army starts invading Germany, says the Government, the neutron bomb will be exploded over the invaders and they will be wiped out without damage to nearby towns and farms. This is "tactical" bombing.

The illustration asks us to believe the Russians might be dumb enough to expose their army in an invasion of Germany, all the time knowing that they were marching into the jaws of the neutron bomb. For thirty-five years the Russians haven't made a military move into Western Europe, despite the fact that our best deterrent has been that old pussycat, the H-bomb.

One should never exclude madness as a factor in foreign affairs, but the likelihood of Moscow's risking the ultimate mess by advancing an army to be neatly dispatched with N-bombs seems farfetched, particularly since after the hypothetical liquidation of the invaders an exchange of H-bombs would remain a lively possibility.

One suspects that what the bomb people have in mind is something else. If all parties to the H-bomb were to be armed with N-bombs, and if the present understanding that the H-bomb can be used only at the brink of doom remained effective, the tidiness of the N-bomb would make it possible for big powers to develop nuclear weapons which they could use as real bombs in real wars of the kind we used to enjoy in the days of the great old wars.

The threat of the neutron bomb is that it makes nuclear war thinkable at last. Do we really need that? Possibly. Bombs seem to be embedded in the psyche of the race, and something in us is soured by the fact that the H-bomb has never been any good for expressing ourselves on ourselves.

That's Show Biz

I went into show business. Why not? Everybody said, "You can never call yourself a writer until you've written a musical that never gets produced." Anyhow, it looked more interesting than politics, which had turned into accounting.

In less time than it takes to say, "There's no business like show business," I was in conference. We were all in conference. The composer brought music. The lyricist brought words for the music. The producer brought his powerful critical judgment, and I brought a script that would never get produced.

We conferred for a year or two. It was exhilarating. I could understand why all the old theater professionals say, "There's no business like show business." We conferred and drank coffee and threw away the script and dreamed of pulling a coup to make *My Fair Lady* and *Grease* look like financial trifles.

Now and then great directors, paladins of the Great White Way, men so eminent one scarce dared shake their hands without permission, would come by, grant us a smile, then a scowl, then a sneer, then stalk out in swirling capes, and we would order coffee and confer.

"Buck up!" the composer always cried. A composer of infinite ingenuity and relentless optimism, he would go back to the keyboard and produce melody more beautiful than he had ever produced before.

"There's no business like show business," the lyricist would tell me, and recharge her nimble wit to produce lyrics not dependent on rhyming "moon" with "June."

Over the coffee I dreamed of millions. In the theater, people talk of millions the way the Pentagon talks of billions. Just one more script and that island in the Aegean would be mine for the buying. I wrote another script.

This one would never get produced either, as it turned out, nor the next one, nor the one after that, but we were getting there. No longer were we doing a musical about a paraplegic cabdriver who falls in love with a tollbooth collector at the Lincoln Tunnel. Somehow, inexorably, because there's no business like show business, the musical had turned into the story of a fast-food-chain heiress who falls in love with a Marine corporal during the Boxer Rebellion.

One day a great director emerged during coffee in a swirl of cape. He had a Mephistophelean smile and beard to match. We all conferred. The director loved it, but of course it was all wrong. The script needed "a lot of work." So did the music. So did the lyrics.

"There's no business like show business," he explained, while proving indisputably that the show was really about an aristocratic Roman girl, illegitimate daughter of Augustus Caesar, who falls in love with Attila the Hun and sires the House of Romanov, which later ruled Imperial Russia.

At this point, the producer became eligible for Social Security and retired. It was the first sensible act any of us had committed.

When I proposed to follow his example, the composer and lyricist and director cornered me behind a cup of coffee and said, "There's no business like show business."

Indeed there isn't. In what other business is it possible to labor three years to earn a total of $90 while spending $465 for coffee? It was no surprise, then, that a second producer emerged from a Rolls-Royce. He loved the show. He even paid for the coffee. It was cloud nine, except for the script, which had to be rewritten to turn it into the story of Abraham Lincoln's granddaughter falling in love with John L. Lewis and inspiring him to found the United Mine Workers of America.

There being no business like show business, the producer canceled the coffee after discovering another show he liked even better. "Come now," the director said, happening upon me as I was about to leap from the Brooklyn Bridge, "there's no business like show business."

What was this we saw before us? Yet another producer? Yes, yes. Now there would be whole urns of coffee. Back to the keyboard went the composer, back to the solstice moon for the lyricist, back to the Plotto Board for the craver of island property in the Aegean.

Who could possibly balk at changing the script again? Of course what the world was waiting for was a musical about a Chicago flower girl who falls in love with Marconi and inspires him to invent radio. Why hadn't we seen it all along?

Orgies of dramaturgical rewriting! A ringing telephone. Will I take a cut in pay, like a good chap?

But I am receiving no pay to be cut—in fact, have earned nothing since three years ago, when somebody paid me $90. "But of course," the telephone explained. "There's no business like show business."

Role Models

Anita Bryant's triumph over homosexuality in Miami reminded me of schoolteachers. There was a lot of discussion in that dispute about teachers and whether their sexual proclivities do or do not influence children and, if they do, whether homosexual teachers can divert the young from the heterosexual path.

People who took Miss Bryant's view that they may talked about teachers as "role models." Lacking fluency in the sociological tongue, a language almost as difficult as Basque, I am unclear what a "role model" is, but those who used the term seemed to be saying that teachers are people children tend to emulate. In any event, many Miamians must have thought their children would become homosexual if subjected to homosexual teachers.

That prompted me to ponder teachers I haven't seen, and scarcely thought about, for decades, and for the first time I reflected on how their sex lives had affected my own. My first

Role Models

thought was that it was curious, perhaps perverse, that I have not turned out to be a spinster.

Nowadays, I know, spinsters have been eliminated from society by the lexicographers of the feminist movement, but there were still quite a few forty years ago, and most of them seemed to gravitate to school-teaching. Until eighth grade, I did not realize that males were permitted to teach school, and my impression was that married females were almost as unwelcome in the trade.

If the teacher was a "role model," parents were obviously unaware of it, for most of them surely did not want their children to grow up to be spinsters. Yet, despite almost constant tutelage by spinsters, I never felt the smallest temptation to indulge in spinsterism. When a group of us classmates sneaked off to somebody's cellar to play, we didn't play "spinster." We played "doctor," despite the fact that in those days you never found a medical man teaching elementary school.

Looking back, it seems we were always at least dimly aware of the sexuality of teachers, or in most cases, the absence of it. Even at an age foolishly thought to be innocent, one made certain assumptions about most of those teachers, and one of the firmest was that they had no sex life whatever. The idea of a teacher in the coils of rapture was as inconceivable as the idea of Herbert Hoover in Bermuda shorts. Yet very, very few of us, I suspect, were seduced by these "role models" into the juiceless life of celibacy.

At age eleven, I and the other males in my class were stirred by the spectacle of a teacher who, though unmarried, was definitely not a spinster. Definitely not. She wore no girdle in the battle against ignorance. I—and, I am sure, fifteen other men my age—still remember her voluptuous chalk movements at the blackboard as she struggled to help us grasp the distinction between a sentence's subject (one chalk line underneath) and its predicate (two lines underneath). Until then I had never seen a teacher fight ignorance without her armor on.

Was she a "role model"? Perhaps. To this day I enjoy lecturing helpless children on the finer points of English grammar, which is almost as difficult as Basque grammar and may, therefore, suggest that that teacher led me down the path to sadism.

High school—it was an all-male establishment—exposed me to masculinity at the blackboard. The teachers wore three-piece suits and smelled of forbidden cigarettes which they were allowed to puff unseen between classes in private hideaways. One assumed them to be married and, therefore, beyond sex. Being for the most part dull, they made marriage seem dull and sexless, yet I already knew that I would someday marry, and knew with equal certainty that even though married I would not turn my back on sex. Sex was what the football captain was up to and, though not yet ready for operations at that rarefied level, I was confident that once I was, I would not wither away as teachers did.

I had at least two homosexual teachers in that school. They didn't tell us they were, but we all knew it. I learned to jeer about them when they were out of earshot and to laugh about "queers," but I learned it from my "role models" in the schoolyard, and not from them.

One of them was largely responsible for encouraging a classmate to pursue a form of art at which he is now one of the world's best practitioners, besides being a family man. The other woke me to the amazing fact that in life there was also wit. The teacher I most wanted to emulate, however, was single, drank wine and had been gassed in World War I. Of his three admirable traits, there was only one I wanted to copy, and sure enough, to this day I love the sound of a popping cork.

Gangland Style

Two Mafia men have been assigned to execute Buck Rackets for giving himself airs, making unauthorized excursions to Jersey City and otherwise getting too big for his britches.

Gangland Style

Crime chieftains have argued for days over the language of the contract. One faction contends that the phrase should be "too big for his breeches." The other argues that using the word "breeches" will make the Mafia sound like a sissy.

A compromise is negotiated. The contract will refer to Buck's lower garment as "britches," but specify that he must be slain gangland-style instead of being bumped off.

The "breeches" faction, with its taste for elegance, is happy with the compromise. They foresee newspaper headlines that say "Buck Victim of Gangland-Style Slaying," which has an official resonance, instead of "Buck Bumped Off," which sounds tacky.

This creates problems for the two Mafia men. Naturally, they would rather bump Buck off. They can manage that when he is on his way to pick up the papers at the newsstand or in a men's shop showing the salesmen he is too big for his britches.

A bump-off is a piece of cake, as they say in the Mafia, but a gangland-style slaying is a bowl of consommé to be eaten with chopsticks.

In the first place, it has to be done in a restaurant if the slayee is a distinguished Mafia official like Buck Rackets. This is written into the Mafia constitution to give all high officials of the organization a sense of security.

This way they know they are never in danger of being slain gangland-style until they eat out. They are also assured of dying on a full stomach.

The two Mafia men have been following Buck for days, but he is too canny for them. Instead of going into restaurants he is content to buy carry-out doughnuts and eat them while walking the streets.

As a man who is giving himself airs, however, he must sooner or later flaunt his pretensions, they know, by going out for an expensive lunch with three martinis, a jug of wine and an avocado stuffed with a blonde.

Buck makes his fatal move in midtown and enters La Chambre de l'Estomac, the most notorious expense-account restaurant west of Zurich.

The Mafia men put on ski masks, stuff their pockets full of side arms and cradle shotguns. They enter La Chambre de l'Estomac and confront Marcel, the maitre d'hôtel, or as he is called in the Mafia, the mayter D.

Marcel immediately sizes them up as small tippers. "Do you have a reservation?" he asks. With an insouciant wave of their shotguns, they intimate that they wish Marcel to stand aside. Instead, Marcel draws a velvet-covered chain across their path.

Others have tried to bluff their way to his tables in the past by a show of arms. Marcel knows from long experience how to teach them that paper bearing Andrew Jackson's portrait does more than shotguns can.

"There will be a thirty-minute wait for a table," he tells them. "Would you like to wait at the bar?"

One of the Mafia men proposes that they bump off Marcel.

Marcel explains that he is too busy to be bumped off and much too important, since being bumped off is tacky. "If you must bump somebody off, I shall see if we have a busboy available," he tells them.

"In the meantime"—indicating a sign that says, "We reserve the right to demand proper attire"—he says, "I must ask you to check your ski masks in the cloakroom."

The second Mafia man is furious. What does Marcel take him for? One of those cheap expense-account chiselers who order $80 meals, pay five bucks to buy back their hats, then charge the whole thing off to Uncle Sam so the poor taxpayer has to pay for it?

"If you'll refrain from making a scene," Marcel says, "I can have a table for two set up in the kitchen."

Look, says the first Mafia man, Marcel does not understand. They are not hungry. They could not afford Marcel's prices if they were hungry. They are here to slay Buck Rackets gangland-style. If Marcel does not lower the chain and honor their shotguns, they will have no option but the trigger. "I will ask Mr. Rackets if he will see you," says Marcel, opening his palm in anticipation of ten big ones for messenger duty.

One of the Mafia men becomes angry enough to shoot the gin on the mirrored wall behind the bar, but he sees reflected in the mirror the face of a world-famous expense-account chiseler cooling his heels in obedience to the law that nobody goes through Marcel's velvet chain without cooled heels if his tips are not up to the mark.

The Mafia man asks the expense-account chiseler for his autograph. "Sure," says the chiseler, "but first lend me your shotgun so I can bump off that headwaiter."

The Mafia man declines, explaining that it would be tacky. They decide to slay Buck gangland-style at the next restaurant but that will probably be unnecessary. Marcel is already presenting Buck's bill. Buck appears to be succumbing to apoplexy, but on a full stomach.

The Golden Apple

Memoirs of old New York.

In those days, everyone lunched at the Round Table at the Algonquin and met under the Biltmore clock. Afterwards, we would take the ferry to Staten Island and watch Cole Porter, who always wore white tie, write "Begin the Beguine," and then go on to Delmonico's for a champagne supper from Lillian Russell's shoe.

This is where I first introduced Tallulah Bankhead to Henry James. They took an instant dislike to each other, for Tallulah was a Giants fan and Henry followed the Dodgers with a subtlety which irritated Tallulah and infuriated Hemingway, who could not stand James's compound-complex sentences. Once, Hemingway met James at Costello's saloon and challenged him to dance in the nude, but Fiorello La Guardia, who was watching a fire across the street, intervened and sent both of them to Europe.

One night on the Great White Way, I asked Nicky Arnstein if he would like to meet Barbra Streisand, but he said he would rather get a massage. I remember it vividly because that same night I was mugged on Columbus Avenue and telephoned the news to Walter Winchell, who was busy arresting Lepke Buchalter for murder and gave me only two lines in his column. It was a heartless town, but there were a million stories on every street corner.

I still remember the day Robert Moses had the idea for covering the whole city with highways because, while shaving that morning, I had thought of an incredibly witty saying about Calvin Coolidge and rushed right down to the Algonquin Round Table to say it for posterity. They were all there—Robert Benchley, Dorothy Parker, Ed Sullivan, Edith Wharton and Thomas E. Dewey—and all looking unaccustomedly glum. And no wonder. Dorothy Parker had taken the witty-sayings recording device home in her purse the night before, anticipating that she was going to say a number of witty things during the evening and wanting to preserve them for the future, and had had her purse stolen on the bus.

George M. Cohan wanted to make a musical of this incident, but unfortunately I was shot soon afterwards by someone who had mistaken me for Frank Costello, and Oscar Hammerstein told Cohan that Broadway was not yet ready for unhappy endings. Things like that happened all the time in Gotham. That's why we called it Baghdad-on-the-Subway.

At the center of all fun, of course, were the fun-loving Fitzgeralds—Scott and Zelda—whose carefree high jinks never failed to keep little old New York gaga with amusement. I almost met them one night at Grant's Tomb, which they proposed to drape in Confederate bunting, but they decided at the last minute to sail for France instead, on the *Berengaria,* and I was robbed at knife point on the Seventh Avenue subway en route to the tomb. When I phoned the news to Winchell from the 116th Street station, he came uptown and arrested me for conspiracy to desecrate a tomb.

The Golden Apple

What a ferment of ideas bubbled through the New York night of that time. I shall never forget the evening Enrico Caruso strode into a small restaurant and instructed the cook to put chicken livers on his spaghetti, thereby inventing spaghetti Caruso. That was the night Harold Ross and I were trying to carry O. Henry out of a speakeasy when it was raided by the police.

Always a glib talker, Ross went free after promising to take the cops to a champagne supper out of Lillian Russell's shoe, but I was arrested for illicit use of alcohol. When I called Winchell to report the news, he said he was sorry he hadn't been there to arrest me himself, but he had been busy advising Franklin Roosevelt on the conduct of World War II.

One night while Eugene O'Neill, Ethel Merman and I were holding the crowd at Toots Shor's enthralled with a discussion of Chekhov, we got news that Elsa Maxwell had arrived in the Hudson with Winston Churchill on a rented yacht. Eugene and Ethel rented a launch to go out to Elsa's party, but after we were waterborne they told the crew that I was a barroom moocher and completely unknown to them—what marvelous jokes we played on each other in those days—and the crew threw me overboard.

Luckily, I was able to swim to the yacht's side and Diaghilev, under the impression that I was Noël Coward, fished me up with a gaff. Elsa had Walter Winchell rush me to Bellevue for stomach-pumping and several inoculations against the Hudson, but the emergency-room nurse misunderstood and I was given six months of electrical shock therapy.

Later, I asked Robert Moses if there had ever been such a golden age in the history of urban civilization and he covered me with a six-lane highway.

Scaling the Heights
of Absurdity

After his recent visit to Tokyo, Vice President Mondale revealed that he and the Japanese had discussed a broad range of issues. Anyone who has ever gazed on this magnificent range can imagine the poetic nature of the Vice President's talk with the Japanese, for it is one of the most moving spectacles nature affords.

Rising majestically out of the bleak Areas of Responsibility, the Broad Range of Issues stretches from the amusing Heights of Absurdity on the north to the historic Peaks of Achievement in the south. It is not clear whether Mr. Mondale has actually seen the Broad Range of Issues or whether his discussions were merely based on study of old *National Geographic*s. The latter seems likelier, for few persons have survived the harrowing journey to that remote paradise.

T. E. Burton, who made the trip in 1923, with nothing more than six camels and a dictionary of clichés, kept a diary of the expedition. Although Burton met a dreadful death on his return journey when he fell into the roaring torrents of the infamous Flow of Information, his diary survived.

At his death, Burton was exploring for the mysterious Reliable Sources, where he believed the Flow of Information originated. Burton's expedition to the Broad Range of Issues started from the east and ran into trouble almost immediately as it passed into the steamy Erogenous Zones. His diary, feverishly sketchy at this point, describes months of struggle to climb out of the squalid Depths of Degradation, which pitted the Zones' landscape.

Indeed, he might have died there had he not seen, one cold winter night, an extraordinary display of the beautiful Rising Expectations light the western sky. Reinvigorated by this atmospheric spectacle, he hauled himself out of the Erogenous Zones and found himself breathing a strangely baffling air.

This, as subsequent geographers have discovered, was the inexplicable Air of Mystery, which blows off the mosquito-infested Miasma of Suspicion and Hate. Luckily for Burton, the sky was clear that night and he was able to navigate safely around the Miasma by following the familiar, if somewhat tired, Aura of Romance, which shimmered in the southern sky.

The southern detour, however, carried him directly into the dreaded Sands of Time, where he wandered for years, surviving only because his camels had taught him how to store water in his hump. One day he stumbled into an orchard. It seemed a mirage, for scarcely a hundred yards distant lay another orchard. Burton sent his camels to explore it for reality, and as they stood there looking at his orchard and he stood looking at their orchard, he suddenly realized the magnitude of his accomplishment. He had discovered the Fruitful Exchange of Views.

Refreshed in spirit, he plunged ahead, ignoring the terrors of the notorious Political Extremes to his left and to his right, and noticed that he was approaching a series of well-defined levels. These, of course, were the well-charted Income Levels—Lower, Middle and Upper.

Then, in a terrifying instant of atmospheric violence, Burton was abruptly picked up into the air and just as abruptly hurled to the ground. We now know that he was in the grip of the whimsical Unanticipated Windfall, which is quite common at the Upper Income Level.

Burton, however, was determined to reach New Heights, an elevation from which, according to ancient lore, one could catch a glimpse of the Areas of Responsibility. Burton spent weeks struggling upward, always upward, and when he at last reached the summit, satisfied that he had reached either New Heights or the equally rewarding Higher Level of Understanding, he fell into a stuporous sleep.

On awaking, he found a graffito cut into rock. It said, "Chauvinist pigs to the wall." This was not New Heights. It was simply

Raised Consciousness, and Burton realized that he was looking out on the world from the Feminist Viewpoint. "At least," he noted in his diary, "it is better than finding myself at the Unorthodox View."

The following year, Burton crossed the Chasm of Misunderstanding, canoed down the Labor Pool and hurled himself through the Language Barrier with such force that he plunged into the fetid Emotional Depression. Only his fierce resolve to enter New Fields of Endeavor kept him going, and when at last he entered the always stimulating New Fields, he met a speechwriter who gave him his first glimpse of the Broad Range of Issues from the ancient Well-Balanced Perspective. "Someday," the awestruck Burton predicted, "this range will be discussed even by Vice Presidents." Not even Burton, of course, could have realized the Japanese would join in.

Elephant's Eye High

Do you ever wish you had it all to do over again, folks? Do you wish you'd taken up the kind of work where you can call people folks, instead of Sir and Deadbeat and Big Shot and Meathead? The kind of life where you can say, "By golly!" and "There's a heap of goodness in this old world of ours"?

But you didn't take that road, did you? You thought you'd be smart, get ahead, see your name up there in lights. So you went and became an airline stewardess, or a cop, maybe a fashion model so skinny you clack like a floating crap game when you walk down the street; maybe one of those systems analysts who are always saying, "Miniaturize the digital circuitry to one ten-thousandth of a megaherz."

Maybe a surgeon hauling out two dozen gallbladders a day. All day long saying nothing but "Forceps!" and "Sterilize that hemostat immediately or the south ventricle will become resected!"

Elephant's Eye High

It isn't all it's cracked up to be, is it? And do you know why? Because, by golly, you've lost touch with nature. Chances are your granddaddy warned you'd lose touch with nature when you told him you were going to become an airline stewardess, or cop, or fashion model.

Remember what he said? "Girl," he said, "there's a heap of goodness in this old world of ours, but all you're going to find up in those airplanes is sore feet and bunions and boozers cussing because they can't have a third martini."

"Boy," he said, "folks like us got a lot to be happy about, but if you go out to the city to pound a beat, all you're going to see of the human race is pipsqueaks, gnats and worms."

Remember where your granddaddy was sitting when he said it? In a rocking chair. Remember where the rocking chair was situated? On the porch.

You don't have a rocking chair, do you? Don't have a porch, either, I'll bet.

Well, what do you have? A cart full of coffee, tea or milk. A nightstick and a .38-caliber revolver. A cup of yogurt in the refrigerator. A few scalpels. A little digital megaherz oscillator cup. It's a long way from nature.

When June starts to roll around, it probably makes you feel like kicking yourself for ever thinking you'd like to be in the big time instead of keeping your feet in the soil. Taking out all those gallbladders may make the nurses think you're as slick as the cat's whiskers, but in your heart you know you'd rather be walking through fields of buttercups, don't you?

Why, by George, you could have been a farmer. Could be getting up these sweet mornings to slop the hogs and check out the cows for hoof-and-mouth disease. Could spend the whole day feeling the honest sweat on your brow while you steer the plow behind old Dobbin.

Have you ever noticed how farmers' sweat is honest? They don't have to choke their pores up with chemical sweat suppressors the way systems analysts and fashion models and surgeons have to do. That's because farmers' sweat is honest. Farmers don't have to be ashamed of it, don't have to treat it like a mad Victorian grandmother that's got to be kept locked in the attic.

How did we all get so far away from nature? "Folly and pride," Granddaddy would have said. That's why my own granddaddy said many years ago, in fact, when I went up to him in his rocker on the porch and told him I was going to the city to take a job stacking groceries on a supermarket shelf.

"Folly and pride, boy," he said. "There's a heap of goodness in this old world of ours, but when you start stacking those groceries you're going to find—"

"I'm sick and tired of picking the ticks off the sheepdog, Granddaddy," I cried. "I want to make it in the big time. I want to be a star."

And what did it get me? What did it get any of us? What good is stardom if you can't call people folks anymore? If you can't see the heap of goodness there is in the world for all the digital circuits and gallbladders and coffee, tea and milk that get in your way?

And all the things we've lost: sitting on the porch swing at sunset, smelling the honeysuckle. Leaning against the silo on hot afternoons and smelling the stable. Walking through the meadow on a dewy morning and dodging the copperheads.

Compared to these, what pleasure can a body get from winning the Nobel Prize for gallbladder removal, from cornering the silver market or dancing all night with Liza Minnelli or handing Prince Charles a cup of coffee, tea or milk and hearing him say, "My dear, if you are not a divorced woman, may I make you, someday, the Queen of England?"

Who among us, folks, wouldn't give up all that for the sweet delight of hoisting a pitchfork and strolling down toward the south forty while picking our teeth with a piece of hay? At least on a sunny day in June? Or maybe just for a few hours of that sunny day, in the soft of the morning, before the sun really gets up there and starts to boil your neck?

I am shaving and it worries me. It has become so compli-
cated. Not like the old days when you smeared a little
soap on your jowls, lifted a razor and scraped your face.
Nowadays you don't have a razor anymore. You have a
shaving system. I am always nervous in the presence of
systems.   —Blade and Blather

Destroying the ethnic characteristics of neighborhoods is
as American as General Custer. It began when the Indians looked down to the beach at Jamestown and Plym-
outh and saw shiploads of Europeans moving into the
neighborhood.
          —A New Kind of American Indian

Celebrities—people who are "new and exciting," who
are famous for being famous, as the old definition goes
—get consumed just as fast as new improved soaps, new
clothing fashions and new ideas. One of the true American horrors is to become "famous," because it almost
certainly means you will be discarded shortly afterward
as outmoded, tiresome and old.
          —The Face Game

There is no business like show business, Irving Berlin
once proclaimed, and thirty years ago he may have been
right, but not anymore. Nowadays almost every business
is like show business, including politics, which has become more like show business than show business is.
          —The Face Game

If all the students now dreaming of law school manage
to get in, the country will suffer a plague of lawyers by
1984. We already have at least ten times as many lawyers
as any rational society can tolerate, which doubtless accounts for the triumph of irrationality in American life.
          —Terminal Jurisprudence

Aunt Ms. Needs You

The feminist movement is the only phenomenon of the age that has produced a bigger literature than Watergate. Of all the "movements" of the discontented which have flourished these past twenty years, it is by far the most devoted to the power of the word.

This may explain why the effort to enact the equal rights amendment is running out of steam. In the mass, American women may read more than men do, but in both sexes an excess of bookishness is apt to be looked upon in America as an elite characteristic. In difficult political fights the elite are usually kept locked in the attic, lest their inadvertent appearance stir the sour juices of public suspicion.

The feminists, violating political usage, have used literature as a heavy assault weapon. In addition to shelves of books, both argumentative and fictional, they have spawned a feminist magazine, *Ms.*, and, at one time or another, feminist counterparts to *Playboy* and *Penthouse.*

Considerable energy has been spent on a campaign to revise the English language with self-conscious neologisms for traditional terms embodying the suffix "-man." Around the country feminist sentinels scan newspapers for "sexist" grammatical constructions and fire off smoking letters calling offenders to order.

There is a certain political sense behind all this, but only to a point. Saul Alinsky states that in the launching stage of a political "movement" the first task is to persuade a group of people that they are aggrieved and abused. After being persuaded that they are victims of injustice and producing the energy that comes from anger, they must be shown an enemy against whom their rage can be directed.

Thereafter, the anger must be sustained until the movement

becomes recognized as a legitimate political force reckoned in the weighing of public arrangements. At this stage, with the movement wielding political clout, the passions that gave birth to the movement become handicaps which interfere with the negotiating process that is politics and governance.

The feminists have entered the final stage of development, but the literature lingers on to afflict them. The enemy they identified in the early stages—the "sexism" of "male chauvinist pigs"—is, obviously, no longer the enemy blocking the equal rights amendment.

The real problem now surely comes from other women, women who feel alienated from a movement whose literature seems elite, disconnected from their daily lives and, often, contemptuous of their aspirations. Except for the indifference or hostility of these women, the equal rights amendment would have sailed through the state legislatures two years ago.

The feminist predicament probably results from the professional and intellectual origins of the movement. Its early leaders were justifiably outraged that they didn't have as much opportunity as men to go to the office and become a success.

The idea that many women might not want to go to the office and become a success seems to have received little attention, although, having seen what happened to most men who were forced to do it, such women, one might have assumed, would number in the millions.

Instead of allowing for a sensible acuity of feminine observation, feminist philosophers took the line that there was something wrong with women who were content with traditional jobs associated with building families. In feminist jargon, their "consciousness" was low. They were trapped in degraded "roles" devised by male "sexists."

It was an appealing argument to women discontented with their marriages, their families and sexual conventions in which they were miserable; but the woman satisfied in her marriage and family, the woman who preferred creating a family rather than going to the office and becoming a success, was made to feel inferior and guilty.

Making people feel guilty is a good way of getting political results in the short run. In the long run, it is a good way of making them despise you. Not surprisingly, the equal rights amendment is failing for want of enthusiasm among women.

In the meantime, feminism has won most of its important battles in Congress and the courts. It has become a political force of considerable weight. If the equal rights amendment fails, it will not be the loss of the war but an occasion to rebuild the army by enlisting the housewives.

Perhaps, to satisfy them, the old revolutionaries who made the movement will have to be purged. That is usually what happens in revolutions that succeed.

The Humble Dollar

The papers keep saying the dollar is very weak. This is nonsense. The truth is that the dollar is absolutely powerless. I sent one out for a pound of cheese the other day and it was thrown out of the shop for giving itself airs.

I used to send the dollar to the grocery with orders to bring back a pound of coffee. I figured this would teach it humility. Instead, it went into a severe depression which psychiatry couldn't cure because it has no way of treating a dollar unless accompanied by 34 others, which I didn't have at the time.

The reason I didn't have them was that one of the children had just stopped by and asked to borrow $470. The measure of how impotent the dollar has become is that children trying to cadge money no longer ask you for a quarter, but for $470. Another measure is that a parent can now borrow a dollar from a child without having to promise to take that child on the roller coaster the following Saturday.

The Humble Dollar

I lent the kid the $470. His grandfather was shocked. "How do you expect children to learn the value of money?" he inquired. I was about to administer a poultice and put him to bed with a nice cup of tea and the latest list of automobile spare-parts prices when the doors caved in.

Not literally, of course. The tax people are nicer than everyone thinks. Still, they were pretty angry in their polysyllabic way and endless subordinate clauses, and you couldn't blame them.

I had sent a dollar to the newsstand for papers. The tax people naturally wanted their share of it, but it had outraced them and been battered down to a mere 35 cents by the newspaper seller before they could reach it. They were getting soft. It was the first dollar that had outrun a tax man since the South Vietnamese ruling families skipped to Switzerland with the United States Treasury.

There was nothing to do but soothe them with dollars, although what they wanted with them I don't know. Neither did Grandfather. "You'd never satisfy me with a dollar that couldn't give you more than 35 cents change after buying three newspapers," he said. "In my day, with a dollar you could buy a Hearst newspaper and weigh yourself ninety-eight times."

Poor Grandfather. He was really out of it. "A penny saved is a dollar earned," he said. The tax people were sympathetic and left without taxing him for being a priceless antique, although they pointed out that if I died before he did his value could create estate tax problems for my heirs.

Tax problems! It was to laugh. I had plans for Grandfather. Curators of the museums of three continents were already dickering for the right to display him. Mounted handsomely behind velvet ropes, running on about the value of money and a penny saved, he would be a bigger museum draw than a petrified dodo egg. If only I could keep him pure, untainted.

For this purpose I had kept him in the dark for years about the price of shoes. Whenever I assembled the dollars required to buy new shoes he would gaze at them disapprovingly. "Buying another new car?" he would ask. "Yes, Grandfather," I would say.

"You just bought a new car last year," he would say. "Nowadays, Grandfather," I would say, "they wear out at the heels faster than they used to."

"No wonder," he would say. "They ought to put tires on 'em the way they used to."

My plan, of course, was not to sell him. I may be cruel but I am no fool. You don't get a priceless grandfather from me for a basket of dollars too weak to stand up to a pound of cheese. No. I intended to trade him for a tract of oceanfront real estate, the perfect hedge against inflation, preferably on the Swiss Riviera.

One day, however, during my absence one of the children who wanted to cadge movie money broke the padlock and braced Grandfather. Grandfather gave him a dime, the sum that had often bought him a double feature plus a cartoon, a Ted Fio Rito short subject, an installment of *The Black Ace Flies Again* and previews of coming attractions.

"Cut the horsing around, Grandpa," the child said. "I need $4.50 plus 35 cents for a candy bar and 50 cents for popcorn." It was the end of my villa in Switzerland. The children wept, of course. I blotted their tears with dollar bills.

How to Rate

I wish I were television people. I'd be cool and have great hair. When I had to shoot somebody with a pistol, I would get him with the first shot, instead of missing him with all six, the way I do now.

Television people are always driving around in cars. I am always driving around in cars, too, but this is because I can never find a parking space. If I were television people, I would always drive right into a waiting parking space and get out of the car and go into a building and get beaten up.

I would look terrific going into the building, all suntanned and beautifully tailored, instead of looking flea-bitten, stoop-shoul-

How to Rate

dered and unpressed, the way I look now going into buildings. If I were television people, I would look cool getting beaten up because I would know that whatever they did to me, my great hair would look terrific just as soon as the beating was over.

If I were television people, my panty hose would never be saggy because little girls would not hesitate to hurt my feelings by telling me if they were, and I would change to improved, unbaggy panty hose. Thanks to a family obsessively solicitous of my hygiene, I would never want for mouthwash or a shampoo to free me from the tyranny of dandruff.

As I drove to my waiting parking space, cool with my great hair, looking terrific in my suntan and perfect panty hose, I would have no fear of coming embarrassingly close to the people waiting to beat me up. Not with my mint-fresh breath and my great surfer's dandruff-free shoulders.

If I were television people I would solve all murders in fifty minutes, which is only one-tenth the time it now takes me to solve the crossword puzzle.

All the women in my life would look like high school prom queens in training for a centerfold portrait in *Playboy,* but they would be nice, clean, wisecracking girls with *magna cum laude* diplomas from the police academy, and whenever somebody tried to beat them up I would shoot him with my pistol and not miss with the first bullet.

Afterward we would go to our favorite hangout and I would tell them, with a cool little laugh line, how I got there in time to do the shooting. We would not hang around long over our ice cream sodas, of course. No, siree, because I'd have to rush right back in time to tell everybody that I was going to tell them some news right after these messages.

Not being television people, I always blurt out my news without prefatory messages, and it goes over like a lead cloud. Not long ago, for example, I was being beaten up by two bionic people who had been irritated because I had missed hitting them with all six bullets in my pistol. I rushed right home, burst into the kitchen and said, "Guess who I just got beat up by!"

"Don't tell us before the important messages!" screamed the children.

"Two bionic people!" I cried, ignoring their pleas. They were disgusted and looked it. If I were television people, I would have winsome, darling, irresistibly charming children who had never been disgusted with their good old dad in their sweet little lives, and never needed $1,500 worth of orthodontic braces or suffered from neuroses created by sinister schoolteachers either.

Television people have all the luck. They are always playing games and winning prizes. If I were television people, I would probably win an armchair that looked like a lot of beer kegs nailed together. And I would not tell the host that any sponsor who tried to palm off that chair as a prize would try to sell mediciney breath, either, the way I would now. Not on your life. If I were television people I would jump up and down in ecstasy, clapping my hands and squealing with joy, and then kiss the host right on top of his great hair.

Most of us, alas, cannot be television people. As F. Scott Fitzgerald remarked to Ernest Hemingway in their famous conversation, "Television people are different from you and me."

"Yes," said Hemingway, "their panty hose never sag."

This enraged Fitzgerald. He challenged Hemingway to put on the gloves and they went three rounds without either one beating up the other. It was duller than Shakespeare on public television, and ever since then "Charlie's Angels" has easily beaten both of them in the ratings.

Revolters, Spare the Waste
[1978]

The United States is the home office of waste and always has been. The country was built on waste. We wasted land, wasted people, wasted resources and wasted fortunes that were built on wasting land, people and resources. Large parts of the country stretching from the South Bronx to Los Angeles shopping centers are now pure wastelands.

I respect waste. Waste made America what it is today. Some people talk about the Constitution, some about the Conestoga wagon, some about the Colt .45 and some about the railroads—and, indeed, all played their role in building the country. But what good would they have done without waste?

It behooves Americans to cherish waste as part of our heritage. Yet, what began a few weeks ago as a decent old-fashioned tax revolt has now degraded into an attack on waste.

A poll conducted by *The New York Times* and CBS News suggests that three of every four citizens want Governments to stop waste. Most of these people want to have their taxes cut, which is natural, but don't want to lose any Government services they now enjoy, which is equally natural.

The question with which they then struggle is how Governments can take in less money without reducing services. The answer is to end waste, which is thought to be rampant in Government, and probably is.

The trouble with this solution is that it offends the American character. Any Government that did not practice waste on the grand scale would be a poor representative of the American people.

Here let me now make a confession. I have just thrown out a half bottle of carbonated water. It had gone flat because I forgot to put a stopper in it. I wasted that water and did not feel the smallest pang of guilt about doing what Government does every day.

What's more, I wasted the bottle it came in, and I wouldn't be surprised if the bottle cost more than the water I wasted. The company that makes these bottles insists that I waste them. So does the union that works for the company that makes the bottles. Both management and labor believe waste is good for business.

This is not an isolated case. The supermarket is selling tomatoes lovingly wrapped in molded plastic. You know that costs something, but what do you do with the plastic after eating the tomato?

You waste it, right along with the paper bags in which the super-market packages the carbonated water with the bottles designed to be wasted and the tomato wrapping which isn't fit for anything but wasting.

I do not quarrel unduly even with such conspicuous waste. Cannier people than I, people who are geniuses of commercial enterprise, find waste a profitable undertaking, and I respect their judgment. I buy their cars, designed to be wasted, and their pens, built to be thrown away. What puzzles me is why they expect Government to behave differently from the people who buy their merchandise.

We had some people in to dinner the other night and they got going on the terrible taxes and from there took off against the evils of Government waste. In fact, they became so absorbed in deploring waste that most of them neglected dessert, thus wasting the better part of a strawberry pie.

Most of them, like me, drive automobiles whenever the impulse strikes, thus contributing to the national wasting of gasoline, which has created the balance-of-payments deficit, which has led to the decline of the dollar. None of us worked up any heat against ourselves for indulging in this traditional American waste. In fact, I didn't even hear it mentioned.

Anybody who did mention it would've been considered a bore. It's boring of me to mention it now. We all looked energy-wasting squarely in the eye a long time ago and decided to keep it as part of the American tradition. Right now, I'll bet, there are thousands of people writing letters to editors and Congressmen about the viciousness of waste while running air conditioners that waste power at a prodigious rate.

Wasting power on air conditioning is an accepted American tradition, even if Abraham Lincoln did do his letter-writing with only a cardboard fan to cool his brow. The chances of persuading Governments to stop waste are probably not a bit better than the chances of forcing ourselves to kick the habit. If the tax revolt deteriorates into an attempt to make Governments behave more sensibly than we do, it is surely doomed.

A Tale of Reproduction

Cutting taxes depends upon forcing Government to do less for us. If we truly want lower taxes we shall have to learn to back politicians into the corner and snarl, "What's the idea of trying to do something for me lately?"

A Tale of Reproduction

Copying machines are revolutionizing the way we live. With recording tape plugged into the radio, a person can now create a private musical library far more cheaply than by buying records. With print duplicators, a fetching piece of writing can be quickly reproduced and circulated among hundreds of acquaintances without the expense of paying the writer for his labor.

It is the miracle of the loaves and the fishes made commonplace, and naturally it creates problems. The *Journal of the American Duplicating Association* reports a typical copying problem experienced by Myra Goltz in one of the Midwestern states.

Mrs. Goltz was so fond of her husband, Hector, that she had four copies of him run off on an experimental machine under development by Spectronics Laboratories. Since the machine is still imperfect, the four additional Hectors were blurred somewhat around the edges and the color was slightly off.

Hector did not resent this. He was, after all, such a splendid husband that he rarely made a fuss about trivialities. He was such a splendid husband, in fact, that Mrs. Goltz was the envy of all the women in town, both nubile and long-married.

Women whose husbands came to the dinner table in their undershirts, snored through the Miss America pageant on television and said that a woman's place was in the home were galled to see Mrs. Goltz suddenly blessed with Hectors four time over.

Inevitably, while counting her Hectors one night at bedtime, Mrs. Goltz had noticed one was missing. He was not one of the better copies, having come off the machine with a decidedly green tinge to his cheeks and a badly blurred nose. When Mrs. Goltz learned that a divorcee in the next block had left town hurriedly during the night, she was not alarmed.

"Nothing to worry about," she told the four remaining Hectors at breakfast next morning. "With those green cheeks and that blurred nose, the stolen Hector will be duck soup for the police to locate before the day is out."

It was not the case. The divorcee took him in disguise to Nervtron, the giant Texas conglomerate which had been developing a high-resolution horse-copying machine. Its plan was to copy the ten fastest horses on the continent and give Nervtron's sagging stock a shot in the arm by cleaning up at the racetrack.

The engineer in charge of the project was the divorcee's former husband. In return for being relieved of alimony, he agreed to see if the new horse-copying process could be used to reproduce the stolen Hector in natural color with a neat nose.

When the divorcee picked up the finished copy, she was delighted. His color and nose were so good that Mrs. Goltz herself could not have distinguished him from the original Hector. It was only later that the divorcee discovered the one flaw in the job. Her brand-new Hector with the wonderful color and nose also came with a full-length horse tail.

Severe cropping and some restitching in Hector's trouser seat dealt very nicely with this difficulty, and the divorcee lived happily ever after, as all wives blessed with a Hector were bound to do.

Unbeknownst to her, however, the engineer had been so entranced by the spectacle of a perfect husband that he had run off several thousand copies, thinking they would make nice presents to his women acquaintances for Christmas and birthdays. The expense of feeding them, however, soon became intolerable. Moreover, the sound of horse tails slapping at flies and mosquitoes kept him awake at night, and he soon turned them loose.

Thinking as one—they were all copies of the same Hector, after all—they slowly gravitated over the years back toward their old hometown for a look at the old homestead.

Mrs. Goltz was out of the country, seeing the Yucatán with the original Hector. Her three remaining copies had long since been hauled off in the night by marriageable women. Imagine her surprise, on returning, to find half the marrying female population of the town enjoying bliss with Hectors.

And such beautiful Hectors. Their charm was not simply in the rich, gracious swelling with which they filled the seats of their trousers. Whereas her own Hector had gone a bit gray and extraneous around the abdomen with the passing years, these were crisp, taut, young Hectors remembered from the early days of marriage when her own Hector was so splendid that she had made four copies of him.

Mrs. Goltz became disgruntled with her own Hector and furious with the women of the town. What right did they have to salad-days Hectors while she, Mrs. Goltz, was left with nothing but the eroding original? Her unhappiness infected the original Hector, who died of a broken heart.

His obituary observed that he had been famous throughout the country as the only Hector in the region to lack a horse tail.

The Electronic Cadger

I went to a mail-order store to order a tire pressure gauge.

"I want to order a tire pressure gauge," I said to a woman at a computer terminal.

"What is your telephone number?" she asked.

"218-2676," I said.

She played the phone number on the keyboard, then studied the results on the computer screen. "Your name is Herman Irving," she said.

"How did you know that?" I cried.

"You live at 723 Elm Street," she replied.

"Astonishing," I said.

She looked pleased.

"I'll bet you could get that machine to tell how old I was when I had the mumps and whether my liver is enlarged," I said.

She played the keyboard again.

"You've never had the mumps," she said. "Just measles, whooping cough and scarlet fever. Appendix removed when you were seventeen. Eighteen stitches to close a bad cut resulting from an automobile accident when you were thirty-nine. Afterward you were charged with drunken driving."

I smiled boyishly. "We were all young once," I said.

Privately, my mind's alarm system was going off. Here was something about Herman Irving I hadn't known. Drunken driving at thirty-nine, eh? That was a bit late in the day for a man to be operating machinery with a snoot full of gin.

"How's my credit?" I asked.

"What do you want to order?" she asked.

"A tire pressure gauge. The catalog lists the price at $4.19."

She tapped the keyboard, then studied the screen.

"You're good for the $4.19," she said, "but don't try to order anything over $4.99."

"You mean I'm not good for $5?"

"Well," she said, "considering that the surgeon who took your appendix out when you were seventeen is still waiting for his payment and that you bounced three checks just last week at the Acme Liquor Store, Ned's Auto Repair and the Patience of Job Dry Cleaning Shop, I'm surprised we're willing to trust you for the $4.19."

"Let me see that screen," I demanded.

She touched a button, and the screen went blank before I could vault over the counter.

"Computer bank information is held in the strictest confidence for your protection," she said. "We cannot permit you to look at it."

I did not make a scene, but stalked out of the shop, walked across the parking lot and got into my car. Herman Irving was waiting in the front seat.

The Electronic Cadger

"Did you get the money?" he asked.

"No."

"I thought you were going to the bank."

"Herman," I said, "I did not go to the bank. I just walked around and consulted my navel. It has advised me not to lend you the fifty bucks which you promised to pay back at the end of the month."

Herman said he was desperate for the money.

"Not a chance," I said. "Something tells me you're a deadbeat, Herman. Something electronic."

"If I don't get that fifty bucks by sundown," said Herman, "there are two guys who are going to fracture the knuckles of my betting hand."

"I'm sorry, Herman."

"Think how much sorrier you'd be if your wife found out you bought a zircon necklace three years ago on the six-month payment plan."

Herman and I studied each other.

"Your wife doesn't have a zircon necklace," Herman said. "I took the trouble of asking her. Now what kind of woman would a man buy a zircon necklace for?"

"You can't prove a thing."

"Pal," said Herman, "I know for a fact you made the purchase at Benny's Cut Glass Jewelry Bazaar in Chicago, because Benny had to complain to the Credit Bureau that you were ninety days behind in your payments."

I did not feel so good. "You must have ordered a tire pressure gauge recently," I said.

"A jack handle, actually," he said. "All they asked me for was my phone number. I gave them yours. I never knew you'd been arrested as a kid for shoplifting bobby pins at the five-and-dime," he said.

"I wanted to give my mother a Christmas present," I said.

"We've all got our painful little secrets," he said, "and fortunately they're all in the data bank. And speaking of banks—"

I slid out of the car and walked over to the bank and withdrew

$50, which was electronically recorded while I was being photographed by the seeing-eye camera for the record.

Cheesy

For eighteen months I studied the depravities of Times Square. They are extensive, as everyone has reported, but what everyone has generally overlooked is how inferior, how banal, how lower-class they are. Compared to the depravities of Paris, London and Southern California, which I have also studied, Times Square's are decidedly bottom-drawer. It is a pity the word "cheesy" has disappeared from American slang because there is no other that so adequately describes the depravities of Times Square. Its depravities are the cheesiest I have ever encountered.

This I believe is why so many otherwise sensible people are turned into raving moralists when exposed to Times Square. It is not because they are really offended by depravity; it is because the overpowering ugliness of the depravity there offends their sense of taste.

George F. Will, a vastly civilized writer for *The Washington Post,* passed through not long ago and wrote a dismayed column about it which intimated that the place foreshadowed the fall of civilization. He had seen the Eighth Avenue flesh salesmen, the narcotics vendors and the peep-show creeps, I gather, and had seen *Snuff,* a piece of bush-league Grand Guignol purporting to entertain with filmed autopsies on living bodies, and had been overwhelmed by the vulgarity of it all. As every person of refinement must naturally be.

I do not know Mr. Will's attitude on depravity as a fact of society, but most Americans seem able to temper their distaste for it in proportion to the amount of elegance in which it is conducted. The general rule seems to be that depravity, to be socially acceptable, must have class.

Cheesy

Generations of Americans have gone to Paris in search of the aesthetically ultimate offense to puritan sensitivity, and if they have usually been disappointed one would never guess it from the amount of winking and leering that goes on when they come home.

By any precise definition, Washington is a city of advanced depravity. There one meets and dines with the truly great killers of the age, but only the quirkily fastidious are offended, for the killers are urbane and learned gentlemen who discuss their work with wit and charm and know which tool to use on the escargots.

On New York's East Side one occasionally meets a person so palpably evil as to be fascinatingly irresistible. There is a smell of power and danger on these people, and one may be horrified, exhilarated, disgusted or mesmerized by the awful possibilities they suggest, but never simply depressed.

Depression comes in the presence of depravity that makes no pretense about itself, a kind of depravity that says, "You and I, we are base, ugly, tasteless, cruel and beastly; let's admit it and have a good wallow."

This is how Times Square speaks. And not only Times Square. Few cities in the country lack the same amenities. Pornography, prostitution, massage parlors, hard-core movies, narcotics dealers —all seem to be inescapable and permanent results of an enlightened view of liberty which has expanded the American's right to choose his own method of shaping a life.

Granted such freedom, it was probably inevitable that many of us would yield to the worst instincts, and many do, and not only in New York. Most cities, however, are able to keep the evidence out of the center of town. Under a rock, as it were. In New York, a concatenation of economics, shifting real estate values and subway lines has worked to turn the rock over and put the show on display in the middle of town.

What used to be called "The Crossroads of the World" is now a sprawling testament to the dreariness which liberty can produce when it permits people with no taste whatever to enjoy the same right to depravity as the elegant classes.

The case against Times Square, then, is not that it is depraved, but that its depravity is so common, so low, so ugly, so vulgar, and because of all these things, so unutterably depressing. Of all the world's great centers of depravity, Times Square is the slum.

The incessant talk about cleaning it out is meaningless, as the Civil Liberties Union notes, unless City Hall is prepared to abrogate the Constitution, which grants the tasteless of the earth equal rights with the elegant in the pursuit of depravity.

Libertarians may resent the elitist tone of all this and insist, with their usual passion for uplift at any cost, that vulgarity must be permitted full expression. Of course it must, but does its expression have to be so leaden?

A Pub Crawl

Calvin from out of town came by and said let's duck into a bar and have a beer. Sure. Good old Calvin. He headed into Bradberry's Strawberry. I stopped him. "It's a swinging singles bar, Calvin. If you look unsingle and can't swing without getting your feet tangled in the vine, they treat you like 135 years old."

So he crossed the street toward the Hollow Crown and I rushed ahead and blocked the door. "This is a gay bar, Calvin. Go in there and they'll treat you like you're an unbribed fire inspector."

Irritated now, Calvin barged on to the next block and the O.K. Corral. He stopped outside. "How come all that neighing and whinnying in there?" he asked.

"That's the horses being coy. They get that way when the big spenders buy them champagne."

"Are you saying this is a bar for people who like to pick up horses?" asked Calvin.

"You'd hate it, Calvin. And if you came in and didn't make a play for one of the horses, they'd hate you."

"Why don't we go to a bar for people who like to beat their

mothers?'' asked Calvin. In his rustic fashion, he fancied he was being sarcastic about the sophistications of New York society. Little did he know that at the Forty Lashes, just around the corner, pre-theater mother-beating hilarity was probably reaching its peak.

Instead, I suggested a leather bar, for people who were into leather. Calvin refused, being into polyester. So I took him toward a tweed bar, for people whose fantasies centered on women—or men—swathed in thick layers of tweed of the most lascivious cut.

Calvin refused again, stating loudly that he detested "tweed freaks." He also hated everybody who was into camel's hair, which eliminated fifty of the raciest bars on the East Side. What's more, he said, he couldn't see why bars had to be segregated according to the customers' taste in romance. What kind of bigoted city was New York turning into anyhow? And so forth.

I recognized the symptoms of a man who was desperate for beer, and down in the next block was the Village Belfry. "Calvin," I said, "the Belfry is a bar we can live with. For one thing, it's stag. . . ."

"For men who want to be bats and have come out of the closet, I'll bet," said Calvin.

"Out of the attic," I said. I explained that they were really quite gentle, and all we would have to do to pass muster was hang from the rafters and squeak. Calvin said he couldn't stand heights.

My opinion of him was going down fast, so naturally I didn't suggest we go to a theater bar and rave to each other about how great we were. "Listen," said Calvin, "in New York every other person you meet is congratulating himself on his self-fulfillment, right?"

"As well as self-gratification, self-respect, self-esteem and self-service, Calvin."

"Well," said he, "then there must be bars for people who are in love with their selfs, right?"

Of course there were. The notorious self bars . . .

"And we can go there and be alone with our selfs and have a nice quiet beer, right?"

This time I did the refusing. I had made the mistake of going to a self bar two years ago and fell head over heels in love with my self the first time it winked back at me from the mirror behind the cash register. The beauty that only I could see behind that plain face could, I knew, be shown to the whole world if I opened my purse for face lifts, hair transplants, dental caps, custom tailoring, voice lessons, manicures and world travel to obtain brilliant international manners.

It had been a passionate affair. Just me and my wonderful self. It would have left me financially ruined if I hadn't realized in the nick of time that our love was a one-way street. No matter what I did for my self it always complained, always whined for more and more self-fulfillment.

"I love you but you don't love me back," I finally told my self, and walked out. I didn't want to risk another involvement by going into a self bar. Not for a beer. I had a better idea.

"Calvin," I said, "we'll do it the Times Square way," and bought two bottles of beer at a grocery and gave Calvin one, and both of us walked around Times Square drinking beer from our bottles in paper bags like everybody else.

O Zone

We are gathered at home to watch the end of the world on television.

It is a special. We are watching it on our old black-and-white set. A touch of sentimentality here.

A neighbor with color invited us over, but we felt the tug of loyalty. "At the end," we said, "we'd rather be with our faithful old black-and-white set that brought the family all the great assassinations."

Nobody can believe the world is really ending. "What will the newspapers have to write about after it's all over?" asks Grandfather.

O Zone

It is 1 o'clock in the morning. For months the networks have tried to persuade the world to end in prime time. "In prime time," they said, "it could top the ratings of the Super Bowl." No dice. The end of the world is not like a Republican National Convention. It is the last thing left that can say no to television.

The President will address the nation in a few minutes. According to NBC, which broke the release date on his speech, he will say that the end of the world is a historic event for all Americans.

The children are restless. They would rather watch *Abbott and Costello Meet Frankenstein* on Channel 8.

Foolish, foolish childhood. Someday, everybody will remember exactly what he was doing the night the world ended. How sad the children would be if they had to say, "I was watching *Abbott and Costello Meet Frankenstein.*"

Someday, they will thank us for this deprivation.

John Chancellor is showing film clips of the events leading to this night's event. Pictures of the last oil well going dry. Of the earth's vitally essential ozone layer breaking down under aerosol-can gases. Of well-dressed men carrying briefcases paying $5 admissions to pornographic movies. Of the rapidly mounting birthrate.

"I always told you that credit cards and automobiles would be the end of you," says Grandfather.

Mother wants to switch to CBS. She feels that so long as Walter Cronkite is handling the end of the world everything will turn out all right.

Marvin Kalb is entering an airplane with Henry Kissinger. Kissinger is smiling. Why? Kalb says Kissinger believes the end of the world may make the Arabs and Israelis more receptive to peace negotiations.

There is an Exxon commercial. Exxon is working to build a better life for everyone after the end of the world.

The cats are bored. We see film of San Clemente. Richard Nixon is watching the end of the world in seclusion with a few old friends.

An interruption for a live shot from Zurich. We see the dollar collapse. Grandmother says the end of the world is very dull. She has expected a big bang.

"This is not a rocket launching from Cape Canaveral," I tell her. "It is the end of the world."

The children are fractious. If there is nothing more to the end of the world than collapsing dollars, mounting birthrates, dry oil wells and well-dressed men carrying briefcases going to dirty movies, they would prefer to watch *Abbott and Costello Meet Frankenstein.*

I want to tell them to shut up, the end of the world is important, but I cannot, because I am a niceguy. You get to be a niceguy by growing up in a world you know can never come to an end. My entire life has been spent mastering niceguyism.

"Is this the way the world ends?" asks Mother.

"Not with a bang, but a whimper," says Cronkite, showing film of the last car in the world running out of gas.

"Just think" says Mother. "When we all get up tomorrow morning the world will have ended."

"Just like yesterday morning," says Grandmother.

The cats are asleep. We turn off the TV. It is so quiet I can hear the police steaming open my mail at the post office to make sure I still believe in the future of America.

Fragments of the last of the vitally essential ozone layer fall on the roof with the sound of small icicles breaking. The children plead to see the end of *Abbott and Costello.* Why not? They ought to have some way to remember the night the world ended, or else how will they ever believe it?

The New York Experience

Our friend Winokur, who is ill at ease in New York, arrived from Iowa for a visit recently and immediately noticed two cucumbers on the sidewalk in front of our house. Apparently

The New York Experience

he had never seen cucumbers on a sidewalk before.

"Should I bring in these cucumbers?" he asked. We all smiled at his rustic simplicity and advised him to let sidewalk cucumbers lie. "Why are there cucumbers in front of your house?" he asked.

Nobody tried to answer that. We are New Yorkers. In New York different things turn up lying in front of your house. Sometimes they are cucumbers. Who knows why? Who cares? "This is New York, Winokur," I said. "Enjoy it, and don't get bogged down in cucumbers."

We gave him a potion to calm his anxiety and bedded him down on the first floor. Having stayed with us in the past, he refuses to sleep upstairs for fear of being crushed by objects falling off the Emperor, the forty-six-story apartment building across the street. The last time he visited, the Emperor shed an entire window of thick plate glass and crushed a car in front of our house. We assured him that the Emperor was always doing that sort of thing, that nobody had been killed yet and that when somebody was, the police would do something about it, since this was the high-rent district and in New York the upper-income folks got action from the law.

Winokur was not reassured. In Iowa, I gather, they don't have buildings that litter. He insisted on the downstairs sofa, but we had scarcely snuggled down for the night when he was upstairs rapping at the bedroom door.

"It sounds like somebody's stealing hubcaps out front," he said. Why did he think law-abiding New Yorkers went to bed at night, if not to allow hubcap thieves the right to work in privacy? Winokur was unhappy with this explanation. "Why don't you go to the window and look?" he suggested.

He was clearly uneasy about going to the window himself, and sensibly so, since you can never tell when the Emperor will send some plate glass sailing out from the thirty-fifth floor, across the street and right into the window where you are investigating a hubcap theft.

So I went to the window. Sure enough, a man was removing the rear hubcaps from a red sedan parked under the Emperor. He was a short, elegantly dressed man with a mustache, and his work was being admired by a large, heavy, well-dressed woman, obviously his wife or companion. I described all this to Winokur.

"Why is a well-dressed man removing hubcaps at midnight?" he asked. "Why is a well-dressed woman watching?"

"Why are there two cucumbers lying on the sidewalk in front of my house?" I explained.

Dissatisfied, Winokur came to the window. "The elegantly dressed man is now putting both hubcaps on the wall at the base of the Emperor," he whispered. "And now, he and the well-dressed stout woman are walking away."

"This is New York," I said.

"Somebody is going to come along and see those hubcaps and take them," said Winokur.

"Not necessarily," I said. "One night when I parked my car out there somebody came along, lifted the hood, stole the radiator hose and didn't even touch the hubcaps."

"Something very funny is going on here," said Winokur. "Fancy-dress couple take off hubcaps. Leave hubcaps where they're sure to be stolen. Obviously, they don't need the hubcaps, they don't want the hubcaps, they just want the hubcaps to be stolen."

Predictably enough, the loose hubcaps were spotted by two very civilized-looking men who seemed to be out for a stroll. They stopped, discussed the hubcaps and, picking them up, walked away with them, one hubcap per stroller. They didn't look like men who really needed hubcaps.

Winokur's Midwestern sense of decency was so offended that he threw up the window and shouted, "Put those hubcaps down." They didn't, of course. Winokur was baffled by this example of white-collar street crime, which was not at all mysterious to a New Yorker.

The man who removed the hubcaps, I explained, hated the owner of the red sedan for having a free parking place at the curb while he had none. In fact, he regarded that curb space as his very own and had taken vengeance, possibly at his wife's urging, by promoting the theft of his enemy's hubcaps.

"Ridiculous," said Winokur.

"This is New York," I said.

I sent him out for the papers next morning. "Somebody has stolen the cucumbers," he said, returning, "and now there's a slice of pizza lying where the cucumbers were yesterday." Life must be very strange in Iowa.

Let 'Em Eat and Eat and Eat

"Business and pleasure don't mix," the old folks used to say, which proves once again that the old folks never did understand the income-tax law. Thanks to that bizarre document, business and pleasure have been mixing happily for so long that you can hardly tell one from the other anymore. Cocktails on a yacht, opening night on Broadway, box seats for the World Series, a suite at the Plaza—these things may sound like good old 100 percent pleasures, but nowadays they are often just business.

A Manhattan restaurant owner whose lunches cost from $20 to $30 a person told *The New York Times* that his customers were "94, 95 percent expense accounts," which is to say people who engage in fancy eating as a way of doing business and deduct the cost on the income-tax return.

Since elegant dining is not most people's idea of work, politicians periodically inflame the liverwurst-sandwich lunchers of America with visions of tax reform which will cut the expense-account aristocracy off the tax dole. The flaw in this otherwise fetching idea is as follows:

The tax law's encouragement for business and pleasure to mix has long since created a new business. Its workmen and entrepreneurs provide pleasures for the expense-account set. As business became increasingly indistinguishable from pleasure, we had one of those odd character transpositions which sometimes occur in long marriages, and pleasure turned into business. Cut the business deduction for pleasures, and what have you gained?

On the positive side, there is the emotional gratification of seeing the expense-account princes paying their own way for a change. This is worth plenty, but is it worth the heavy damage that will be suffered by the pleasure industry?

Some businessmen doubtless will continue buying $25-a-plate lunches for four even though the bill has to be paid out of the children's college fund, but many will quickly discover they can do just as much business over pastrami on rye at the desk.

Almost immediately a lot of waiters, busboys and dishwashers are going to become unemployed. Linen-laundering companies will fold, putting more people out of work. Doormen, hat-check attendants, bartenders and makers and sellers of glassware, plate and silverware will join the unemployed.

These are not the most depressing consequences. With the closing of restaurants, a little more life goes out of the center of cities as they are replaced with the modern equivalent of the Egyptian tombs—banks, airline offices, parking lots. Pressed rigorously against the entire pleasure industry, the campaign against entertainment deductions bleeds hotels, taxis, theater—all the unessential amenities of life which distinguish cities from suburban shopping malls.

This is why the New York restaurant lobby as well as the taxi, hotel and airline industries are resisting the Carter Administration's tax-reform proposal for a 50 percent cut in allowable expense-account deductions. New York, the home office of Federally subsidized high living, is the city that can least afford a wipeout of the expense-account set.

Somewhere there may be liverwurst lunchers who cry, "Hear, hear!" when President Carter says it's an outrage that "a business executive can charge off a $55 luncheon on a tax return and a truck driver cannot deduct his $1.50 sandwich," but not in New York. Too many liverwurst lunchers here depend on the expense-account splurges to keep them in liverwurst.

This is a small illustration of the social absurdities created by an absurdist tax law, and also an effective lesson in why it will be almost impossible to restore any sanity to it. The law has created an inequity—the right of privileged groups to deduct the cost of fancy living—and has simultaneously made the preservation of this inequity a matter of vital economic importance to the people against whom it discriminates.

Irrationalities like this abound throughout the country, thanks to the Government's practice of shaping tax law to influence the way people lead their lives. Thus, people who would like to live in city apartments inhabit suburban houses because the tax law was designed to make people buy houses. Actors who would like to play King Lear go into ranching because the tax law was designed to make people treasure cattle over Shakespeare.

People who would like to herd the expense-account nobility into tumbrels for the guillotine defend them, instead, against the mob because the tax law, willy-nilly, has created a loophole-service industry they need for their livelihood.

Everybody may agree with President Carter that the tax law is a "national disgrace," and most of us surely want it reformed, except for that small part of the disgrace on which each of us has built his private calculations for survival.

Rich Peter, Poor Paul?

Q: Are you really the Wizard of Oz?
A: No. I am the Wizard of Economics, but the two Wizard-hoods, being dependent on a talent for projecting an illusion of wisdom from a miasma of doubt, are actually interchangeable.

Q: Would you prefer to talk about the Straw Man or the Carter Administration?
A: Is there any difference?
Q: I'll ask the questions, thank you. Why are my taxes about to go up?

A: Because Congress has just learned about penicillin.

Q: Nonsense, Wizard. Penicillin has been around more than thirty years. Congress would have learned about it before now.

A: Not at all. Communication is very slow in Washington. It took almost ninety years for Congress to learn that slavery had been abolished.

Q: What does penicillin have to do with my taxes?

A: Thanks to penicillin almost everybody now lives long enough to collect Social Security. Congress didn't count on penicillin when it invented Social Security, so it didn't worry where it was going to get the money for Social Security payments to all those folks penicillin was going to conduct into their seventies, eighties, and nineties. Last week Congress heard the system was broke. This week they're preparing some new taxes to patch it up.

Q: Will they be very steep taxes?

A: As the Royal Executioner told the gentleman who was about to be drawn and quartered, you, sir, will know pain.

Q: Aren't there also going to be heavy new taxes on my oil and gas, after the energy bills are passed?

A: As you seem to be a glutton for bad news, yes.

Q: Is there no good news?

A: Of course. The Senate is proposing to reduce your Social Security tax by making your boss pay a lot more than you do.

Q: What's good about that? If the boss pays more taxes he's got less money to give me a raise to meet the ever-rising cost of living. Don't I end up paying the boss's share, too?

A: The Senate proposal is based on the assumption that you're too dumb to know things like that. If you're not, you lose the tax benefit of the Senate plan.

Q: Can't anything be done to save me from these taxes?

A: Of course, and the Administration is dedicated to doing it. Its aim is to create more jobs. With more jobs, more people will pay taxes and the individual burden will be reduced.

Q: How do you create more jobs by raising the tax employers have to pay on every jobholder? Won't this encourage employers to hold down the tax bill by holding down the payroll?

A: You don't understand economics. Of course a big rise in the Social Security payroll tax might hold down employment. That is why the President proposes to compensate for raising the Social Security payroll tax by cutting the income tax.

Q: Let's see if I have this right. The Government proposes to take from my left pocket and add to my right pocket. Wouldn't it be easier just to leave both pockets alone?

A: You forget that more lucre is needed to keep Social Security afloat. What is returned may not be so great as what is taken away.

Q: Then why doesn't the Government take only what it needs from the left pocket and let it go at that, instead of taking too much from the left pocket and then having to put some of it back in the right pocket?

A: Because, you see, the President has promised tax reform. With the extra income-tax forms you'll have to fill out to recover what's due your right pocket, not to mention all the new forms you'll need to cope with the new credits and deductions in the new energy bill, the President figures you'll finally become angry enough to write a letter to Congress demanding tax reform.

Q: Would that do any good?

A: Does a flea scratch dogs?

Q: Can't you give me something, Wizard, to help me make sense of it all?

A: That, alas, is medicine which does not exist. But here—take two of these dumbness pills every four hours, and it won't hurt so much.

Washington at Parsippany

In television they're called "docudramas," at the movie house they're "epics," at the bookshop they're "historical potboilers." Who can resist them?

"General Washington, sir, we have been marching for weeks. The men are exhausted. Can't we establish winter quarters in that town ahead?"

George Washington looks at the town. It is all wrong. He knows it is all wrong because he does not know its name. Its name, in fact, is Parsippany, New Jersey, though Washington does not know that. "Colonel Travers," he says, "I know not yonder town."

"It is Parsippany, New Jersey, sir."

George Washington looks at Colonel Travers with disgust, knowing Travers must be ad-libbing lines, for towns such as Parsippany, New Jersey, are never mentioned in docudramas, epics or potboilers. "Parsippany, New Jersey, Colonel Travers," he says, "will never become a historic old tourist attraction in the centuries to come."

Colonel Travers stares at Washington in awe. "Someday, General," he says, "generations to come will call you the father of our tourist attractions. How far must we search before we rest?"

"We march, Colonel, until we come to a place called—VALLEY FORGE!"

The army of the Israelites is gazing at a distant city. "Hath yonder city a name, O Joshua?"

"That, Sergeant, is a place called—JERICHO!"

Behind his desk in the Oval Office, Franklin Delano Roosevelt glances up from dispatches. "Well, bless my soul," he says to a man entering, "if it isn't Harry Hopkins, the most controversial figure in the New Deal!"

"I hear there is bad news, Chief."

"True, my controversial but close friend. The Japanese have bombed a place."

"What place, Chief?"

"A place called—PEARL HARBOR!"

Washington at Parsippany

Colonel Travers has sought an audience with General Washington. "The men are suffering miserably here at Valley Forge, General."

"Sit down, Colonel, sit down. Do you ever dream?"

"Yes, General. I dreamed just last night that I was approaching a small town in England with William the Conqueror and I asked, 'What is the name of that town, William?' and he replied, 'If you must know, it's Wimbledon, but if you had any dramatic sense you wouldn't ask me the name of any town until you know very well I can reply: "That is a place called—HASTINGS!"' "

"Perhaps you are in the wrong line of work, Travers," General Washington says. "Perhaps you should have gone into mapmaking instead of docudrama."

Joshua stands brooding in the ruins of Jericho. "Why dost thou brood, O Joshua, at the moment of the great tumbling down of the walls?" asks a sergeant.

"I fear, Sergeant, that our victory this day does not yet assure a future of peace for—THE TROUBLED MIDDLE EAST."

Eleanor Roosevelt is helping Franklin pack his suitcase. "So," she says, "you are going to a place called—YALTA!"

Franklin nods.

"Why?" asks Eleanor.

"To meet a man called—STALIN!"

Joshua wakens by his campfire. "I have just had a dream most passing strange, Sergeant. It was of a man of the distant future wearing a wig who will bring a great nation into existence."

"I, too, have had this strange dream, O Joshua. Was it of a man called—GEORGE WASHINGTON?"

"It was he," says Joshua, "and it did seem that all the people rose up and hailed him as the father of our tourist attractions and it was in a far place, a place called—AMERICA!"

"General Washington," asks Colonel Travers, "what is that town ahead?"

"Scaggsville, Maryland, if you must know, and hereafter I'll thank you not to ask me that question again until we come to a certain place in southeastern Virginia."

"Do you mean a place called—"

"That's my line," says Washington. "A place called—YORKTOWN!"

"Do you ever dream of the future, General? Of a strangely dressed man called—ROOSEVELT?"

"My dream, Colonel, is of a great country, a place called—THE UNITED STATES OF AMERICA—a place where fourscore and seven years from now we will be called—OUR FOREFATHERS!"

Colonel Travers does not ask, "How can we be our forefathers?" He is afraid of being expelled from the Screen Actors Guild and the Authors League.

The Flag

At various times when young, I was prepared to crack skulls, kill and die for Old Glory. I never wholly agreed with the LOVE IT OR LEAVE IT bumper stickers, which held that everybody who didn't love the flag ought to be thrown out of the country, but I wouldn't have minded seeing them beaten up. In fact, I saw a man come very close to being beaten up at a baseball park one day because he didn't stand when they raised the flag in the opening ceremonies, and I joined the mob screaming for him to get to his feet like an American if he didn't want lumps all over his noodle. He stood up, all right. I was then thirteen, and a Boy Scout, and I knew you never let the flag touch the ground, or threw it out with the trash when it got dirty (you burned it), or put up with disrespect for it at the baseball park.

The Flag

At eighteen, I longed to die for it. When World War II ended in 1945 before I could reach the combat zone, I moped for months about being deprived of the chance to go down in flames under the guns of a Mitsubishi Zero. There was never much doubt that I would go down in flames if given the opportunity, for my competence as a pilot was such that I could barely remember to lower the plane's landing gear before trying to set it down on a runway.

I had even visualized my death. It was splendid. Dead, I would be standing perhaps 4,000 feet up in the sky. (Everybody knew that heroes floated in those days.) Erect and dashing, surrounded by beautiful cumulus clouds, I would look just as good as ever, except for being slightly transparent. And I would smile, devil-may-care, at the camera—oh, there would be cameras there—and the American flag would unfurl behind me across 500 miles of glorious American sky, and back behind the cumulus clouds the Marine Band would be playing "The Stars and Stripes Forever," but not too fast.

Then I would look down at June Allyson and the kids, who had a gold star in the window and brave smiles shining through their tears, and I would give them a salute and one of those brave, wistful Errol Flynn grins, then turn and mount to Paradise, becoming more transparent with each step so the audience could get a great view of the flag waving over the heavenly pastures.

Okay, so it owes a lot to Louis B. Mayer in his rococo period. I couldn't help that. At eighteen, a man's imagination is too busy with sex to have much energy left for fancy embellishments of patriotic ecstasy. In the words of a popular song of the period, there was a star-spangled banner waving somewhere in The Great Beyond, and only Uncle Sam's brave heroes got to go there. I was ready to make the trip.

All this was a long time ago, and, asinine though it now may seem, I confess it here to illustrate the singularly masculine pleasures to be enjoyed in devoted service to the Stars and Stripes. Not long ago I felt a twinge of the old fire when I saw an unkempt lout on a ferryboat with a flag sewed in the crotch of his jeans.

Something in me wanted to throw him overboard, but I didn't, since he was a big muscular devil and the flag had already suffered so many worse indignities anyhow, having been pinned in politicians' lapels, pasted on cars to promote gasoline sales and used to sanctify the professional sports industry as the soul of patriotism even while the team owners were instructing their athletes in how to dodge the draft.

For a moment, though, I felt some of the old masculine excitement kicked up by the flag in the adrenal glands. It's a man's flag, all right. No doubt about that. Oh, it may be a scoundrel's flag, too, and a drummer's flag, and a fraud's flag, and a thief's flag. But first and foremost, it is a man's flag.

Except for decorating purposes—it looks marvelous on old New England houses—I cannot see much in it to appeal to women. Its pleasures, in fact, seem so exclusively masculine and its sanctity so unassailable by feminist iconoclasts that it may prove to be America's only enduring, uncrushable male sex symbol.

Observe that in my patriotic death fantasy, the starring role is not June Allyson's, but mine. As defender of the flag, I am able to leave a humdrum job, put June and the kids with all their humdrum problems behind me, travel the world with a great bunch of guys, do exciting things with powerful flying machines and, fetchingly uniformed, strut exotic saloons on my nights off.

In the end, I walk off with all the glory and the big scene.

And what does June get? Poor June. She gets to sit home with the kids the rest of her life dusting my photograph and trying to pay the bills, with occasional days off to visit the grave.

No wonder the male pulse pounds with pleasure when the Stars and Stripes comes fluttering down the avenue with the band smashing out those great noises. Where was Mrs. Teddy Roosevelt when Teddy was carrying it up San Juan Hill? What was Mrs. Lincoln doing when Abe was holding it aloft for the Union? What was Martha up to while George Washington was carrying it across the Delaware? Nothing, you may be sure, that was one-tenth as absorbing as what their husbands were doing.

Consider some of the typical masculine activities associated with Old Glory: Dressing up in medals. Whipping cowards, slackers, and traitors within an inch of their miserable lives. Conquering Mount Suribachi. Walking on the moon. Rescuing the wagon train. Being surrounded by the whole German Army and being asked to surrender and saying, "You can tell Schicklgruber my answer is 'Nuts.' " In brief, having a wonderful time. With the boys.

Yes, surely the American flag is the ultimate male sex symbol. Men flaunt it, wave it, punch noses for it, strut with it, fight for it, kill for it, die for it.

And women—? Well, when do you see a woman with the flag? Most commonly when she is wearing black and has just received it, neatly folded, from coffin of husband or son. Later, she may wear it to march in the Veterans Day parade, widows' division.

Male pleasures and woman's sorrow—it sounds like the old definition of sex. Yet these are the immemorial connotations of the flag, and women, having shed the whalebone girdle and stamped out the stag bar, nevertheless accept it, ostensibly at least, with the same emotional devotion that men accord it.

There are good reasons, of course, why they may be reluctant to pursue logic to its final step and say, "To hell with the flag, too." In the first place, it would almost certainly do them no good. Men hold all the political trumps in this matter. When little girls first toddle off to school, does anyone tell them the facts of life when they stand to salute the flag? Does anyone say, "You are now saluting the proud standard of the greatest men's club on earth?" You bet your chewing gum nobody tells them that. If anyone did, there would be a joint session of Congress presided over by the President of the United States to investigate the entire school system of the United States of America.

What little girls have drilled into them is that the flag stands for one nation indivisible, with liberty and justice for all. A few years ago, the men of the Congress, responding to pressure from the American Legion (all men) and parsons (mostly all men), all of whom sensed perhaps that women were not as gullible as they used to be, revised the Pledge of Allegiance with words intimating that it would be ungodly not to respect the flag. The "one nation indivisible" became "one nation *under God,* indivisible," and another loophole for skeptics was sealed off. The women's movement may be brave, but it will not go far taking on national indivisibility, liberty, justice and God, all in one fight. If they tried it, a lot of us men would feel perfectly justified in raising lumps on their lovely noodles.

Philosophically speaking, the masculinity of the American flag is entirely appropriate. America, after all, is not a motherland—many places still are—but a fatherland, which is to say a vast nation-state of disparate people scattered over great distances, but held together by a belligerent, loyalty-to-the-death devotion to some highly abstract political ideas. Since these ideas are too complex to be easily grasped, statesmen have given us the flag and told us it sums up all these noble ideas that make us a country.

Fatherland being an aggressive kind of state, the ideas it embodies must be defended, protected and propagated, often in blood. Since the flag is understood to represent these ideas, in a kind of tricolor shorthand, we emote, fight, bleed and rejoice in the name of the flag.

Before fatherland there was something that might be called motherland. It still exists here and there. In the fifties, when Washington was looking for undiscovered Asiatic terrain to save from un-American ideologies, somebody stumbled into an area called Laos, a place so remote from American consciousness that few had ever heard its name pronounced. (For the longest time, Lyndon Johnson, then Democratic leader of the Senate, referred to it as "Low Ass.") Federal inspectors sent to Laos returned with astounding information. Most of the people living there were utterly unaware that they were living in a country. Almost none of them knew the country they were living in was called Laos. All they knew was that they lived where they had been born and where their ancestors were buried.

What Washington had discovered, of course, was an old-fashioned motherland, a society where people's loyalties ran to the place of their birth. It was a Pentagon nightmare. Here were these

The Flag

people, perfectly happy with their home turf and their ancestors' graves, and they had to be put into shape to die for their country, and they didn't even know they had a country to die for. They didn't even have a flag to die for. And yet, they were content!

The point is that a country is only an idea and a fairly modern one at that. Life would still be going on if nobody had ever thought of it, and it would probably be a good deal more restful. No flags. Not much in the way of armies. No sharing of exciting group emotions with millions of other people ready to do or die for national honor. And so forth. Very restful, and possibly very primitive, and almost surely very nasty on occasion, although possibly not as nasty as occasions often become when countries disagree.

I hear my colleagues in masculinity protesting, "What? No country? No flag? But there would be nothing noble to defend, to fight for, to die for, in the meantime having a hell of a good time doing all those fun male things in the name of!"

Women may protest, too. I imagine some feminists may object to the suggestion that fatherland's need for prideful, warlike and aggressive citizens to keep the flag flying leaves women pretty much out of things. Those who hold that sexual roles are a simple matter of social conditioning may contend that the flag can offer the same rollicking pleasures to both sexes once baby girls are trained as thoroughly as baby boys in being prideful, warlike and aggressive.

I think there may be something in this, having seen those harridans who gather outside freshly desegregated schools to wave the American flag and terrify children. The question is whether women really want to start conditioning girl babies for this hitherto largely masculine sort of behavior, or spend their energies trying to decondition it out of the American man.

In any case, I have no quarrel with these women. Living in a fatherland, they have tough problems, and if they want to join the boys in the flag sports, it's okay with me. The only thing is, if they are going to get a chance, too, to go up to Paradise with the Marine Band playing "The Stars and Stripes Forever" back behind the cumulus clouds, I don't want to be stuck with the role of sitting home dusting their photographs the rest of my life after the big scene is ended.

Crawling Up Everest

On July 18 the two of us set out together to read *Remembrance of Things Past* by Marcel Proust. We have been reading it fairly steadily ever since, thanks to our stocked kits of smelling salts, and are determined to keep on reading until we either finish or die in the attempt.

Our first diary entries— of a Shackleton's expedition in literature—are presented below because this is a moment that cries out for public examples of heroism to remind us again of the greatness of which Americans are capable.

Few deeds can be more heroic than an attempt to read *Remembrance of Things Past* from beginning to end. Some persons will quarrel with this. Some will argue that true heroism lies in sitting through all of Wagner's *Die Valkyrie*. Others will hold that it consists in enduring a festival of Andy Hardy films. Every man has his Everest. None is so formidable as *Remembrance of Things Past*.

Remembrance of Things Past is longer than Everest is tall. When all seven volumes are piled together the stack is more than six miles tall. This great length is due not only to the incredible number of strained similes contained in the novel's seven volumes, but also to the dense layers of tedium packed into almost every paragraph.

Reading it is a feat to test Hercules, Washington, Lindbergh, John Glenn or John Wayne. "Life is too short and Proust is too long," Anatole France is said to have explained when asked why he had not read it. Perhaps so.

To help in the struggle I have retained a Sherpa reader who is highly praised among his countrymen for his ability to read anything. His name is Tenzing. Once Tenzing read the inaugural address of Warren G. Harding in its entirety, and to show that this was not a fluke, went on to read *The Last of the Mohicans* almost halfway through.

To protect ourselves against the temptation to cheat by skipping several volumes, we are reading aloud, every last word. The opening diary entries follow:

July 18: Would anybody believe 12,000 words about a man who had a hard time going to sleep when he was a boy? We read twenty-two pages of this before Tenzing gets ugly and says I have betrayed him by not telling him that this is a plot to bore him to death. Fortunately, I am asleep by this time and cannot take offense.

July 19: Another twenty pages today. The narrator—Proust, I suppose—still couldn't get to sleep. In a sudden flurry of narrative action Proust drinks a cup of tea and eats a cookie, which remind him of his boyhood, especially an aunt and a church he associates with that age, and an inability to go to sleep.

July 20: Only six pages tonight. Proust remembers the church again and, in a plot complication, recalls a stained glass window. Tenzing revives my heartbeat with brandy after seven hours of reading the paragraph on pages forty-nine, fifty and fifty-one. Our medical team pleads with us to turn back.

July 22: Our first crisis last night. Lifting the book to begin, I was seized with acute indolence, which the doctors say is common in the tertiary stage of tedium gravis. It was brought on by my conviction that Proust was going to remember the church's steeple while my life ebbed away.

Recovered enough tonight to read again. Proust tells absolutely everything about a meal that was prepared when he was a boy—asparagus, chicken, potatoes, marrow, spinach, apricots, roast leg of mutton, biscuits, preserves, coffee, cream, pepper and salt, bread, butter, knives, forks, spoons, table cloth . . . Tenzing says I must get a grip on myself.

July 23: Tonight we read for three weeks and finish nine pages. Proust reads in his garden and remembers veal.

July 24: Hurrah! Seventeen pages in just thirty-two hours tonight! Proust thinks of an invalid aunt and a musician who rather thinks he would like to play for some guests but is too shy to mention it.

July 25: Tenzing is in a deep depression. "That rotten Proust is going to think of the church again," he predicts at dinner. "Compared to Proust," he tells me, "Uncas, Chingachgook and Warren Harding are as much fun as Mae West." I take Tenzing to see an old Terry Thomas movie, which reminds us both of brussels sprouts.

July 26: Refreshed by our night off, we plunge through twenty-seven pages about Proust's boyhood passion for hawthorn blossoms. Tenzing collapses in hysteria, cursing hawthorn blossoms, spinach, church steeples and stained glass windows.

Our medical team orders us to take a week off. With 60,000 words behind us we have barely dented the book, but we feel heroic and American. Next week, says Tenzing, who has peeked ahead, the plot will thicken. He believes Proust is about to take a walk in the country. I already begin to look forward to it. Or is it merely anticipation of the ticker tape parade up Broadway?

The Late, Late, Late Movie

There is a time in the depth of night, somewhere between the hour of euphoria and the hour of the wolf, in which one sinks as listlessly and inexorably into the pit of hopelessness as a spoon falling through a barrel of molasses. This is the hour of the car dealer.

It is known only to insomniacs and night people who, as if those two afflictions were not sufficient curse, are also addicted to post-midnight television and particularly to television reruns of old movies. For reasons known only to the cash-register keepers in charge of television programming, the good movies are almost

The Late, Late, Late Movie

always held back until the hour of the car dealer, when all of life's winners are sound asleep.

The good movies rarely start before 12:30 A.M., and the true greats most commonly cannot be seen before 2:20. Is this because persons of taste and discernment spend the early hours of night doing such interesting things that they have no time for television until the pit of night?

I do not know. What every movie lover does know, however, is that the stuff available before midnight is usually low-quality. On the other hand, the commercials that intersperse the early-night trash are high-quality, often higher-quality than the movie they are disrupting.

Lavishly produced, cleverly acted, smartly written, beautifully photographed, the early-night commercials often provide a fresh breath of entertainment to relieve the air of heavy labor emanating from the movie. True, these uptown commercials are repeated until the viewer feels like an imbecile in the power of an automaton determined to teach him the multiplication tables.

After the fiftieth or sixtieth exposure to the bacon commercial, one wants to shout to the picture-book wife, "Yes, honey, this really is great bacon," to show that the lesson has been learned before the picture-book husband can say, "Honey, this is great bacon."

You shout the line. The husband goes ahead and repeats it anyhow. "Honey, this is great bacon." All right, he may still be treating you like a boob, but you know you have passed a test, have made progress, have mastered the lesson. Great bacon.

Now, the great old movie begins, and for a few minutes television is aesthetically balanced. The movie is high-quality; the commercials are high-quality. "Honey, this is great bacon." Yes, this miserable wife is guilty of inflicting unclean collars on her husband. And this intolerable seizure of gastric distress—is it not amusing to see it so ingeniously foiled by the perfect stomach alkalizer?

One settles back, feeling television a complete harmony of acquisitory impulse and art, as beguiling salesmanship matches

Cary Grant, Frederic March and Katharine Hepburn flawlessly with great bacon, marvelously laundered collars and chastened gastric distress.

Then—the hour of the car dealer. The elegant commercials retire for the night and Gary Cooper's scene is followed abruptly by a man strolling among his automobiles howling about upholstery. This man is to Gary Cooper as Soupy Sales is to Charles de Gaulle.

His whole commercial is illuminated with a five-watt bulb. His voice is on loan from a bus station loudspeaker. But the terrible thing about him, the truly terrible thing which begins to eat into the soul, is the knowledge that he will be back after this commercial. Lord, will he be back!

You could endure him once, twice, three times, as the price of seeing Miriam Hopkins, Carole Lombard, Irene Dunne. But he's going to put patience to the trial of rack and bastinado before this night is out. Not only will he reappear time and time and time again, but these reappearances will happen at increasingly closer intervals.

The car dealer, of course, is only a metaphor for the entire plague of pitchmen who infest the movie. There is the carpet king, incessantly walking through his gigantic warehouse. The suit salesman. The party with the fantastic new vegetable slicer. It dices, slices, cubes, chops, peels, and all for the incredibly low price of ——.

And now, back to Gary Cooper after this fantastic record bargain. The eighty-seven greatest hits of the Ozone Beach Accordion Choir, yours today on this two-record set for only ——.

I never make it to the end of the great movies. It's a case of low tolerance to torture. At 1:15 A.M. you may get ten minutes of the movie and ten minutes of the world's most resistible salesmanship.

It may be that the movie never ends, but simply fades away into unbroken hours inhabited only by the car dealer, the carpet king, the suit salesman, the vegetable slicer, the suspiciously underpriced records.

It is safer to surrender before the hour of the wolf arrives. This leaves time for a morning which gives you the chance to say, "Honey, this is great bacon."

The Beer Culture

The people of Beer World are named Buck, Mike, Al and Mac. There are no Algernons in Beer World, no Marmadukes, no Gaylords. Beer World has hair on its chest.

Yes, there are a few women in Beer World. They are named Gladys, though there is one named Elvira. You have seen the woman who brings a tray of beer to Buck, Mike, Al and Mac while they are sitting in the beer parlor in their mackinaws being rugged and jolly? Of course you have seen her. That woman is Gladys.

You may also have seen Buck recently having his beer at a distinctly sissifed ski lodge in company with a lissome young woman. That woman is Elvira. Buck sometimes takes Elvira to these sissy places in order to experience the perfection of beer without sweating.

Buck often feels guilty after these perspiration-free outings with Elvira, for in Beer World it is man's duty to heave and grunt until his pores open and let the honest body juices cascade freely. Only then does he truly deserve beer. Beer is the reward for manly toil in Beer World.

How often have you seen Buck, Mike, Al and Mac exhausted at the end of an honest day's work on the firing squad, sleeves rolled up, shirt collars opened, perspiration dampening their cheeks as they labor to rid the world of malcontents, looters and sissies—how often have you seen them joyfully throw down their tools as the sun sets, embrace each other merrily and tramp over to Gladys's place for their beer?

Now comes beer time. The beer has been created for Buck,

Mike, Al and Mac in recognition of their labor, in recognition of all they do. The beer is for them. Not for Algernon. Not for Marmaduke and Gaylord. Someone will object that we never really see the boys putting in a full day's work on the firing squad, that all we ever see are the final few executions at sunset. But of course; in Beer World, sunset is the only time of day. The sun stands eternally in the setting position. Shortly after Buck, Mike, Al and Mac throw down their rifles, or their scythes or their big tractor-trailers, and receive their beer from Gladys, they tramp out into the sunset again and finish building a skyscraper so they can throw down their rivet guns and march back to Gladys's place for another round of well-earned beer.

Why does Buck occasionally sneak away to sissified places with Elvira to drink his beer in dry clothing? Surely Buck would rather be with Mike, Al and Mac arriving at Beer World's cottage by the lake in their plaid fishing shirts.

Of course Buck would. It is much more fun racing to the refrigerator with Mike, Al and Mac and discovering four bottles of chilled beer than it is sitting across a table from Elvira. Is Buck —let us phrase the question as delicately as possible—is Buck soft on women?

The question is often raised by Mike, Al and Mac when they are all having dinner together in order to deserve a beer, or jogging twenty miles together just at sunset in order to earn the right really to enjoy a beer. Once they even asked Doc—Beer World's psychiatrist—to put Buck on the couch, give him a bottle of beer and find out if he was really one of the boys.

Doc had just finished whipping a massive superego down to size and was headed to Gladys's place for his beer when he conducted the examination. He pronounced Buck a perfectly normal beer guy with a slight woman problem.

It seems Buck had a mother, which is very rare in Beer World. In his youth, "Old Moms," as Buck called her, used to send him to the corner saloon to buy her what she called "a bucket of suds." "Old Moms" had since been deported under Beer World's rigid legal code, which denies citizenship to most women, especially if, like "Old Moms," they sit around the house in dresses made from flour sacks drinking beer out of tin buckets.

The law was necessary because people like "Old Moms" created a bad image of Beer World, which wanted to be viewed as a sweaty but clean-cut place full of boys whose beer had fewer calories and whose mothers, if they must have mothers, wouldn't be caught dead wearing flour sacks. In short, Buck felt bad about the old lady's deportation; when he took Elvira out for beer, he was really taking out his mother who had learned to dress expensively and to drink her beer out of a glass.

Elvira actually despises beer and would much prefer a drink with Amaretto in it, but doesn't dare order it for fear Buck would accuse her of not being one of the boys and walk out of her life forever. The women of Beer World do not have much opportunity to get out for a good time. Elvira has often asked Gladys to go out and have some Amaretto with her, but Gladys is afraid that if the boys learned about it they would call her a sissy.

Great American Ailments

We have all heard that America is a sick society, but nobody has been very specific about what precisely ails us. To fill this gap in the medical sciences, I have completed six hours of research by sitting in front of a television set, as a result of which I can now offer the following Complete Encyclopedia of Leading American Ailments.

Nagging backache: A mysterious affliction suffered by at least fifteen of every hundred Americans; possibly associated with tired kidneys, or moving the piano.

Rough, chapped lips: A winter ailment which takes half the fun out of kissing. Not to be confused with cracked, ugly hands, which result from washing dishes in inadequately advertised detergents.

Cracked, ugly hands: A scourge peculiar to women. (See "Rough, chapped lips" above.)

Razor nicks: All males who use safety razors sold before 1980 suffer at least three per shave.

Medicine-y breath: This common ailment invariably attacks persons who, upon being told their breath is offensive, rush off to gargle their own mouthwash. Can be cured only by using a second mouthwash recommended by the person who diagnosed the case in the first place.

Everyday aches and pains: A malaise whose origin still defies medical science, but believed by many to result from getting up in the morning, or being mugged.

Sleepless nights: Characterized by intense tossing and turning after retirement. Probably caused by large accumulations of cracker crumbs or problem dandruff (see "Problem dandruff" below) in the bed sheets. Medication: three pages of *Remembrance of Things Past* by Marcel Proust, or three ounces of gin, or pill prescribed by television.

Unneutralized stomach acid: A nasty business in the digestive tract resulting from taking a pill which neutralizes only half as much stomach acid as it ought to.

The wet look: A ghastly head ailment in which the patient's hair becomes tightly plastered to his skull. Peculiar to males.

Headache: Another nasty head condition in which nerves that look like steel wires tighten around the sides of the skull, forcing the infamous headache pain to strike, thus producing severe wrinkling around the eyes, tart language to beloved family members and an appalling loss of cosmetic makeup on the facial planes.

Great American Ailments

Cold miseries: A terrifying mechanical assault on the upper torso in which a fire rages inside the throat, a shower runs at full volume inside the skull and a rope, inserted into the chest cavity, attempts to strangle the lungs.

Problem dandruff: A new and more dreadful form of the male's ancient curse, discovered just last year at the world-famous Dandruff Clinic in Zurich. Unless patient submits to radical shampooing, no rug in his house can be saved.

Unsightly dandruff: Sometimes called the Italian disease because Columbus is thought to have brought it with him from Genoa, unsightly dandruff, if not treated rapidly, invariably leads to loss of job promotion and severe social embarrassment, such as losing the girl.

Offensive foot odor: A hideous pedal ailment secretly suffered by males, who live under unbearable psychic torment because of fear they may be taken to Japanese restaurants where their terrible secret will become known when they are asked to remove shoes.

Cellulite: An affliction in which fatty deposits resembling subcutaneous Jell-O pockets accumulate on female hips. Can be cured only by buying a book from Ann Miller, the famous doctor of tap dancing.

Iron deficiency: Are you aware that women require twice as much iron as men? Very few of them are getting it, and for this reason they suffer from sluggishness, midafternoon fatigue and inability to put up with small children. Treatment: a large bowl of shredded jail bars at breakfast every morning.

Wetness: Glandular affliction common among Americans who run five miles to the supermarket on August afternoons. Fortunately, home diagnosis is easy: you have only to ask a pair of your talking overalls if you need treatment. If overalls say yes, spray yourself with chemicals. Wetness is not to be confused with "The wet look" or "Offensive foot odor." (See above.)

Acid indigestion brought on by overindulgence: This dreaded medical mouthful is believed to afflict up to 60 percent of the entire American population on any given day and results from being alive.

Sluggishness brought on by irregularity: More commonly known as the ailment that dares not speak its name, S.B.O.B.I., as scientists call it, most commonly strikes retired men who are about to undertake ladder jobs around the house. It is always accompanied by a more youthful adult who knows precisely what to prescribe.

Another edition of this encyclopedia will deal with other American ailments, like "Dull-old-nonvibrating-shower-head depression," which is just emerging.

A Heap of Seeing

The old-timer was sitting on the porch talking to the boy when Earl came home from work. Earl was tired of the old-timer with his stories about all he had seen in the old days. Earl had heard them all hundreds of times.

"Hi there, Earl," said the old-timer.

"I guess you're telling the boy about all the things you saw in the old days," said Earl.

"Guess what, Dad?" cried the boy. "The old-timer was just telling me about the time he was watching television in a motel room and saw a woman win a Naugahyde den chair shaped like a beer keg."

"I've heard that story," said Earl. "It was a game show."

"That woman was so happy she jumped up and down in the air squealing like a pig in his first pair of spats," the old-timer said to the boy.

A Heap of Seeing

"Did you really see Joe Namath wearing panty hose?" asked the boy.

"Sure did, son," said the old-timer. "Right there on television. Joe was wearing the panty hose and grinning like a boll weevil in deep cotton."

Earl scowled. He didn't like this attachment between the boy and the old-timer. He wanted the boy to grow up and learn how to beat the income tax, not spend his life exploring the marvels of the world as the old-timer had done. "It's time to come in and study your tax shelters, boy," he said.

"Earl," said the old-timer, "did I ever tell you about the time I happened to wake up in front of the television set and see two people squeezing toilet paper?"

"Dozens of times," said Earl.

"Gosh," said the boy. "What did you do, old-timer?"

"Didn't do nothing," said the old-timer. "Just sat there playing it real cool and keeping my eye on that toilet paper. Pretty soon, along comes some jasper, tells them to stop that squeezing and they leave. The fellow's all alone, see, and what do you think he does?"

"What?" asked the boy.

"He squeezes the toilet paper himself."

"You're kidding!" cried the boy.

"Just as sneaky as a mole in the pea patch he was," said the old-timer.

"You must have seen it all," said the boy.

"I wouldn't say that," said the old-timer. "There was a heap of seeing to do in those days. There wasn't time enough to see it all. Take the time they killed the President's killer on television. I missed that. My tube was in the shop that day."

"Boy," said Earl, "if you don't get in the house and start studying investment credits, you're going to grow up to be tax poor."

"Earl," said the old-timer, "did I ever tell you about the time I saw them shave sandpaper with a razor blade?"

"You told me just last night," said Earl. "It was a fraud."

"That's right, boy," said the old-timer. "It turned out they weren't really shaving sandpaper. It just looked like sandpaper on television. What it was, was they put a lot of loose sand on a piece of glass. There were sights in those days, son."

"If you'd spent your time studying the tax laws instead of sitting around seeing the sights," said Earl, "you'd have enough money now to be telling these stories on the Riviera instead of my front porch."

"I'll bet you saw a lot of people killed on television," said the boy.

"Thousands of them," said the old-timer. "The real killings went on at dinner time during the news shows, then afterward they'd taper off with a few make-believe killings to get everybody's mind soothed down."

"Those must have been the days," said the boy.

"Of course, sometimes you saw people getting born, or people getting divorced. One of my favorites was seeing people who were being crushed under overturned trucks while this television reporter with the microphone would go up to the next of kin and say, 'How does it feel seeing your next of kin being crushed under that overturned truck?' "

"It sure sounds more exciting than tax-free bonds," said the boy. "Daddy," he said, "when I've beaten the income tax, can I see the marvels of the world the way the old-timer did?"

"We'll talk about that later," said Earl, sending the boy inside to his depreciation tables.

"Tell you what, Earl," said the old-timer. "Invite me in for a bite of supper and I'll tell you about the time I saw cigarette packages dance back in nineteen-and-five-naught."

"You already told me," said Earl. "You just go on home and turn on the box, and maybe you'll see something you never saw before."

The old-timer lumbered off unhappily. "Ain't much chance of that," he said. He was right, but he turned on the tube anyhow. He didn't know how to do anything else.

Someone has sent a copy of Alexis de Tocqueville's *Democracy in America,* which reminds me that I have never read it, although I have quoted from it frequently in writings which sought to masquerade as learned. De Tocqueville is so widely unread, even among professors, that anybody who throws out a de Tocqueville quotation is almost certain to put his reader on the intellectual defensive.

—Off the Top of de Tocq

It is astonishing what politicians can find to quarrel about. The Panama Canal, for heaven's sake. With civilization wearing out all over the country, with dogs amok in the streets of New York, with body snatchers menacing the Elvis Presley mausoleum, the best Washington can find to worry about is the Panama Canal.

—It Won't Hold Water

The reason for the high rate of unemployment is Henry Kissinger. Every time a new job opens up, Kissinger grabs it before anybody else can apply. Go to a publisher who needs somebody to work on a book, and he says you are too late. He's already hired Kissinger to do the book. Go to Chase Manhattan where there's an opening in banking, and it turns out they have already hired Kissinger. You've heard that NBC News needs a man? Forget it. They've already hired Kissinger.

—The One-Man Gang

Few public spectacles are more entertaining than Congress hitting the hallelujah trail. True, a writhing mass of Congressmen in the throes of uplift cannot match such superior media entertainments as the Gary Gilmore execution circus, but for connoisseurs of the art of flimflamming the rustics, a Congress in the heat of piety cannot be beat.

—Congress in Pious Heat

A Gloom Full of Spies

Notes on the espionage business, jotted while recuperating from an overdose of spy novels.

Spies are old and tired and sick of it all.

Their home office is in London, but they are very seldom permitted to go there. They are expected to stay out in the cold, looking seedy and lunching on meat pies and bad coffee.

This keeps them in Berlin a great deal of the time and allows them to become involved with *fräuleins*. Afterward they sit alone over meat pies and coffee brooding upon their failed marriages and wondering if their children still love them.

The *fräuleins* usually get murdered or turn out to be spies for the Russians, the Chinese, the Americans or the home office in London, which trusts nobody.

For this reason, spies spend many of their idle hours wondering why they didn't go into more agreeable work when they were young.

One day they are called to London for a meeting with Control. Nobody knows who Control is. Even Control's wife believes he leads a humdrum life as a floorwalker at Harrods. Having lost faith in him, Control's wife has been carrying on for years with a Socialist Member of Parliament.

For this reason, Control is old and tired and sick of it all. There is talk in Whitehall that he is losing his edge, that he has gone downhill since Eton.

When spies are called home to meet with Control, they see the telltale signs of age, fatigue and sickness of it all. Spies are trained to detect such weaknesses.

"Control is old and tired and sick of it all," spies say to themselves.

A Gloom Full of Spies

They have tea in the office and engage in hollow heartinesses. This gives Control the chance to size up spies and see whether life out in the cold has destroyed their character. He notes with sadness that they are old and tired and sick of it all.

For this reason and others, Control does not trust spies. Spies do not trust Control, either, and for good reasons.

Having read as much spy literature as the next man, they know that Control is either (a) a Soviet or Chinese agent, (b) the chap who arranges all those murders of *fräuleins* in Berlin or (c) a man of such unscrupulous fidelity to his country that he will have his own spies murdered whenever necessary to protect his network.

Naturally, their blood runs cold when Control becomes sympathetic and says, "You're old and tired and sick of it all, aren't you, old chap?"

This is the way Control always begins when proposing one last big job, with the promise that when it is over the spy will be given a desk job in the home office reading cables from equatorial backwaters for rotten pay while being kept under surveillance by the secretaries.

When spies hear this from Control they realize that they are probably going to be given the business. If Control has something big in the air, it's a cinch that any small-fry, old, tired and sick-of-it-all spies he chooses to involve will be used only as pawns.

The spies know this, and Control knows they know it. What's more, spies know Control knows they know it.

What spies don't know is why they have stayed with this filthy business all these years. Control doesn't know either. Once there was principle involved in it, duty to crown and self. But that was when they were all young and peppy and had not foreseen that they would get mixed up in the dirty business of murdered *fräuleins*.

And now—now they simply plow ahead, double-crossing each other, watching the *fräuleins* fall like duckpins, living on meat pies and filthy coffee, seeing their wives waltzing around the West End with flashy Socialists.

Living in an unrelieved state of depression, spies always accept the big job, even when it takes them to Macao. It is better than retiring to Bognor Regis with nothing to do but think about what rotten husbands and fathers they have been.

Moreover, even in Macao they are certain to find one last chance at true love, for, though the meat pies of Macao are not much to smack the lips about, the chances are excellent for finding a youthful Eurasian knockout who can restore a spy's sense of simplicity, honor and loyalty.

Afterward, they know, Control's plan may require them to be shot as part of a master scheme to pull an intelligence coup, but on the other hand, maybe Control will only need to have the Eurasian beauty ventilated.

It is a fifty-fifty chance to survive for another bout of *Welt-schmerz*. Maybe even better, since it's altogether possible that Control will be exposed as a Soviet spy back in London and given the chop before the Macao scene becomes messy.

Spies are old hands at computing the odds. Not like the innocent Americans from CIA who do it all with computers and lack all sense of the weariness of absolutely everything as well as the character it takes to become old and tired and sick of it all.

The Incredible Shrinking Life

When we moved to New York we had to get rid of the children. Landlords didn't like them and, in any case, rents were so high. Who could afford an apartment big enough to contain children?

Naturally, we all wept. What made it doubly hard was that we had to get rid of the dining-room furniture too. It made you feel sad. It was like being whittled away.

When the apartment rent went up, we had to settle for something with one room less, which meant getting rid of the trunk with Grandmother's old snapshots and 1899 letters to her grandfather, as well as our favorite easy chair, locks of the children's

The Incredible Shrinking Life

baby hair and the urn containing Uncle Mark's ashes.

"All that junk," said the real estate agent, "belongs in an attic, and New Yorkers can't afford attics." Attics were the past and New York was now. "To hell with the past, and three cheers for now!" we cried, as we got rid of it all.

And yet it made you feel sad. It was like being whittled away.

The rent went up again, and we had to get rid of the guest bedroom. Everybody said we were crazy for keeping a guest bedroom anyhow. It was an invitation for impoverished relatives, deadbeat acquaintances and children to bilk you of a free night's sleep. So we got rid of the guest bed and the sampler that said, "Welcome to our happy home," and we settled into a one-bedroom place with a doormat outside in the hallway that said, "Scram."

The doormat came from one of the chic new doormat boutiques in SoHo and looked so up-to-date that it made us feel almost as trendy as Jackie O. Still, when you got inside, you couldn't help feeling sad. You felt you were being whittled away.

The next rent increase presented hard choices by driving us into a one-room place with a windowless kitchen. The old sofa on which we had sat to watch the Super Bowl of 1964 had to go. So did the old lamps by which we had struggled to read Marcel Proust's *Remembrance of Things Past.* The old bed went, too, and the old rugs, the old mirror and the spare toothbrush.

When we first approached this new, lean shelter, scarcely larger than a procurer's automobile, we felt inexplicably sad until I cried, "Come now, it was just such a cubbyhole as this in which we first set out on the great American adventure of marriage and success."

With that, I scooped my companion into my arms and bore her over the threshold. How thrilling it was to recapture the euphoria of better days and to be young again. And, this time, in New York! And yet, it made you feel sad. It was like being whittled away.

The next rent increase was brutal. We refused to pay, refused to be whittled again.

"You don't want to pay, suit yourself," said the landlord. "This town's crawling with saps who'd give an eye and their front teeth for a place like this." He was apparently right. Entering and leaving the building, we saw half-blind, toothless saps staring at us with slavering apartment lust.

Out we went. Moving down again.

"Why are we always moving down?" I asked friends. "In the old days everybody used to move up. I remember the year I moved up to Kents. That same year I moved up to a three-bedroom house for only $22,000."

Friends assured me that moving down was what you did in New York. Why didn't any of us ever consider moving out? I asked. "You crazy?" they explained. "New York is where it's at."

I moved down. To fit into the smaller space I had to get rid of my companion. "It's just a closet," I said. "You wouldn't really like it." Anyhow, I pointed out, landlords didn't like women in their closets.

Naturally we both wept. It really did make you feel sad. It was like being whittled away.

One night the landlord opened the closet door and showed the hooks to a German with a favorable rate of exchange, a millionaire Italian playboy, an oil-rich Arab and two highly skilled American tax evaders.

There was no doubt what that meant. I called real estate agents. They took me all over Manhattan, looking at warehouse shelves. Not one of them could accommodate anybody more than four feet tall.

The surgeon was reassuring. "I have done hundreds of such operations," he said, "since the real estate boom began. My patients inhabit some of the most expensive shelves in Manhattan."

"Will I regret it afterward?" I asked.

"A touch of sadness is only to be expected," he said, "after you've been whittled away."

Bottom of the World, Ma!

I never watch shows that give a misleading impression of the people they deal with, so naturally I passed up "Death of a Princess" after Saudi Arabia announced that it gave a wrong impression of life in the oil-rich kingdom.

For the same reason, I didn't go to see *Cruising,* which, judging from the public demonstrations against it, gave a bad impression of the homosexual life. I am not going to see the new Charlie Chan movie either because, though it hasn't been made yet, Americans of Chinese origin say Charlie Chan is an affront to Chinese culture.

Unfortunately, I did see some Charlie Chan movies forty years ago, but I was too young to know better. For the same reason, I went to see *Hamlet* in 1947. However, I have never seen it since, and never intend to, now that Danes have told me it gives a very bad impression of life in Denmark.

I walked out of *The Godfather* after the first thirty minutes when I realized it was giving a misleading impression of Italian family life, and dropped *War and Peace* like a ten-pound sack of potatoes after it became obvious that Tolstoy was giving a completely lopsided impression of Napoleonic France.

Does this reflect an undue sensitivity to the feelings of others? It might have seemed so once, but that was before I felt for myself the sting these misleading entertainments can produce. Which brings us to Ralph Bellamy.

I refer, of course, to the movie Ralph Bellamy and not to the stage Bellamy who, as Franklin D. Roosevelt in *Sunrise at Campobello,* swept everything before him with his mighty decency. The movie Ralph Bellamy, as graybeards and late-night TV addicts will remember, never swept anything before him.

In movie after movie Ralph Bellamy was the man who didn't

get the girl in the end. And why? Because Ralph Bellamy was polite and kind and gentle.

It is still embarrassing to confess—such is the grotesque power of movies to make you ashamed of your own culture—but I identified with Ralph Bellamy. I was polite, kind and gentle, too. Not that I wanted to be, mind you. I wanted to be sassy like Clark Gable or sullen like Humphrey Bogart, but my attempts invariably resulted in a punch in the nose. I was forced to take the polite, kind and gentle route as a matter of survival.

Well, the humiliations were constant. As soon as Bellamy walked on the screen and told Irene Dunne, "I have the honeymoon suite on the *Berengaria,* dear," the entire audience broke into snickers. Everybody was thinking: "That poor polite, kind and gentle sap—too dumb to realize that Irene is going to be in Cary Grant's arms when the *Berengaria* sails tonight."

I forced a snicker, too, to show I was a regular guy, but it hurt, friends. It hurt. What that movie was saying to me was: "You are the effete product of an inferior culture."

In one movie Ralph planned to take his mother along on the *Berengaria* because Ralph, you see, liked his mother. He respected her. He called her "Mother," not "Mom." He didn't refer to her as "the old lady." She was "Mother." And everybody laughed. People who had mothers were ridiculous and couldn't get the girl; that's what the movie was saying.

Well, you guess right; I had a mother. What's more, I didn't call her "the old lady." I liked my mother. I respected her. I was, in short, a loser. No girl for me at the end. Nothing but the awful loneliness of that honeymoon suite on the *Berengaria* as Irene and Cary embraced on the dock and my mother asked, "Why in the world did you order all that champagne?" while the audience hooted with delight.

Cary Grant didn't have a mother. Clark Gable didn't have a mother. Humphrey Bogart didn't have a mother. James Cagney, to be sure, had a mother once, but she was a murderous old gunslinger and he called her "Ma," not "Mother," and honored her by getting blown up on top of a gas storage tank while screaming, "Top of the world, Ma!"

Ralph Bellamy movies were as commonplace as Charlie Chan movies, and in the terrible fashion of these things, the unfair and distorted stereotype began to affect my behavior. I became politer, kinder and gentler with the passing years, and lost more and more girls in the end.

Politeness, kindness and gentleness became my way of life and the good times passed me by. Politeness, kindness and gentleness are why I never see a show or read a book that anybody doesn't want me to see or read and why I have to make my own good times playing solitaire and looking for funny names in the telephone directory.

Up Against Those Gallic Wiles

France's refusal to boycott the Olympics was inevitable, of course. Anyone who understands France could have told the President it was inevitable. I could have told the President. My friend Marcel could have told him, I thought when I read the news: "France Refuses to Go Along with U.S. Olympics Boycott."

This reminder of my friend Marcel also reminded me that we hadn't lunched for a long time, so I telephoned him to arrange a lunch date. Naturally, he was irritated by the call.

"Do you want to talk to me?" he asked.

"I most certainly do not," I declared. "I must have dialed the wrong number. Good-bye."

And I hung up. That's because I understand the French. You see, I knew that if I, an American, said I wanted to talk to Marcel, he wouldn't talk to me. Once he suspected that I didn't want to talk to him, however, he would insist on a conversation. The phone rang almost immediately.

"It is absolutely essential that we talk," he said.

Since I wanted to lure him to the luncheon table, I said, "Why don't we get together on a bench in Central Park just before church on Sunday morning?"

"Talking on park benches is a barbaric American cultural deformity," Marcel explained. "Let us meet like civilized men over good food."

"Good," I said, "I'll meet you for dinner at La Grande Addition."

"Dinner is too serious to be eaten with an Anglo-Saxon," he explained. "We shall have lunch at Les Petites Bêtises."

You may think that my cunning grasp of French psychology had at this point helped me attain my goal of setting up a lunch with Marcel. If so, you do not understand the French.

In fact, I didn't even bother keeping the lunch date at Les Petites Bêtises, since I knew Marcel would not show up. I also knew he would expect me to telephone and, in a bumbling Anglo-Saxon rage, demand to know why he had stood me up. This would give him a chance to insult me.

So I phoned and shouted at him and said I had never been so insulted in my life. This put him in fine humor.

"But you must realize, my friend," he said, "that at the last minute when our lunch engagement was due I was suddenly presented with the opportunity to talk to someone interesting, witty and intelligent."

I tried to improve his spirits even more by making sobbing sounds into the telephone and grinding my teeth to suggest I was chewing the carpet, and I concluded by saying, "I shall never lunch with you again."

Now Marcel's glee subsided as his fierce Gallic pride rose to the challenge.

"We will see about that!" he cried.

"Never!" I shouted, slamming down the receiver.

An hour later, a platoon of French caterers arrived at my door with an admirable lunch. Marcel followed before the soup had been ladled out of the tureen.

"You see?" he said. "We have ways of making you lunch."

Gloating silently at the success of my machinations, I told him that the great friendship between France and the Anglo-Saxon peoples could never die and that he was a great human French being.

Naturally, he had to disagree.

"Hah! You would think differently, my friend, if you knew that after this lunch is consumed I shall proceed immediately to a rendezvous with your wife."

Well, don't think I didn't know how to spoil that little tête-à-tête. Without saying a word, I addressed myself to the soup bowl, took up a large soup spoon and began eating.

He was about to attack his own soup, but when he saw me using a soup spoon he realized he was in deep trouble. He was in danger of following an Anglo-Saxon lead.

"But then, old friend," he said, "you truly intend to eat that soup with a spoon?"

"I wasn't raised to know no better," I said, treating him to a few noisy slurps from the upraised spoon.

"Tant pis for you," he said, and began eating his soup with a fork. It took him quite a while and also made a mess of his necktie, shirt and lapels.

I sent him to the dry cleaner, but naturally when he got there he insisted on going into the wet wash, and I called my wife and asked if she was expecting Marcel, and she said she had never heard of any Marcel and why did I ask, and I said it didn't matter since he wouldn't be ready at the laundry until next Thursday anyhow.

Keeping Up with Halpingshtorm

Being petit bourgeois, I try as hard as anybody else to keep up with the Joneses. The man against whose achievements I measure my own is not Jones, however, but Saul Halpingshtorm.

Jones became so angry about my efforts to keep up with him that he moved to New Jersey a few years ago to enjoy his superiority in solitude. "If you want somebody to keep up with, try keeping up with Saul Halpingshtorm and leave me alone" were his parting words.

Halpingshtorm, unlike the testy Jones, enjoyed having somebody try to keep up with him. One evening I came home wearing the lean and costly tweeds of the Ivy League, which I had bought that day because Saul Halpingshtorm wore the lean and costly look of the Ivy League. The children wept.

"What have you done with your green double-breasted suit with white pinstripes, Daddy?" they cried.

That was the suit whose purpose was to keep up with Jones. "Daddy is not keeping up with Jones anymore," I told the tykes. "From now on Daddy is keeping up with Saul Halpingshtorm."

I went to Halpingshtorm's for dinner that evening. He was not wearing his lean, costly, Ivy League tweeds. He was dressed for the Gregory Peck role of white hunter in *The Macomber Affair,* though he seemed to have forgotten the elephant gun. Later, somebody told me this was a safari jacket.

The other guests arrived in similar dress. When dinner was ended, Saul hinted that it would be considerate of me to leave early so everybody could talk about my being so pathetically out of fashion.

It was always that way in haberdashery. When I showed up at Saul Halpingshtorm's wearing a gold necklace because Saul had started wearing gold necklaces, Saul was wearing an ascot. When I bought black Swiss ballet slippers because Saul had started wearing black Swiss ballet slippers, Saul started wearing jogging shoes.

Upon learning that Saul Halpingshtorm dined nightly at Mama Pepita's, I went to Mama Pepita's. "What time does Mr. Halpingshtorm come in?" I asked. "Mr. Halpingshtorm quit coming in after last night," Mama Pepita said. "From now on he dines only at Elaine's."

The next night I went to Elaine's. Elaine gave me a table in the next block. Saul Halpingshtorm, who had the best table in the house, sent me a Mailgram requesting me not to drop by his table, as he did not want to be seen talking to someone who vacationed in Baltimore.

That summer, having learned that Saul vacationed at the seashore, I rented a cottage in Asbury Park. That fall he asked, "Why didn't I see you in Nantucket this summer?"

The next summer, I rented a house in Nantucket and invited Saul to come play pinochle, but he said he was busy. Later, somebody told me Saul Halpingshtorm, who had bought a house in Nantucket, didn't visit with people who merely rented.

The following summer I came into a fortune, thanks to a typographical error in a Rockefeller will, and bought a home in Nantucket before the lawyers could bring action. In the fall, I asked Saul Halpingshtorm why I hadn't seen him in Nantucket that summer. "I only take winter vacations now," he said.

I was not utterly enslaved to Saul Halpingshtorm. There were moments of rebellion, moments when I said, "To hell with keeping up with Halpingshtorm." I would show my independence by refusing to read the books he had read, to see the movies he had seen, to buy the clothes he had bought, to adopt the ideas he had consumed.

This seemed to sadden him. He would speak to me like a father, urging me not to quit trying. Once, because Saul Halpingshtorm never wore a hat, I bought a hat and wore it to his house. I have never seen him so depressed. When I left, he spoke to me with gentle kindness. "Don't wear that hat," he said. "It makes you look like you have a pointed head."

I realized that he needed me, that of all his great circle of friends, I was the only one who could never keep up with him. I threw away the hat. Constant humiliation is a small price to pay for friendship.

In mid-April he phoned to announce that he was taking a spring vacation at St. Bart's. He knew very well that I had never heard of St. Bart's and did not know that St. Bart's was the only place to vacation that spring, and that by the time I could get reservations there St. Bart's would be overrun with McDonald's hamburger stands. Nevertheless, to please him I said, "I'm going to get to St. Bart's myself as soon as it's completely out of fashion."

After hanging up I stood in front of the mirror. My head definitely came to a point.

Let's Go for a Little Ride

B. A. Cornell, an Australian visitor to New York, complains in a letter to the editor published in *The New York Times* that he was bilked by a cabdriver who charged him $40 for transport from the East Side Airlines Terminal to the Port Authority Bus Station.

This seems a strong accusation. To be sure, the cab fare from the airlines terminal to the Port Authority station should amount to no more than $3, provided the passenger can tell the cabdriver how to get there. Mr. Cornell obviously could not give accurate directions. This is understandable. He was a stranger in town. And so he was "taken for a roundabout ride and charged $40" for a $3 trip.

In accusing the driver of cheating him, however, Mr. Cornell assumed that the cabdriver knew how to get from the airlines terminal to the Port Authority station. Why does he not take the Christian attitude and assume that the cabdriver had no better notion than he, Mr. Cornell, had of how to get there?

It may be that in Australia cabdrivers know how to get from Point A to Point B without directions from their customers. This is not the case in New York. In New York no person may be licensed to drive a taxi until examination by the authorities proves that he cannot find his way around the city.

Now and then, if Mr. Cornell comes back to New York and is lucky, he may find an old-timer who can drive unerringly from Central Park to the Empire State Building. I myself found a cabbie last November who knew how to get from Rockefeller Center to Christopher Street in Greenwich Village.

Let's Go for a Little Ride

His name will not be disclosed here, since the taxi authorities might haul him into court and revoke his license on charges of competence. Let us all hope that Mr. Cornell will come back to New York and, next time, bring a large, detailed street map so he can enjoy directing our famous cabs and learn to love New York as the rest of us do.

A ready map can make all the difference in the world, particularly if the cabdriver speaks English. If he does not, some very amusing fares may result. One night, wishing to go from Sutton Place on the East Side to Prince Street in SoHo, I produced my map and began reciting directions, only to learn that the cabdriver understood only Macedonian and a few snatches of demotic Turkish.

Did I accuse the poor wretch of cheating me when he overshot Prince Street by a mile and plunged into the Holland Tunnel? Of course not, Mr. Cornell. I enjoyed the sport as, threading his way through the streets of Jersey City in search of a translator, he sought to find a fellow Macedonian by pulling alongside pedestrians and shouting, "Hey, peoples! Hey, you peoples!"

Mr. Cornell will never know the fun of New York until he has tried to get from the 59th Street Bridge to La Guardia Airport in a cab driven by a Chinese who has immigrated just eight hours earlier from the Tibetan frontier and is under the impression that "Turn left at the next corner" and "Step on the gas" both mean "Go back to Astoria and start over."

It may seem that the taxi authorities of New York will not license a person to drive a cab unless his only language is Macedonian, Chinese, demotic Turkish, Greek, Finnish, Urdu, Russian or Arabic, but this is not the case. In fact, there are extraordinary numbers of English-speaking drivers, considering that the taxi bureau will license only English-speakers who are allergic to smoke.

You can always tell whether your driver speaks English, Mr. Cornell, by glancing into the cab before entering. If the interior contains a printed announcement that says, "No Smoking: Driver

Allergic to Smoke," it is a safe bet that he will understand routine directions spoken in English.

No other cab fleet in the world boasts so many drivers allergic to smoke as New York's fleet. In fact, the city is so famed for its vast numbers of cabbies suffering from allergy to smoke that persons allergic to smoke come here from all over the United States so they can drive cabs that advertise their ailment.

Mr. Cornell does not state the time of day his $40 ride took place. If he wants the taxi bureau to take punitive action against the driver, however, he can get results if the ride occurred during the rush hour, immediately after the theater closings or during a rain.

New York taxi industry rules require all drivers during these periods of high public demand for service to switch on their "Off Duty" lights and race through the streets refusing to pick up passengers. If Mr. Cornell got his taxi during one of the "Off Duty" periods, he should find the taxi bureau willing to make the driver cry uncle.

Champion, Beat Thy Typewriter

NEWS BULLETIN: *Norman Mailer has just punched Gore Vidal after a brief verbal exchange at a Manhattan party for the rich and famous. Mailer's punch was followed by a quick glass of alcohol to Vidal's face—whether wine or whiskey has not been determined— and an invitation to step outside. Vidal countered with a flurry of slashing repartee, driving Mailer up against the telephone where he is now trying to set the record straight with the gossip columnists.*

They were calling him an old man now. Henry James could take that. He was old, old in the bone, old in the spirit. All those years of brooding about the significance of the American heiress in Europe had taken it out of him. But, by George!, he was still

Champion, Beat Thy Typewriter

Henry James. The Master. And he could still raise a lump on the jaw of any writer who stepped into the same party with him.

His agent didn't believe it. "Henry," he had said, "it's time to hang up the gloves." By way of reply Henry James had given him a smart uppercut toward the jaw which missed and struck a chandelier, damaging James's middle finger, the one he relied upon to start his famous "which" clauses.

"Look what you've done," said his agent. "Now you won't be able to write any 'which' clauses for a month. You'll start writing like that new Hemingway kid."

James didn't care. Nobody had booked him an opponent since he had floored Mark Twain with a left hook to the kidney at the Baltimore Bachelors' Cotillion three years earlier, and James was hungry. Specifically, he was hungry for William Dean Howells. He had studied Howells's prose with the cunning of the Master and had good reason to believe Howells would be a sucker for a rabbit punch.

"I want William Dean Howells before a white-tie gala in Mrs. Astor's ballroom," barked James. The agent shrugged. "It's your funeral, Hank," he said.

Howells had no intention of pugilizing with Henry James in Mrs. Astor's ballroom or anywhere else. For one thing, Henry James was a name that spelled floperoo at the box office. Nobody had been able to finish the opening chapter of a James novel in fifteen years. Everybody would expect James to use 35,000 words to utter the obligatory preliminary insult, which put the audience to sleep long before he started punching.

Henry was working out on the big typewriter when his agent brought him the news. John L. Sullivan was watching him in deep admiration. Sullivan had been an acolyte to Henry James ever since Henry, in a prefight press conference, had challenged Big John to put up his dukes and step into the ring.

"You ever fight anybody good?" Sullivan had asked him.

"I've gone a few rounds with Mr. Tolstoy," Henry had said.

It was the first existential statement Sullivan had ever heard. In gratitude he took to hanging around James's typewriter urging the great belletrist to discuss existentialism and even gave Henry pointers on the easiest way to break a poet's jaw with bare knuckles.

When John L. Sullivan heard that William Dean Howells had refused Henry's challenge, he urged the Master to accept the refusal as a victory, abandon pugilism and give the world an expensive coffee-table picture book on Lillian Russell, which would not only illuminate the cancer in the soul of theatrical booking agents, but also make him rich.

The crassness of this proposal so enraged Henry James that he smashed a right cross into John L. Sullivan's rib cage and broke every bone in his hand. And so, that night at the Vanderbilts' reception for President Taft, he was unable to counter with a single punch when Theodore Dreiser strode across the ballroom and relieved the agonized boredom of the guests by knocking Henry James to the floor with a quick left jab to the jaw and a right hook to the solar plexus.

James was never quite the same afterward. Joseph Conrad cracked three of Henry's ribs with an indolent left hook one evening in the Boston Atheneum, and A. E. Housman came all the way from England to raise a mouse under James's right eye at a black-tie dinner the Fricks gave for Nellie Melba.

James finally retired from pugilism after Edith Wharton knocked him out for thirty-five minutes with her famous powder-puff uppercut during a chance meeting at Alice Roosevelt's coming-out party. With James's retirement, the great era of two-fisted belles lettres was almost at its end. With World War I and the twenties, a new generation began to dominate American literature, a desperate lost generation which was to abandon the manly art of self-defense and make alcoholism the principal sport of their profession.

The romance had gone forever from the scribbler's trade, gone with the social punch in the nose. It would be a long time ere American letters would again find a real he-man.

All politicians are humble, and seldom let you forget it. They go around the country boasting about their humility. They are proud of their humility. Many are downright arrogant about their humility and insist that it qualifies them to be President.

—**The Big Town**

Whenever someone sets out to solve the Middle East problem, he naturally insists on getting to the crux of the matter and then becomes confused when he can't find the crux. The crux of the Middle East problem is that it has no crux.

—**From Eden to Yemen Sans Camel**

To a Republican, a Republican President is not good enough. He must be The Right Kind of Republican President. The Right Kind of Republican President is the kind for whom independents and Democrats will vote only if the alternative is Attila the Hun.

—**Exorcist Wanted Quickly**

Expanding Memorial Day into the Memorial Day Weekend illustrates the benefits that can flow from the national zeal for excess. Without the spirit of excess, how would America ever have hit on the idea of having the whole country honor its war dead by going on a three-day picnic?

—**The 100 Years' Primary**

Government lies are most dangerous when we believe them to be the truth. Once the Government acquires the honest habit of acknowledging that it lies a lot of the time about very important matters, we will all be better off, for then we can stop listening to the Government with childish credulity and watch it with the skepticism with which one con man watches another, which is not the worst of all possible ways of defining our relationship with it.

—**The Cold War Virus**

Old, Aging Fast and Young

Old: You are named John or Mary, got married in June and can still rhyme "honeymoon" with "Joon" without wincing.

Aging fast: You are named Dirk or Linda, have just decided that a divorce is more trouble than it's worth and wish the Beatles would get together again.

Young: You are named Jason or Jennifer, are living together out of wedlock because you can't afford the punitive income tax on working married couples and don't think of sushi as raw fish.

Old: You miss the *Queen Mary.*

Aging fast: You treasure an old snapshot of yourself being tear-gassed the day the cops routed the SDS from the physics lab.

Young: You remember the good old days when "Charlie's Angels" still had Farrah Fawcett.

Old: Wouldn't trust a computer as far as you could throw one.

Aging fast: Never trust anyone over thirty—oops!—over forty-five.

Young: No nukes!

Old: You are shocked by evidence that Franklin D. Roosevelt was unfaithful to Eleanor.

Aging fast: You find it incredible that Theodore Roosevelt never engaged in premarital sex.

Young: You doubt that anyone engaged in sexual activity before 1975, except when fully clothed.

Old: "When I was a kid, you could buy an ice cream cone for a nickel."

Aging fast: "Remember that summer we flew to Europe and

hitchhiked all the way from London to Lake Como on just $50 a day?"

Young: "I'll need $25,000 a year to start, but first let's talk about the retirement plan."

Old: You want your children to have a better life than you had.

Aging fast: You want your child to have it just as good as you had it, except for the really heavy drugs.

Young: You wouldn't mind having children if you could afford a house to put them in and if the Government rewrote the law to make children a profitable tax shelter.

Old: You are watching another made-for-TV movie about World War II, and all the soldiers are wearing their hair in the thick, long-locks, Los Angeles style popularized by local TV news-show anchormen. You become intensely irritated because whoever made the movie was obviously too young to know that all GI's in World War II wore crewcuts.

Aging fast: While watching the same movie, you are sickened by the tendency of American mass culture to glorify war instead of showing it like it is—namely, as an evil that can make a mess of the most expensive hair styling.

Young: You find the movie very boring if you are male, but continue watching to get some tips about how to shape your hair for a sexier look; if female, ditto.

Old: When you think of the great evils of the twentieth century, what you have in mind are the Great Depression, Adolf Hitler and Josef Stalin.

Aging fast: What comes to your mind, on the other hand, are irrelevance, conformity, the Establishment, Lyndon Johnson and disco.

Young: And what comes to yours? Cholesterol, pollution, nuclear meltdown, the Ayatollah Khomeini and the skyrocketing Social Security tax.

Old: Until this moment, you haven't thought about Warner Baxter in twenty years.

Aging fast: You think it quaint that anyone should ever have thought about Warner Baxter. This is because you have forgotten that you haven't thought about Sam the Sham and the Pharaohs in ten years.

Young: You feel very smug in this department because you still think about Johnny Rotten and Sid Vicious every now and then. But just you wait a few months, young-timers.

Pocket Money

A curious side effect of inflation is the psychological change that occurs in the human attitude toward money. It is as if we have a built-in psychological defense to protect us against the mental ravages threatened by declining currency.

Recently, for example, without even noticing it, I abandoned the habit of carrying all paper money in my wallet and took to stuffing bills of $1 and $5 denominations into my trouser pocket, which in the past had been habitually reserved for items of small value, like coins.

In my rigidly organized psychological system, the wallet was the repository for things of value—paper money, credit cards, permits issued by the more terrifying bureaucracies, lists of clothing sizes of persons who might retaliate if holidays and their birthdays were not observed with gift presentations, instructions for shipment of the remains in case of abrupt demise in some remote location and so forth.

The pants pocket, more easily, more thoughtlessly accessible to the right hand, has always been the place for things whose loss would not be a disaster. Toothpicks collected from the delicatessen counter, coins, chewing gum wrappers, lint and messages to telephone editors, lawyers and press agents immediately.

Pocket Money

The fact that coins were relegated to this pocket reflected an earlier inflation that must have occurred during the 1940's. Before World War II, I distinctly remember treating coins with great respect. In fact, I can still remember every detail of a day in 1935—the sun was shining and there was a slight autumn nip —when I looked down and saw a dime gleaming up from the sidewalk. I have never felt so rich again.

In any case, at that time coins were stored in one of those small fake leather coin purses associated with caricatures of the miser. By 1945, however, they had been relegated to the pocket with the toothpicks and lint.

By that time my psychological organization had been expanded to include a wallet, an accessory so alien during the prewar years that it was associated only with bankers and gangsters. The wallet was the place for what was then known as folding money. "Real money," it was called. Real money was a dollar.

A year or so ago, I began noticing dollar bills turning up among the coins and lint, having been stuck there thoughtlessly, with casual contempt, as stuff not worth the dignity of a place in the wallet. Obviously, my psychological system was undergoing a change of which I was scarcely aware. Without any conscious thought at all, I had marked the dollar down to the value of flotsam or, perhaps, only jetsam.

Then, a couple of months ago, reaching in the pocket for a dollar to buy a magazine that used to cost 25 cents, I was startled to come up with a $5 bill.

The thing was obviously spreading, like one of those monstrous diseases from outer space that bemuse writers of science fiction thrillers. Several times after that I had the same experience— going into the pocket for a dollar and coming out with a $5 bill.

At first, somewhat alarmed, I stuffed the big bill into the wallet, but it left me uncomfortable. What, after all, was a $5 bill anymore? Did it deserve the dignity of the wallet? Every time you hopped out of a cab after sitting motionless for twenty minutes in rush-hour traffic, you had to come across with a $5 bill.

The wallet should be reserved for more powerful stuff than this. At the rate people were demanding $5 bills, you could wear out a wallet in two weeks if you had to manhandle it for each demand.

The $5 bill went permanently to the pants pocket along with lint, toothpicks, the ridiculous pennies and quarters and the wretched, bloodless, decaying, unworthy $1 bills.

This created immense psychological relief: When one stopped thinking of $5 bills as "real money," the pain and outrage occasioned by being charged $1.25 for a copy of *Newsweek,* $6 for a pound of veal and $3.50 to sit twenty minutes in a taxi without shock absorbers or springs became almost tolerable.

Not long ago when a waiter brought me a $135 bill for dinner for six, I scarcely even screamed, and I no longer look with awe upon fellow New Yorkers who pay $110 a month for parking space for their cars. The people across the street who rent two-bedroom apartments for $2,200 a month still leave me agape in such wonder as will be dispelled, I suppose, only when I shift the $20 bills from wallet to pocket.

And indeed, why not? Those things, after all, aren't really dollars anymore. They're lire.

Impressions of America

Impressions of America:

Atlanta: An entire city surrounded by an airport.

Maine: Two men in plaid shirts snowbound in a cabin in the woods with a moose in the guest room.

Chicago: Four ward heelers in rented tuxedos meeting in an opera-house lobby during an intermission of *Rigoletto* to discuss the rising price of embalming.

Impressions of America

Virginia: A group of beautifully mounted hunters galloping behind baying hounds in pursuit of a union organizer.

Oregon: Eighty billion gallons of water with no place to go on Saturday night.

Indiana: A mammoth basketball court with one hoop in Lake Michigan and the other in the Ohio River.

Philadelphia: A lonely widow, no longer young, composing an essay on Marlowe's superiority to Shakespeare for publication in the Chamber of Commerce magazine.

Montana: A grizzly bear praying for the early arrival of cable television.

San Francisco: Marcel Proust editing an issue of *Penthouse.*

Florida: The complete works of the Marquis de Sade after being bowdlerized by Gerald R. Ford.

Boston: Ludwig van Beethoven being jeered by 50,000 sports fans for finishing second in the Irish jig competition.

The New Jersey Turnpike: A man sealed in a metal cage has the complete writings of St. Thomas Aquinas, James Fenimore Cooper, Dale Carnegie and Edgar A. Guest read aloud to him in a metallic monotone by a machine invented by the telephone company.

Dallas: A custom-built limousine with a built-in table large enough to permit six millionaires to play Monopoly in the backseat en route to a revival meeting.

Iowa: Four Republicans meeting clandestinely in a cornfield to practice a Haydn quartet.

New York City: Two armed men strolling through yesterday's battlefield and shooting the wounded fall into a heated argument about which of them is the nobler human being and shoot each other, but not gravely enough to deter them from continuing their work.

California: Four tennis rackets with expensive teeth-capping jobs discuss the latest thing in religion while being massaged beside a swimming pool.

Houston: The twenty-fifth reunion of an Ivy League class debating whether abandoning tweeds for ten-gallon hats constitutes a sellout is interrupted by the arrival of an oil tanker which pumps them all full of gold.

Cleveland: The Venus de Milo with the torso missing.

Las Vegas: Sammy Davis, Jr., lecturing Benjamin Franklin on the old American virtues.

Reno: A set of false teeth buried in the arm of a slot machine.

Washington, D.C.: Dinner at Lucrezia Borgia's house with Tartuffe as the guest of honor.

The Grand Canyon: Zeus and Moses each telling the other, "And I thought I'd seen everything!"

Los Angeles: A car with an incredible bosom and a $50 hair styling auditioning for the lead in a new television comedy series about a hermaphroditic automobile that is constantly being pressured by friends to choose one sex or the other, submit to the necessary surgery and quit being an embarrassment to its neighbors.

Denver: A mad industrialist cackling happily over his chemical retorts as he dreams of strangling the Rocky Mountains to death in a noose of fumes.

Utah: Johann Sebastian Bach composing "Brighten the Corner Where You Are."

North Dakota: Henry James with writer's block.

Golden Oldies

By midnight I knew that Lana Turner would be killed, that Clark Gable would return to his wife, that his wife would forgive him and that Clark would join his old pal, John Hodiak, in doing medical good works in slummy Chester Village. I explained all this to the young people and went to bed. The young were impressed next morning. Skeptical of my forecast, they had sat through a cascade of commercials only to discover shortly before dawn that I had been absolutely correct at midnight. How? Had I seen the movie back in the Jurassic period of the late 1940's when it was new?

No, and yes. Although I had missed this particular movie *(Homecoming)* when it came out in 1948, I had seen it a thousand times under other titles, and knew the rules the script must obey. Everyone who went to the movies to learn how to live in that time learned that life was lived by rules almost as rigid as the rules for constructing a sonnet.

These were prescribed by a censorship code accepted by the American film industry, and, for a nation growing up in movie houses, created illusions that still affect our attitudes toward the world. A film like *Homecoming* is a typical example of the movie as social sermon.

Clark is a rich uptown surgeon who, having lost touch with humanity, sees people only as a procession of livers and gallbladders. Married to the beautiful Anne Baxter, he has selfishly neglected to reproduce. He is too busy repairing rich people's innards to have children. He throws flossy cocktail parties for his swell neighbors and becomes huffy when his old pal, Hodiak, chides him for being insufficiently attentive to malaria and hookworm in the local slum.

Given these circumstances, children of the 1930's and 1940's know immediately what must happen to Gable by film's end. He must learn humility. He must build a family. He must relent in his insensate passion for surgeon's wealth and sweeten his character by doing good works. Fortunately, World War II is available, and Clark is pressed into battlefield surgery. Enter Lana Turner, a brilliant charming widow and mother, a woman of wit and compassion and, what is more, the best darn scrub nurse in the whole United States Army.

Poor Lana. We know from her first entrance she is doomed by the censors. Clark will fall in love with her. At a moment of battlefield crisis they will share a chaste kiss. The kiss of death. In this harsh world, romantic trifling between married men and widows of even the highest moral nobility is a sin punishable by death. Since Clark has a wife to return to for forgiveness, and familial duties to perform and humility to learn, and since Lana is a mere widow, it is clearly she who must pay the penalty.

This is all silliness, to be sure, and mature people who sat through twenty years of these movies surely found little correspondence between their own lives and what was happening on the screen. Everybody knew arrogant men who died in happy senility, thieves who lived happily ever after and adulterers who did not suffer instant punishment by enemy shrapnel.

Nevertheless, even the most sophisticated moviegoers of that time were constantly exposed to the image of a well-ordered society in which the Ten Commandments were violated only on pain of terrible punishment, and social harmony always prevailed in the end. Crime, violence, carnality and even desire were treated as social aberrations. Blacks, when visible at all, were invariably wise, comic or soothing pillars of a well-ordered social system.

Among what are now called "ethnics" only the Irish seemed to exist in any numbers. They were warm, lovable and full of wisecracks, with a strong predilection for holy orders, and usually came from the poorer neighborhoods. Englishmen existed as butlers and silly asses encountered at the country club. Country clubs seemed to exist all over the place. Persons of the Alpine complexion existed as gangsters and pirates who, unlike Errol Flynn, showed none of the social graces to their female captives.

One may speculate whether the contemporary idea of American society in decay is not a false notion which has been created, at least partially, by this old movie portrait of a society that was once stable, orderly and governed by the immutable justice of the Hollywood censorship code.

This is the ever-popular myth of the golden age which persuades so many generations that there was once a wonderful moment in the past when the world was sound and good people ruled and evil was justly punished. After Camelot came chaos and despair, except, of course, that Camelot never existed, any more than the world portrayed by those old Hollywood films existed.

In all probability there was just as much crime, just as much violence, just as much injustice and sin on a per capita basis during the 1930's and '40's and '50's as there is today, though the nature of the hellishness may have changed a bit.

Those of us old enough to have fed on those old movies, however, are burdened with the illusion of a golden past that makes it hard to accept the disorder of the present age as the social normality. It is hard to live at ease with present sexual ethics when you have been conditioned to believe that Lana must die for making goo-goo eyes at Gable.

The Marrying Kind

For three years Pietro and Tess lived together without marrying. Such an arrangement had ceased to be scandalous when they took it up, had even become fashionable. It expressed the partners' reevaluation of the culture, or their liberation from tired old values, or something. It doesn't matter what. Pietro and Tess did it.

They were married a few weeks ago. "It had got to the point

where it didn't matter," Tess explained at the reception. "For all practical purposes we were married anyhow, and very happily, but it was starting to go sour because we didn't have the marriage certificate."

The canker in the love nest was the English language. Though English is the world's most commodious tongue, it provided no word to define their relationship satisfactorily to strangers. When Tess took Pietro to meet her parents the problem became troublesome. Presenting Pietro, she said, "Mommy and Daddy, this is my lover, Pietro."

Pietro was not amused. "It made me sound like a sex object," he said. "What's more, Tess's dad kept taking me off alone and trying to pump me for tips about how to become a lover."

Pietro felt demeaned and cheapened. Afterward, he quarreled with Tess and accused her of not respecting him as a person who had a fine mind and was a first-rate stockbroker. "Next time," Tess said, "I'll introduce you as my stockbroker." Pietro stormed out of the house.

A few weeks later, they were invited to meet the President. Entering the reception line, Pietro was asked by the protocol officer for their names.

"Pietro," he said. "And this is my mate."

As they came abreast of the President, the officer turned to Mr. Carter and said, "Pietro and his mate."

"I felt like the supporting actress in a Tarzan movie," said Tess. It took Pietro three nights of sleeping at the YMCA to repair the relationship.

"Why don't we call a spade a spade?" Tess suggested. Pietro pointed out that it was all very well to call a spade a spade, but it sounded ridiculous to call a relationship a relationship. Tess insisted they try it anyhow, so when Pietro bumped into Mayor Rizzo one day in Philadelphia, he said, "Frank, let me introduce you to my relationship, Tess." The Mayor said he was delighted, but he looked more like a man who suspected somebody was trying put one over on him and fled without wishing Tess a nice day.

"Let's get down to basics," Pietro told Tess. "I'm your man and

The Marrying Kind

you're my woman. Why don't we just come out and say so?" And so, when Pietro ran into Sammy Davis, Jr., at a party, he said, "Sammy, this is my woman, Tess." Whereupon Sammy seized Tess, whirled her into a fast fox-trot and brought down the house by shouting, "Tess, you is my woman now."

Back to the drawing board, on which they kept the dictionary. "This is my beloved" was no good. Sounded like a bad poem. "This is my companion"? Worse. Invalids, octogenarians, wealthy lunatics and kleptomaniacs had companions, but not persons who were young, enlightened and progressive enough to take turns washing the dishes. "Boyfriend" and "girlfriend" might have worked if they hadn't sounded so 1926. Pietro and Tess were 1976; yes, and 1977, too, and also 1978. For Pietro, this eliminated, "This is my chick, Tess," "This is my bird, Tess," and "This is my sweetie, Tess."

For Tess it eliminated, "This is my beau, Pietro," as well as, "This is the man in my life, Pietro." For a while they tried "my friend." One night at a glamorous party, Pietro introduced Tess to a marrying millionaire with the words, "This is my friend, Tess." To which the marrying millionaire replied, "Let's jet down to the Caribbean, Tess, and tie the knot."

"You don't understand," said Pietro. "Tess is my friend."

"So don't you like seeing your friends headed for big alimony?" asked the marrying millionaire.

"She's not that kind of friend," said Pietro.

"I'm his *friend,*" said Tess.

"Ah," said the matrimonialist, upon whom the dawn was slowly breaking. "Ah—your—*friend.*"

As Tess explained at the wedding, they couldn't spend the rest of their lives rolling their eyeballs suggestively every time they said "friend." There was only one way out. "The simple thing," Pietro suggested, "would be for me to introduce you as 'my wife.' "

"And for me," said Tess, "to say, 'This is my husband, Pietro.' "

And so they were wed, victims of a failure in English.

The Don Juan Experience

I was about to start writing my big book on Don Juan, the world's most tireless lover, when the interviews with Gay Talese began appearing. Talese had just finished a *magnum opus* of his own, a book called *Thy Neighbor's Wife,* all about America's sex life, and in the interviews he said he had immersed himself so thoroughly in the subject that he had actually forced himself to experience many of the activities he was writing about.

This seemed like carrying things a bit far. If he did a book about somebody getting lynched, would Talese insist on being strung up from a cottonwood tree? Possibly so, for I know him to be the most conscientious of writers. This is probably why he has never done a book about a lynchee.

Well, a few days after the first Talese interviews, the publisher of my Don Juan book phoned and asked when I was going to Spain.

"Not going to Spain," I said.

"Do you want to be big time and make millions like Talese, or are you a mouse who's satisfied to write a dinky little worst-seller?"

"Erma Bombeck is making millions, and she never leaves her kitchen in Arizona," I said.

"That's because Erma is writing about burning up the skillet and finding her kids' tennis shoes in the salad bowl," said the publisher. "Go to Spain. Immerse yourself in the Don Juan experience."

I had done enough research already to know what he was getting at. According to Mozart's excellent study of Don Juan, the Don had treated Spain like a motel on the outskirts of town. According to his faithful servant Leporello, he had seduced 1,003 women in Old Castile. Country damsels, waiting-maids, city ladies, countesses, duchesses, baronesses, viscountesses, fat girls in winter, thin girls in summer, women of every condition.

My doctor was not encouraging. "This seems to be a very demanding book," he said. "Can't you write something about knitting?"

I was miffed to think he considered me not up to Talese's standards of research.

"One thousand and three," he mused. "In your condition that would be like smoking three packs of cigarettes an hour."

He agreed, however, it would make a great book.

"Isn't there another country where Don Juan took life a little easier?" he wondered.

We consulted the Mozart libretto and studied Leporello's statistics. In Italy the Don had seduced only 640.

"But you'd be gorging on pasta between engagements," said the doctor. "Devastating to your blood pressure."

In Germany, 231. "More like it," said the doctor, "but in Germany you'd be tempted to cool off with the beer, and we know about your liver, don't we?"

"Aha!" I cried. "France! Leporello says in France, only 100."

"Be realistic," said the doctor. "Think of the cost of buying dinner for 100 women in Paris."

Eventually, I chose Turkey. Don Juan's triumphs there numbered a mere 91. What's more, since I didn't speak any Turkish, there would be no need to spend a lot of money taking the ladies to movies and nightclubs so we could get to know each other better.

I bought a hookah and a fez and was all packed for Istanbul when my publisher phoned again. He wanted me to come by his office and pick up a false goatee. He said I would come closer to experiencing the real Don Juan with a goatee on my chin, but the beauty part was, it had a small recording device built into the whiskers.

"That way," he said, "everything will be on record just as it happens."

"Why do we want that? I thought this was a book, not a transcribed recording," I said.

"How are you going to write a book after the statue comes to dinner?" he replied.

He was referring to the end of the Don Juan story, in which the Don invites a statue to dinner, and the statue shows up, and the Don and the statue sing at each other, and then the statue takes the Don down to hell.

"It would be great if you could write a terrific inside book about conditions in hell," said the publisher, "but frankly, once you get down there, I'm not sure we can count on your getting the manuscript out. Just leave the goatee behind when the statue grabs you, and we can have all the tapes transcribed into a book right here in the office."

I told him I wasn't going to have the statue to dinner. He said I wasn't fit to touch the shift key on Talese's typewriter. My new book is about a guy who sleeps until ten every morning. The research is terrific.

Dangerous Mutant at Large

Here is a letter from an unauthorized person. He is angry and confused. While driving a rural road in New England recently, he was stopped by a sign which said, "No Unauthorized Persons Permitted Beyond This Point—Violators Will Be Prosecuted." The rest of his letter follows:

Although I had been seeing this odiously discriminatory sign all my life, it was not until this moment that I realized how sick and tired of it I was.

Where was it written that the authorized persons of the earth had the right to prosecute the unauthorized? What, in the final analysis, was so terrible about being an unauthorized person?

Dangerous Mutant at Large

If I had deliberately set out in life to become an unauthorized person and had pursued this ambition through the fens of depravity, there might have been some excuse for excluding me from uninteresting roads, the parking lots of bureaucrats, airport locker rooms and all the other fascinating places to which only authorized persons are admitted.

But I had not deliberately sought my miserable status. It had simply happened to me. As some people are born with turned-up noses and some with silver spoons in their mouths, I was born an unauthorized person. At my birth the doctor came to my father and said, "Congratulations! You are the father of a bouncing seven-pound unauthorized person."

My parents were delighted. Both of them had been authorized for as long as they could remember and were jaded with years of going anyplace they wanted to go without being prosecuted. For me they dreamed of a different life, and heaven knows I have had one.

Three times convicted of being an unauthorized person, I had escaped prison only through the boon of plea-bargaining, under which prosecutors had agreed to recommend mercy if I pleaded guilty to conspiracy to circumvent the use of zip codes on my outgoing mail.

The fourth time I was not so lucky. At National Airport in Washington, I had barged into the co-pilot's coffee shop for a doughnut to get me through an early-morning flight to Cleveland and was trapped in a police stakeout. The judge gave me three years for being an unauthorized person with a doughnut, but the prison wouldn't let me in, as unauthorized persons were not permitted except on visiting days.

I offered to camp outside the walls, but the warden said he would prosecute me if I tried it since unauthorized persons were not permitted to tent within a thousand yards of the barbed wire.

There was nothing to do but go home and face the ignominy of telling everybody I was unqualified for prison. Instead, I decided to see the country. The trip was a disaster. Police everywhere had seen mug shots of me on post office walls and were alerted that I was a dangerous unauthorized person capable of trespass without warning.

They were waiting for me all over Washington where I seemed to be the only unauthorized person in town. They were waiting for me when I tried to see the President, the Congress, the Pentagon and the Supreme Court, as well as my dossiers at the FBI and the CIA.

When I went to New York to see Frank Sinatra, they were waiting for me as I stepped off the elevator in Frank's hotel. At each stop, they surrounded me while smug, authorized persons en route to see the President, Congress, Pentagon, Supreme Court, CIA men, G-men and Frank smiled the superior smiles of the authorized.

Two can play at this game, I said to myself, and went home, and posted signs on my street which said, "No Authorized Persons Permitted Beyond This Point."

Authorized men appeared at my house. "Are you authorized to post signs?" they asked.

I asked if they were authorized to ask questions.

They said they'd ask the questions.

I said I wasn't authorized to answer questions.

They said who was authorized to answer questions on my behalf.

I said I wasn't authorized to tell them.

They said what was I authorized to do.

I said I wasn't authorized to do anything.

They had never seen an unauthorized person before. They went for their guns.

The judge is tired of seeing me back in court. He promises to drop the charges if I agree to become authorized, but we are in a stalemated position. I went to the Authorizing Office today. Unauthorized persons are not permitted past the receptionist.

The notion that the all-conquering power of love can prevail over the inexpressible difficulties of marriage with its monstrous weekly bills dates from the era of plenty when the single "breadwinner" could still support unemployable women, children and grandparents, usually without resorting to armed robbery.

—Two-Income Zones

A no-nonsense letter from the National Academy of National Academies puts the question crisply: "The 1980's will be here before you know it. What should America do about it?"

They have asked the right man. If there is one thing I have firm convictions about, it is what this country should do in the 1980's. The first thing it should do is reduce output of no-nonsense letters, as well as no-nonsense executives and no-nonsense politicians. Look where all this no-nonsense nonsense has got us in the 1970's. In a nonsensical pickle, that's where.

I say let's cut out the no-nonsense in the 1980's. While we're at it we should also cut out the habit of letting computers and desks write letters to living human beings.

Just yesterday I had a letter From the Desk of Wilmer Bainbridge urging me to subscribe to a twelve-month course in home insulation. This letter was written by a computer, which apparently serves as amanuensis for Bainbridge's desk. Why can't Bainbridge's desk write its own letters? Why doesn't Bainbridge's desk fire Bainbridge and cut expenses?

Better yet, why don't we fire all three of them in the 1980's and restore the peace of mind that my grandmother, rest her soul, knew in the halcyon days of William Howard Taft? She lived to a splendid old age, my grandmother, in large part because she never absorbed the shock of receiving a letter written by a machine at the behest of furniture.

—Stranger than Orwell

Saturdays on Planet Libido

Far away on the gray planet Uxor the Emperor Zung, with evil incarnate written all over his goatee, is confronting the luscious Velma Suttee, U.S. space-traveling sex object. Yes, space fans, it is 1937 and we are watching a Saturday afternoon movie serial, and we know what is about to happen now, do we not?

Emperor Zung's dilated nostrils leave no eleven-year-old in doubt about what is on his mind, but Velma, apparently unaware of the effect a miniskirt and tight silk can have on an imperial libido, has to inquire, "What do you want of me, you swine?"

At this point, let us interrupt the action for a nostalgia quiz. What, in fact, does Emperor Zung want of luscious Velma Suttee, space fans of 1937?

To help you toward the answer, here are some additional facts. Velma is not only bound in chains but also surrounded by four Nubian slaves. Velma obviously thinks Zung wants her to ask why he imports slaves all the way from Nubia, especially when he has such a surplus of chains, but she is determined not to give him the satisfaction.

Moreover, Aces Norton, U.S. space hero with whom Velma travels from galaxy to galaxy to make the universe safe for democracy, is at this very moment drugged and shackled in an impenetrable dungeon crawling with man-eating bill collectors. Zung has just explained to Velma that she is completely in his power and that Aces Norton will not live to see the dawn.

In *Star Wars,* which does a creditable job of re-creating the feel of these Saturday afternoon thrillers, Velma's plight is recapitulated in the character of the captured princess, but what happens to the princess is odd and disturbing. The evil powers which have her at their mercy have no desire to do anything but pick her brain for secrets and then kill her.

Saturdays on Planet Libido

The people who made *Star Wars* are very young, and so, while they have otherwise done a fine job of re-creating Saturday afternoons in 1937, they have failed to include one ingredient that made those afternoons so delicious. They have left out the sex.

This may result from the natural tendency of the very young of all generations to assume that sex was not invented until they came to puberty. In fact, however, sex already existed even in children's entertainments in 1937, having been invented during the previous year. And, of course, it was a prime ingredient of such space thrillers as *Flash Gordon, Buck Rogers* and all the other films in which square-jawed heroes wandered the cosmos in form-fitting union suits in company with ladies of ample bosom and graceful calf.

When the Emperor Zung leered at the helpless Velma we all knew too well what he wanted. He wanted to get married. This news invariably produced pandemonium in Velma's breast, signified by enchanting heavings of same, and all over the theater eleven-year-old boys briefly forgot to chew their Jujubes.

Nowadays it will strike eleven-year-olds as odd that anyone could have regarded getting married as the equivalent of a fate worse than death. The contemporary moviegoer, accustomed to more directness in libidinal transactions, could understand Emperor Zung indulging in a brisk bout of rape, but would be flabbergasted if the old rascal ordered Velma to prepare to get married at once.

In 1937, however, nobody in the audience was in any doubt about what was going on. By threatening to marry the poor girl, Zung was—in the movie code of the time—declaring his intention to have his way with her.

Dale Arden, who traveled with Flash Gordon, seemed forever to be threatened with marriage, as did Wilma Deering, Buck Rogers's spaceship companion. Curiously, although Buck and Wilma presumably lived together constantly in their travels, as did Flash and Dale, no one ever suspected them of being up to anything for the simple reason that they were not married. It wasn't until late in life when Dick Tracy finally married Tess

Truehart that it even occurred to any of Dick's fans that he might be capable of a sex life.

On occasion, space emperors had luscious daughters—always brunettes—who plotted on marrying the captive hero. Though memory may trick me here, I seem to recall one instance when Emperor Ming threatened to marry Dale Arden and his daughter threatened to marry Flash Gordon in the same adventure.

One reason marriage may have seemed such a dreadful fate to audiences of that day may have been the clean-movie code, which specified that once a movie character got married, she or he could never get divorced, or, if they did, that they would have to die at the end of the show.

Whatever the reason, the moment when marriage threatened the helpless female lead was indispensable to a well-rounded Saturday afternoon adventure thriller, and *Star Wars* would have been even better than it was if its makers had realized that even to the kiddies the prospect of sex is almost as interesting as a talking robot.

The Search for Loneliness

Greta Garbo wanted to be alone, but most people didn't. They thought it exotic. That one of the great beauties of the age should choose loneliness when all humanity was available for her companionship seemed spooky and probably added to Garbo's allure by suggesting a dark preference in tastes that was utterly alien to the American zest for human commotion.

This was in time past, in the 1930's and 1940's, when Sweden and solitude were still as remote as Cambodia and sheriffs campaigning for the homosexual vote. In time present, loneliness seems to be the aspiration of depressingly large numbers of Americans. Looking at the growing numbers of persons proclaiming happiness from the solitude of private burrows, you wonder whether we are becoming a race that is simply afraid of people or whether we are finding such joy in self-love that it can only be spoiled by human contact.

Youth is reluctant to marry. When it does, it is reluctant to produce children, but quick to divorce. When men and women live together, in wedlock or out, the arrangement is often formalized as a "relationship." Sometimes this is defined in legal contracts, as though it were a deal for an exchange of services between parties who distrust each other.

These "relationships" are commonly designed to provide the parties with escape clauses to be invoked when long-term human involvement produces its inevitable messiness. The distaste for the messiness of human relationships is not new, of course. It has always been a characteristic of one of the stock comic figures of American society, the crotchety bachelor who avoids entangling alliance because he can't stand babies' diapers and women's stockings drying over his bathtub.

What made the bachelor comic was his willful refusal to undertake life's interesting complications, the sterility of the life he deliberately chose because he was too timid to try the water. Nowadays, however, the bachelor is no longer the source of comic literature and film but a figure of admiration whose example is celebrated as a happy adjustment to the exigencies of a mean-spirited society.

The women's movement attempts to lionize the female bachelor. Newspapers, books and magazines recite happy tales of women who, having successfully skirted the perils of husbands and nest building, have found contented anchorage in private harbors alone with their TV sets, their books, their wine, their pictures, their telephones and their self-fulfillment.

This is a long remove from the day when settlers traveled heavy miles a few times a year to escape the loneliness of prairie solitude in quilting bees and harvest feasts. A long distance even from a not-so-distant time when Americans pulled out of one-horse towns and dusty backwaters and poured into New York seeking people, life, adventure, love and the messiness of human connections.

Nowadays Americans come to New York to be alone, and the drift toward loneliness is nowhere better illustrated than in the changing sexual customs. A recent report in *The New York Times* tells of a spreading "asexuality" among New Yorkers. Increasing numbers of persons, it states, are finding that abstinence from sex develops into atrophy of sexual appetite, which makes it quite easy for them to live contentedly without sex.

Not long ago a man told me of a woman who went to an "asexual bar" to pick up men because she could be sure there was no risk of any human involvement. I thought he was joking, but now it seems entirely probable that "asexual bars" will sprout throughout the city to accommodate the growing demand for places where people who want to be alone can do so with people like themselves.

"Asexuality" was preceded by "solosexuality," a practice, heavily dependent upon machinery, which permitted people to subdue the natural instinct for human companionship with the aid of mechanical devices and illustrated manuals on the art of being your own irresistible lover.

"Solosexuality" developed out of "omnisexuality," a product of improved contraceptive technology which permitted people to satisfy the craving for human relationship almost as readily as the craving for an afternoon newspaper, and without much more risk of human involvement. "Asexuality," however, opens the possibility of a society in which perfect loneliness can finally be achieved.

There is a rather elegant nursing home I visit from time to time. In a certain wing almost everyone is totally alone except, now and then, for the occasional visit of someone like myself, the small residue of long-forgotten, messy human relationships. Minds wander in the past here, coming to rest briefly in a moment in 1910 when a younger brother got a thrashing from his daddy, then lurching forty years ahead to the moment of a son's marriage, a husband's death. Loneliness is almost absolute to the visitor, unable to cross into those dead worlds. He realizes that he may very well end here if he jogs assiduously and avoids tobacco. And if so, will there be people out of the past, people who have to be married, people who have to be buried, day after day, to pass the time? If not, what a loneliness.

Schlemiel

Next door lives Anna Karenina. She has been carrying on with a count named Vronsky.

Next door to her lives Emma Bovary. Emma leaves the house after her husband has gone to work and goes to a nearby hotel. Not long ago I saw her leaving the lobby with a man named Kugelmass.

It is an interesting neighborhood.

One day at the supermarket I encounter Anna. "Have you read the latest about Farrah?" she asks. No? She tells me. Farrah's planet is in conjunction with Arcturus, or vice versa; as a result, Farrah cannot decide whether it is a propitious time to change hair sprays.

I tell Anna some real news. Emma Bovary's in conjunction with Kugelmass, and if Chuck Bovary finds out about it, he will probably change wives.

"Kugelmass?" says Anna. "You mean that professor who looks like Woody Allen?" Her boredom is intense. She opens a magazine. "Would you believe it?" she asks, suddenly animated. "Robert Redford believes profoundly in the environment."

Next day I run into Emma Bovary on the street. She cannot wait to tell me the news. Farrah secretly went to a drive-in for hamburgers and caught a three-day virus. The news has been kept secret until now.

"Emma," I say, "poor Emma, let me tell you some real news."

It is good stuff. Anna's husband is sick and tired of Count Vronsky. He is going to move out and take the child with him.

Emma replies that I don't know what misery is until I have read the latest about Jackie's suffering. Jackie has gone to a horse show and been unable to get into the paddock because so many people wanted her autograph.

"Emma," I tell her, "that is not suffering. If it is suffering you enjoy, think of poor Anna. She is planning to throw herself under a moving train."

Emma says that is silly, since there aren't any trains anymore, and have I heard the news? Liza Minnelli is deeply in love with her husband. Moreover, there is absolutely nothing between Chris Evert and Jimmy Connors.

Poor Kugelmass. How long those hotel afternoons must seem. No wonder he looks like Woody Allen.

I shake Emma at the delicatessen, and whom should I see ordering a half pound of Danish fontina but Isabel Archer, who looks like Henry James in skirts, and no wonder, the poor girl having given up Lord Warburton for that rotter Gilbert Osmond.

"Poor old Isabel," says the counterman, when Isabel Archer has gone. "With that beard, she looks more like Henry James every day."

"You've heard about that rotter Gilbert Osmond, I suppose," I say to him. The counterman's eyes become glazed. If there is one thing that bores him it is the interesting problems of interesting people.

"I don't know from Gilbert Osmond, but I've got the late scoop for you, buddy," he says. He produces a fresh edition of *Schlemiel,* the gossip journal published for, by and about schlemiels.

" 'It is the real thing at last for Liz,' " he reads. " 'Happiness. Love. Caviar at the Iranian Embassy.' "

I am sitting home. Through the walls I can hear Anna next door practicing throwing herself under train wheels. In the street, Chuck Bovary is in tears, begging Emma not to leave him for a professor who looks like Woody Allen. Across the street, I can hear Gilbert Osmond playing the cad in the living room with a very loud horsewhip.

The telephone rings. It is my old fraternity brother Count Vronsky. He is bored. "What's new?" he asks.

I tell him: Farrah may or may not change hair sprays. Robert Redford cares about fresh air. Farrah once had a three-day virus. Jackie is suffering. Liza is enjoying conjugal bliss, it's cooled off between Chris and Jimmy, and Liz is very happy with the caviar in Washington.

Vronsky is shattered by these disclosures. Being Russian, he is so high-strung. I hear him weeping. "What threadbare lives we commonplace people lead," he sobbed.

I tell him Anna is practicing throwing herself under train wheels. "No wonder, the poor girl," says Vronsky. "Her brute of a husband has canceled her subscription to *People, Them, You, Me, National Enquirer, The Star, Ear, Eye, Nose, Throat* and *Schlemiel.*"

I hear moving train wheels. Or is it the presses rolling? And if so, why?

East Side Reject

One of the worst things that can happen to a New Yorker is to be tossed out of the East Side. I know too well, having just suffered this humiliation.

I was not booted completely out of New York, although it was a close thing. I was able to get a finger grip on a few feet of real estate down west by the Hudson River within sniffing distance of Hoboken. I comfort myself that I am the luckiest person alive, because when I was a child I had an uncle who lived in Hoboken by the gas works, and everybody said that living near the gas works was good for you because it prevented whooping cough.

In the predawn hours, however, when the meat packers arrive

for work and begin slamming sides of beef against my bedroom wall, I awaken and face the truth: evicted from the East Side.

The East Side is where the swells live, and I wanted to be as swell as the next swell when I settled in New York. I wanted to wear a mink coat to the supermarket when I went to buy a jar of peanut butter.

I wanted to have a tiny little thoroughbred poodle, no bigger than the back of my little finger. I wanted to walk my tiny little poodle through streets choked with limousines until he defiled sidewalks right in front of the town houses of multimillionaires and internationally famous courtesans.

I wanted to shop in boutiques with signs in the window that said, "English Spoken Here."

I wanted to eat the perfect artichoke.

I wanted to rub shoulders with famous expense-account swindlers' limousines and trade secrets with the world's great tax evaders about where to find a pasta more perfect than the perfect artichoke.

All this, and more, I enjoyed on the East Side, and it seemed it would never end. But it did.

It was the inflation that got me. The landlord telephoned one day suggesting that I get out. He intended to sell my residence. Perhaps I could buy. "What are you asking?" I inquired.

"One million dollars," he said. "You are insane," I said. "Maybe an Arab will come along," he said. I should point out that everybody on the East Side lived in a fever of greed inflamed by dreams that an Arab would come along.

The price of poodles no bigger than the back of your little finger had risen astronomically in anticipation that an Arab would come along. One day in a stomach boutique where I finally found the perfect watercress, the owner refused to sell it to me. "Maybe an Arab will come along," he said.

I telephoned real estate agents to plead with them to keep me on the East Side. They all answered the phone by saying, "Is this the Sheik of Araby?"

"I'll take anything, even a black hole," I said, "as long as it's

East Side Reject

on the East Side." They ordered me to quit tying up their phones. "An Arab may want to call," they said.

I offered to surrender my life insurance and sell five of my children into slavery in return for a single bedroom within walking distance of a perfect asparagus. Useless. Useless. I had been priced out, ejected, evicted, humiliated.

The cockroaches in our million-dollar property wept when the movers came, but they were crococile tears. Yes, it's true: East Side cockroaches can weep crocodile tears. This is because they are perfect cockroaches. Our cockroaches were not the kind to give up the East Side for immunity from whooping cough.

East Side friends were too embarrassed to show up for the farewell. They were perfect friends who had dined on the perfect lamb chop, and they did not want to stand around feeling superior to friends who were being snubbed by their cockroaches.

Hardest of all was bidding adieu to the Emperor, the mighty apartment house, taller than the Washington Monument, which had blotted out our light perfectly for five dark years. From high in the clouds, the Emperor amused itself over the years by pelting us with its plate-glass windows (it was perfect plate glass) and by sending its tenants to the balconies to bombard us with marbles, eggs, potatoes and soda-pop bottles.

But when we pulled away for the last time, the Emperor did not weep so much as a single piece of garbage on us. It had neither window frames, marbles, eggs, potatoes, soda-pop bottles nor garbage to waste on people who couldn't afford the East Side.

"Funny," I told the mover. "That building usually tries to kill me."

"It's probably waiting for an Arab to come along," he said.

What a Man's Got to Do

Why do I continue to ride the subways? Even the police now say they are too dangerous for a cop to patrol without a companion cop to protect his back. I can best answer with other questions.

Why does the torero confront the bull? Why does the hunter face the charging lion? Why does the bomber crew rise again to face the flak over Bremerhaven? It is not easy to feel like a hero these days, but when I head for the subway, I feel myself walking a little bit straighter, my jaw setting in a firmer line, my primitive animal reflexes becoming tauter.

In five years in the subways I have acquired skills—professionalism—of which I am proud. I am an aging man, like Willie Stargell, but there is a fine pleasure, as there must be for Stargell, in testing myself to find whether the wisdom and experience are still enough to compensate for the loss of quickness.

I feel confidence as I submerge at 42nd Street and brush past the man at the foot of the steps with his chant of "Acid and grass, acid and grass, acid and grass."

Inside I am cautious about avoiding eye contact, which can lead to critical encounters with roving maniacs. On the platform, I cunningly stay back from the rails pretending to notice no one, but sizing up everyone. I keep distance from men carrying paper bags which may conceal meat cleavers or .357 magnums. If someone runs, I slide discreetly behind an upright steel pillar and grasp it firmly against the possibility of being shoved onto the rails.

When the train arrives, I do not enter the cars in which the lights are out or in which too many of the doors refuse to open.

At my destination, confronting a 300-yard walk along an abandoned tunnel illuminated with a ten-watt bulb, I roll my newspaper so tightly it becomes a murderous spear and, swinging it

aggressively, stride through the gloom like Bogart walking down a mean street. When I emerge whole, I feel complete and alive again and a true New Yorker.

Just Plain Nice

President Carter is nice. Ronald Reagan is nice, too, but in a different way. You know: President Carter is really nice—nice family man, nice smile, nice to people, nice church man; but Ronald Reagan has such a nice sense of humor, and a nice grin, and a nice way of presenting himself.

You just can't help thinking Mr. Reagan is so nice all around that it would be nice to be with him, but of course it would be nice to be with President Carter, too, only in a different way.

I was thinking about this yesterday morning while shaving. It was nice to shave. Not terrific, mind you—don't get me wrong —but, still—nice.

I guess what got me thinking along these lines was the day. It was a nice day. Not one of the great days, to be sure, but not really rotten either. It was the kind of day when it doesn't really rain, but the sun doesn't really make much show either, the kind of day when you feel stiff all over and ten years older than you really are, but not like you might have to go into the hospital right away. In short, a nice day.

Downstairs for breakfast the usual question arose: "How did you sleep?"

"Nice. How about you? Did you sleep nice?"

"Very nice."

Actually, I had not had an astonishingly pleasant night. There had been a medium-weight nightmare sometime during the hour of the wolf, but on the other hand it hadn't waked me with such terror that I had to get up and go into the parlor and read myself

back to sleep in the *Autobiography* of Benjamin Franklin. Not a really awful night's sleep, and not a wonderful one either. Just nice.

To make conversation I said that breakfast was nice. It was, too. There was frozen orange juice and ersatz cholesterol-free bacon followed by caffeine-free coffee. It was pretty artificial but still a good deal tastier than no breakfast at all. It was nice to have a breakfast when you considered that the alternative was hunger. I could see I was going to have a nice day.

This proved to be the case. The people on the subway were nice. Nobody you would want to meet, but nobody trying to kill anybody else either. Just nice people. The subway was nice, too. Filthy, as usual, but most of the lights were working. It wasn't one of the dazzling subways such as come along every few months or so, but it wasn't one of the really unspeakable subways either. It was just a nice subway.

Things at the office were also nice, which wasn't terribly interesting, but on the other hand didn't leave you with heartburn or indigestion or an urge to ask the widow in accounting to run away with you to Macao and start a new life.

"It's very nice at the office today," I remarked to a nice vice-president, and he was so pleased that he invited me out for a nice lunch.

We had a nice talk. "Whatever they say about President Carter," he said, "nobody can say he isn't nice."

"The President is nice, all right," I pointed out, "but have you noticed how nice Ronald Reagan is, but in a different way from President Carter?"

"That's a nice concept," he said. "It's nice for the country having two nice men to guide our destiny."

"I don't think niceness is too much for the American people to ask for," I said.

Walking back to the office we saw a nice madwoman. Not a wonderful madwoman who thrusts $100 bills into your pocket and disappears into the crowd, and not a dreadful madwoman who accuses you of kidnapping her babies and slaughtering her

cattle, but just a nice madwoman who was walking through the streets screaming to herself about a volcano erupting in her kitchen sink.

It was like that all day. Arriving home, being asked, "How was your day?" and replying, "Nice. How was yours?" I received the reply, "Very nice."

Then we had some martinis and got out the pistol and shot out the tube in the television set. The woman downstairs came up to see if anyone was hurt. "We just shot the television set," I explained. "That's nice," she said. "Not really great because you could have missed and hit the wall and not have to buy a new telly. But not really terrible either, since you didn't shoot each other. Just nice."

I made us all another martini and propounded the theory that the 1980's were going to be The Nice Decade and we all had a nice chat. It was a nice evening. I mean, it wasn't V-J Day in Times Square, but it wasn't London in the thirteenth century either. Just nice, so nice, like President Carter and Ronald Reagan, only in a different way.

Not Much to Brag About
[1979]

I intended to summarize the decade today, as a dull journalist should at this turn of the earth, but fell instead to thinking about my grandfather, who was born 125 years ago. That was in 1854, and though he is dead now and beyond the tedium of journalists' year-end and decade-end summations, I wonder what, if anything, that happened from 1970 through 1979 would have struck him as worth reading about.

Very little, I suspect, at least if he could be treated to a century-and-a-quarter roundup covering the three generations which the two of us bestride. Perhaps the California custom of holding group assemblies in tubs of hot water would bemuse him briefly, or the frequency of public demonstrations by homosexuals, but even these seem small chaff compared to the eerie curiosities of the 1920's.

Prohibition, women wearing stockings rolled below the knees, gangsters running about with tommy guns—such stuff would surely strike him as stranger and more entertaining than anything that happened in the 1970's.

Would the near-impeachment of Richard Nixon interest a man who had only an hour to read a summation of the past 125 years?

It seems doubtful. How many people today are interested in the impeachment of Andrew Jackson, which occurred when my grandfather was an adolescent? In fact, the politics and the diplomacy of the 1970's would surely be skipped entirely in my grandfather's precious hour of reading time, for except to scholars and Washington's pundits, they have been as complex, incomprehensible and dull as any politics and diplomacy since the maneuvers of the Whigs and Tories in the reign of Good Queen Anne.

Who of us alive today would linger during a 125-year roundup over the Hayes, Garfield, Arthur, Cleveland and Harrison Administrations? Yet they were at least as engrossing as the Nixon, Ford and Carter years.

My guess that Grandfather would have had an hour to devote to a 125-year roundup may be on the liberal side. He did heavy work with his hands and had only kerosene lamps to read by. Eyeglasses were not very sophisticated even by the time of his death, and night comes early in December to tempt a tired man to bed.

If he could have had the entire 125-year record set before him, he would probably have considered news of the electrification of Morrisonville, the village in which he lived, more absorbing than stories of 1970 oil profits, the troubles of the equal rights amendment or the 1976 debates between Gerald Ford and Jimmy Carter.

The story of the mass-produced automobile replacing the horse would have been read with particular dismay, for he was a blacksmith. But that truly weighty development occurred long before the seventies. He might have lingered a moment with pleasure over the tale of the automobile's decline in the otherwise uninteresting seventies.

He might even have said a good word for the Arabs, though this is speculative, for he believed in supporting his own Government so firmly that, though a Virginian, he sided with the Union during the Civil War.

The 1970's did not produce any bellicose event in a weight class with the Civil War, or the World War for that matter, or World War II, or the Korean War, or the Vietnam war. In fact in any list of the ten most vital events, moments in history, startling occurrences or earthshaking developments, the seventies would be hard-pressed to get into a 125-year summation.

In this period Germany became a nation, the British Empire disappeared, revolutions in Russia and China reshaped the nature of world power, a hundred colonial enclaves became independent nations and the United States became the most powerful state on the planet, but none of these happened in the 1970's. In the seventies, the United States quarreled with Cuba about who had the right to do what in Africa.

During the 125 years since my grandfather's birth, the American continent was joined by rail, slavery was abolished, the atom was cracked, the world was linked by airborne machinery and men traveled to the moon. But none of these things happened in the 1970's. In the seventies the television set was adapted for the playing of electronic games in the home.

It appears that the 1970's claim to distinction will be that it was the time when the United States became poorer. I cannot imagine my grandfather wasting much time over this development when other decades have so much to tantalize the reader's eye. Until his death, he lived in a community without plumbing, central heating, electricity, a radio, a telephone, a paved road, a car or a grocery with a frozen-juice department, and he sent his sons to work after fourth grade for $5 a month, and it is doubtful that he ever felt poor, and it is doubtful that he would have much time for a nation that does feel poor because a lot of people can't afford to keep the parlor heated to seventy-two degrees.

My hunch is that he would have dropped off to sleep before reaching the 1970's, but that, if he hadn't, he would have said, "This story starts off real good, but it sure does get dull in the last chapter."

Losing Speed

"I cannot pinpoint with certainty the moment at which I lost touch," writes a middle-aged friend. "It wasn't when everybody was eating Colonel Sanders's Kentucky Fried Chicken because I distinctly remember eating the stuff with some regularity in those days and thinking nothing of it.

"But somewhere between there and here, if I may use Joseph Heller's ominous title, something happened. Driving up the East Coast last year, I suddenly realized that I had never eaten a Big Mac. By that time Big Macs had been eaten by precisely told hundreds of millions, but I still hadn't consumed my first.

"Pausing outside Baltimore, I ate one, hoping to reestablish community with the American reality. It obviously didn't work because I haven't eaten a Big Mac since, although as hamburgers go, the Baltimore Big Mac was not a total loser. It just seemed, well, unnecessary.

"Too many things had begun to seem unnecessary. All America was watching Archie Bunker, and I was still asking people who Archie Bunker was. It's not that I'm a television snob either. When still in touch with American reality, I never missed an installment of 'Perry Mason' and though 'Gunsmoke' never really fetched me, I could do a passable imitation of Festus being laconic with Matt Dillon.

"I could even make weak gags based on television commercials, had a hundred switches on 'Mother, I'd rather do it myself' and knew the distinction between an Excedrin headache and twice as much stomach acid. But something happened. Just the other day, reading a list of the most popular shows on the tube, I suddenly realized that I had never seen 'Laverne and Shirley,' 'Three's Company,' 'Happy Days,' 'Mork and Mindy' or 'Love Boat,' had never heard anybody talk about them and, in fact, hadn't the least idea of what any of them was about.

"Worse, I didn't want to know. I didn't want to go to the King Tut exhibit either, despite the fact that it was all sold out. When I was in touch with American reality, I always wanted to go to shows that were all sold out, even if I didn't want to see them, because I enjoyed lording it over people who hadn't been able to get in.

"I have seen shows that were all sold out at which the only available seat aimed my line of sight straight into the theater wings and, though I saw more of the stagehands than the actors, I was satisfied because I had been present at the show everybody was talking about. Then something happened.

"Nowadays, the minute I hear a show is all sold out, I instantly decide that I don't want to see it and never think of it again. Same thing with greatest games ever played. Before losing touch, I used to dote on greatest games ever played. I can still tell you about Johnny Unitas and the Colts beating the Giants in overtime; about the Bobby Thompson home run, the Don Larsen perfect game. Then something happened.

"Reading about the forthcoming Super Bowl the other day, I realized that I had gone out of my way to avoid every single greatest game ever played for four or five years. Recently a man in his forties got to talking about the Yankees–Red Sox playoff game in the fall of 1978 and pronounced it the greatest game ever played. I had seen the game, which was excellent in fact, but hadn't realized it was the greatest ever played and found myself disliking it a little now that it had been reduced to the status of the King Tut exhibit and 'Laverne and Shirley.'

"I didn't see *Jaws,* either. Not that I didn't revel in film blood at one time. Randolph Scott pumping lead into the Dalton boys left me ecstatic before I lost touch. But something happened. For several years I have carefully avoided paying $3 to witness realistic imitations of people being eaten by beasts, tortured by sadists or beheaded in close-ups by guillotines, Samurai swords or speeding automobiles.

"There are several dangers in being out of touch with the country. Children hold me in contempt, I've lost the ability to talk to the masses of people who are in touch—how is it possible for anybody to sustain a conversation about the Carter Administration? Yet, in-touch people do—and I worry a lot about the world's passing me by.

"To be out of touch, after all, is a kind of death. Here are all these things that engross millions—Big Macs, 'Laverne and Shirley,' greatest games ever played, *Jaws,* King Tut—and my ability to share the excitement is dwindling to zero.

"When television is the subject and I say, 'Mother, I'd rather do it myself,' people break off the conversation abruptly. When everyone else is talking about *A Chorus Line* and I have to drag in *Oklahoma!* I feel myself being silently scratched off invitation lists. Never had a Big Mac? This bird must be an elitist. Never mind about that Kentucky Fried Chicken, that was then, Buster —now is now.

"It's almost enough to make me tune in 'Laverne and Shirley' next time around, but not quite. Why is staying in touch such hard work once you're grown up?"

Summer Beyond Wish

A long time ago I lived in a crossroads village of northern Virginia and during its summer enjoyed innocence and never knew boredom, although nothing of consequence happened there.

Seven houses of varying lack of distinction constituted the community. A dirt road meandered off toward the mountain where a bootleg still supplied whiskey to the men of the countryside, and another dirt road ran down to the creek. My cousin Kenneth and I would sit on the bank and fish with earthworms. One day we killed a copperhead which was basking on a rock nearby. That was unusual.

The heat of summer was mellow and produced sweet scents which lay in the air so damp and rich you could almost taste them. Mornings smelled of purple wisteria, afternoons of the wild roses which tumbled over stone fences and evenings of honeysuckle.

Even by standards of that time it was a primitive place. There was no electricity. Roads were unpaved. In our house there was no plumbing. The routine of summer days was shaped by these deficiencies. Lacking electric lights, one went early to bed and rose while the dew was still in the grass. Kerosene lamps were cleaned and polished in an early-morning hubbub of women, and children were sent to the spring for fresh water.

This afforded a chance to see whether the crayfish population had multiplied. Later, a trip to the outhouse would afford a chance to daydream in the Sears, Roebuck catalog, mostly about shotguns and bicycles.

With no electricity, radio was not available for pacifying the young. One or two people did have radios that operated on mail-order batteries about the size of a present-day car battery, but these were not for children, though occasionally you might be invited in to hear "Amos 'n' Andy."

All I remember about "Amos 'n' Andy" at that time is that it was strange hearing voices come out of furniture. Much later I was advised that listening to "Amos 'n' Andy" was racist and was grateful that I hadn't heard much.

In the summer no pleasures were to be had indoors. Everything of delight occurred in the world outside. In the flowers there were hummingbirds to be seen, tiny wings fluttering so fast that the birds seemed to have no wings at all.

In the heat of midafternoon the women would draw the blinds, spread blankets on the floor for coolness and nap, while in the fields the cattle herded together in the shade of spreading trees to escape the sun. Afternoons were absolutely still, yet filled with sounds.

Bees buzzed in the clover. Far away over the fields the chug of an ancient steam-powered threshing machine could be faintly heard. Birds rustled under the tin of the porch roof.

Rising dust along the road from the mountains signaled an approaching event. A car was coming. "Car's coming," someone would say. People emerged from houses. The approaching dust was studied. Guesses were hazarded about whom it might contain.

Then—a big moment in the day—the car would cruise past.

"Who was it?"

"I didn't get a good look."

"It looked like Packy Painter to me."

"Couldn't have been Packy. Wasn't his car."

The stillness resettled itself as gently as the dust, and you could wander past the henhouse and watch a hen settle herself to perform the mystery of laying an egg. For livelier adventure there was the field that contained the bull. There, one could test his courage by seeing how far he dared venture before running back through the fence.

The men drifted back with the falling sun, steaming with heat and fatigue, and washed in tin basins with water hauled in buckets from the spring. I knew a few of their secrets, such as who kept his whiskey hidden in a Mason jar behind the lime barrel, and what they were really doing when they excused themselves from the kitchen and stepped out into the orchard and stayed out there laughing too hard.

I also knew what the women felt about it, though not what they thought. Even then I could see that matters between women and men could become very difficult and, sometimes, so difficult that they spoiled the air of summer.

At sunset people sat on the porches. As dusk deepened, the lightning bugs came out to be caught and bottled. As twilight edged into night, a bat swooped across the road. I was not afraid of bats then, although I feared ghosts, which made the approach of bedtime in a room where even the kerosene lamp would quickly be doused seem terrifying.

I was even more afraid of toads and specifically of the toad which lived under the porch steps and which everyone assured me would, if touched, give me warts. One night I was allowed to stay up until the stars were in full command of the sky. A woman of great age was dying in the village and it was considered fit to let the children stay abroad into the night. As four of us sat there we saw a shooting star and someone said, "Make a wish."

I did not know what that meant. I didn't know anything to wish for.

Spaced Out

I am sitting here 93 million miles from the sun on a rounded rock which is spinning at the rate of 1,000 miles an hour,

and roaring through space to nobody-knows-where,

to keep a rendezvous with nobody-knows-what,

for nobody-knows-why,

and all around me whole continents are drifting rootlessly over the surface of the planet,

India ramming into the underbelly of Asia,

America skidding off toward China by way of Alaska,

Antarctica slipping away from Africa at the rate of an inch per eon,

and my head pointing down into space with nothing between me and infinity but something called gravity which I can't even understand, and which you can't even buy anyplace so as to have some stored away for a gravityless day,

while off to the north of me the polar ice cap may

be getting ready to send down oceanic mountains of ice that will bury everything from Bangor to Richmond in a ponderous white death, and there, off to the east, the ocean is tearing away at the land and wrenching it into the sea bottom and coming back for more,

as if the ocean is determined to claim it all before the deadly swarms of killer bees,

which are moving relentlessly northward from South America, can get here to take possession,

although it seems more likely that the protective ozone layer in the upper atmosphere may collapse first,

exposing us all, ocean, killer bees and me, too,

to the merciless spraying of deadly cosmic rays.

I am sitting here on this spinning, speeding rock surrounded by 4 billion people,

eight planets,

one awesome lot of galaxies,

hydrogen bombs enough to kill me thirty times over,

and mountains of handguns and frozen food,

and I am being swept along in the whole galaxy's insane dash toward the far wall of the universe,

across distances longer to traverse than Sunday afternoon on the New Jersey Turnpike,

so long, in fact, that when we get there I shall be at least 800,000 years old,

provided, of course, that the whole galaxy doesn't run into another speeding galaxy at some poorly marked universal intersection and turn us all into space garbage,

or that the sun doesn't burn out in the meantime,

or that some highly intelligent ferns from deepest space do not land from flying fern pots and cage me up in a greenhouse for scientific study.

So, as I say, I am sitting here with the continents moving, and killer bees coming, and the ocean eating away, and the ice cap poised, and the galaxy racing across the universe,

and the thermonuclear thirty-times-over bombs stacked up around me,

and only the gravity holding me onto the rock,

which, if you saw it from Spica or Arcturus, you wouldn't even

Spaced Out

be able to see, since it is so minute that even from these relatively
close stars it would look no bigger than an ant in the Sahara
Desert as viewed from the top of the Empire State Building,
    and as I sit here,
    93 million miles from the sun,
    I am feeling absolutely miserable,
    and realize,
    with self-pity and despair,
    that I am
    getting a cold.

About the Author

Russell Wayne Baker was born in Loudoun County, Virginia, in 1925. He graduated from The John Hopkins University in 1947 and that same year began his career as a reporter with *The Baltimore Sun.* In 1954 he joined *The New York Times* Washington bureau, for which he covered government and national politics. He began writing his "Observer" column for *The Times* in 1962; his "Sunday Observer" appears in *The New York Times Magazine.* In 1979, Mr. Baker received the George Polk Award for Commentary and the Pulitzer Prize for Distinguished Commentary.